Language, classrooms and computers

As computers become more widely used in schools, it is clear that they have
the potential not just to support the achievement of conventional goals, but
also to redefine what we mean by reading, writing and discussion. The
contributors here, all with experience of teaching about language and computers for the Open University, use teachers' accounts, together with their
own research, to examine how the use of computers in schools can affect the
ways in which children learn and teachers teach. The first section looks at
some generic aspects of computer use, focusing particularly on class management: individual and group learning, the role of the teacher as facilitator
and co-learner and the problems of limited access. The second section
examines the contribution of specific sorts of software package: word
processing, e-mail, hypertext and so on to language learning. This is a book
for everyone who wants IT to add a new dimension to their teaching.

Peter Scrimshaw is Lecturer in Education at the Centre for Language and
Communications, the Open University.

Language, classrooms and computers

Edited by Peter Scrimshaw

London and New York

428.0078
2269 —

First published 1993
by Routledge
11 New Fetter Lane, London EC4P 4EE

Simultaneously published in the USA and Canada
by Routledge
29 West 35th Street, New York, NY 10001

© 1993 Peter Scrimshaw

Typeset in Garamond by
LaserScript, Mitcham, Surrey

Printed and bound in Great Britain by
Biddles Ltd, Guildford and King's Lynn

British Library Cataloguing in Publication Data
A catalogue record for this book is available from the British
Library.

ISBN 0-415-08574-8   ISBN 0-415-08575-6 (pbk)

Library of Congress Cataloging in Publication Data
has been applied for

ISBN 0-415-08574-8   ISBN 0-415-08575-6 (pbk)

Contents

Figures and tables

FIGURES

TABLES

Contributors

Dr Eunice Fisher was Senior Research Associate for the ESRC-funded Spoken Language and New Technology Project, and was previously a Staff Tutor at the Open University. She is now Senior Lecturer in Psychology in the Faculty of Humanities and Social Sciences at Nene College.

Dr Ann Jones is Lecturer in the Institute of Educational Technology at the Open University. She was a member of the EH232 Computers and Learning Course Team, and co-edited 'Computers in Education 5–13'. She is co-author of a forthcoming book entitled *Personal Computers for Distance Education*.

Dr Diana Laurillard is a Senior Lecturer in the Institute of Educational Technology at the Open University. She chaired the Course Team that produced EH232 Computers and Learning and is currently engaged in three CALL projects at the Open University. She is a member of a consortium within the Teaching and Learning Programme led by the Modern Languages department at the University of Hull.

Prof. Paul Light works in the Department of Psychology at the University of Southampton, and was previously Director of the Centre for Human Development and Learning in the School of Education at the Open University. He is currently co-directing a Leverhulme research project on collaboration and feedback in children's computer-based problem solving.

Giorgio Marullo is Head of Modern Languages at Holland Park Comprehensive School. He is also a part-time student at the Institute of Educational Technology of the Open University, engaged in postgraduate research on CALL.

Dr Neil Mercer is Director of the Centre for Language and Communications in the School of Education at the Open University. He is Co-Director of the Spoken Language and New Technology Project and the author, with Derek Edwards, of *Common Knowledge*.

Bernadette Robinson is a Staff Tutor in the School of Education at the Open University. She was a member of the EH232 Computers and Learning Course

Team, and has written widely on distance education, including the role of new technologies.

Peter Scrimshaw is a Lecturer in the School of Education at the Open University, and chairs the Language and Communications Research Group there. He has written and edited a number of books and articles on curriculum issues and on the use of computers in schools.

Acknowledgements

The contributors to this book were nearly all involved in the production of the Open University Course EH232 *Computers and Learning*, which first came out in 1991. While preparing the material for that course it became clear that for some of us the specific issue of the role of the computer in language teaching and learning was of particular interest. We decided therefore to develop this line of thought further; this book is the result.

We are grateful to our colleagues on the EH232 Course Team: Helen Boyce, Oliver Boyd-Barrett, Jenny Chalmers, John Chapman, Ruth Hall, David Hawkridge, Andrew Law, Tim O'Shea, Jon Rosewell, Eileen Scanlon, Serena Stapleton, Helen Thompson and Tom Vincent. We are also grateful to the Open University for kindly agreeing to our drawing upon parts of the course for this book. These remain © 1991 the Open University.

In addition we would like to thank Sally Tweedle and Carol Fine for their helpful comments on an early version of Chapter 10, and the NCET for permission to reproduce extracts from teacher's accounts of their classroom experiences with computers. These were produced as part of the work of the PALM Project, which was funded by NCET in association with Cambridgeshire, Essex and Norfolk LEAs, at the University of East Anglia.

Finally I am particularly grateful to my colleague Pam Powter, who has handled the production and collation of the chapters for this book with characteristic professionalism, calm and good humour throughout.

Part I

Computers in context

Chapter 1

Teachers, learners and computers

Peter Scrimshaw

I have come increasingly to recognise that most learning in most settings is a communal activity, a sharing of the culture. It is not just that the child must make his knowledge his own, but that he must make it his own in a community of those who share his sense of culture. *It is this that leads me to emphasise not only discovery and invention but the importance of negotiation and sharing.*

(Bruner, 1986, p. 127)

Part I of this book explores a set of related questions about the role of computers in learning, and the implications of this for classroom activities and the teacher's role. The questions we are concerned with are these:

- What theory of computer supported learning would best help teachers to understand how best to promote learning in their classrooms?
- What practical research methods does such a theory require?
- What classroom roles does it suggest for the individual pupil, his or her classmates, the teacher and the computer, if learning is to be encouraged?
- How is access to computer supported learning distributed, and how might it be distributed more equitably?

Not all of these questions are addressed in every chapter, and we are by no means entirely of one mind as to the way in which they should be answered. Chapters 2 to 6 explore these questions, and the interrelationships between them in some depth, while this chapter gives an overview of the account that they provide, and some of the problems that this account presents.

THEORIES OF LEARNING AND THEIR IMPLICATIONS

In Chapter 2 Ann Jones and Neil Mercer begin by arguing that any teaching is based upon a model of learning, either consciously or not. Educational software, therefore, being a resource designed to support teaching and learning, will likewise incorporate such models. They then look critically at three theories of learning, and trace out some of the ways each can be identified in educational software.

Taking B. F. Skinner as a key exponent they first discuss behaviourism. The emphasis in this approach upon observable and measurable behaviour, and the systematic reinforcement of desired responses they see partially reflected both in the old teaching machines that predated the use of computers in education, and in many of the drill and practice programs that are still widely available and used. They argue that Skinner's picture of behaviour as a series of discrete fixed responses does not fully reflect the reality. In language use, for instance, people often have to produce quite novel sentences, the construction of which implies that speakers are using general rules and principles rather than selecting from a fixed repertoire of specific responses.

If Skinner's position is inadequate as a universal explanatory account of learning, it does not follow that there are not some kinds of learning for which it is both adequate and pedagogically informative. The learning of low level (but still important) specific facts and motor skills are the obvious examples. If this is accepted, it could be that software based upon the theory would in fact be of value, provided it was used only to develop those capacities. Perhaps the problem here is not that there are not such uses, but that by endorsing the use of computers for such purposes we may inadvertently encourage a view of education in which such an approach is taken to endorse an atomistic and inadequate conception of higher order capacities too.

If learning theory has to explain the capacity to employ higher order principles, it must also imply an active view of learning, for the learner is now not seen as making automatic responses to external stimuli but as actively reviewing experiences and interpreting them in terms of more general ideas or categories. Jones and Mercer take the work of Seymour Papert as an exemplar of this kind of constructivist perspective. His ideas may be seen as part of the line of development that runs from Piaget through Bruner. Papert not only extended Piaget's ideas in a distinctive way, but also applied his theories systematically to educational computing. He accepts Piaget's emphasis upon the importance of children working through concrete experience to develop conceptual understanding, and his most famous contributions to educational software have been the Logo programming language and the floor turtle, which together provide young learners with tools with which to construct new understandings in areas such as mathematics and physics.

Jones and Mercer consider this version of constructivism as being not so much wrong as incomplete. They observe that what Papert provides is a theory of learning but not a theory of teaching. This perhaps arises naturally from the highly active conception of learning that constructivism embodies, together with the perhaps over optimistic expectations that Papert initially had for the capacity of suitable software to provide whatever structuring and support the learner might need. If the capabilities of at least current software is seen as more limited, then a gap opens up for the teacher to fulfil a mediating role between learner and program. Indeed much of the evolving debate and research about Logo has been concerned to identify what that role might be.

Finally Jones and Mercer turn to communicative theories of learning, taking the work of Lev Vygotsky as their exemplar. They argue that any individualistic theory of learning, whether constructivist or behavourist, will be inadequate. One reason for this is that nearly all learning with computers involves other people, either directly as co-learners or teachers, or indirectly as the authors of the program or the supporting documentation. Thus to understand what is learned and how we must take this social context into account; what is required is a theory of teaching-and-learning, not just of learning alone.

Vygotsky's communicative theory of learning has this social dimension. He emphasises the role of language in cognitive development as a tool for teaching and learning, and as language is a socially constructed tool its use requires the learner to interact with others. The authors (following Griffin and Cole) argue that this means that the teacher must be seen as an active communicative participant in learning, with the computer acting as a medium that creates new possibilities for learning and communication between teachers and learners. This they contrast with an approach that sees the computer as a surrogate teacher, itself entering into dialogue with the (usually individual) learner, and eventually perhaps replacing the teacher entirely.

Why Jones and Mercer support this view of the computer's role is unclear. If, as they argue earlier, the computer or other curriculum resources are themselves social constructs, why does the social nature of learning require the direct presence of another person, rather than just contact with the sorts of social artifacts from which, as a matter of observable fact, people sometimes can learn independently? We will return to this problem later.

TEACHING AND THE CONCEPTUALISATION OF INFORMATION TECHNOLOGY ACTIVITIES IN THE CLASSROOM

In this chapter Neil Mercer further develops the case for using a communicative theory of learning and teaching when dealing with the educational role of computers. He favours observational research methods rather than experimental ones, and in particular the detailed qualitative study of videotaped and directly observed lessons, backed up by interviews with the teachers and learners observed, to find out how they perceived the activities that took place, and the reasons they give for what they did. The reason for favouring such an approach emerges naturally from a commitment to a communicative theory. This requires the detailed study of the communications that take place, but also requires that these be set within the pattern of perceptions and intentions that the various actors bring to the situation, for it is these which give the talk and the other actions the meanings they have. A concern with communication also requires that the researcher looks at more than speech, for there are other non verbal kinds of communication taking place which only direct observation or videotaping can pick up. In short, the talk that takes place has a crucial role in promoting (or preventing) learning, but to understand what that role is we need to interpret the talk both within the context of the total setting in which it occurs, and within the context of the prior experiences and intentions of all the actors involved.

Mercer suggests that when this notion of context is given its full weight, it has three important implications for how we view computers and learning. One is that it implies that the process of learning about or through computers is about the context within which the computer is being used. It is not therefore primarily about the relationship between learner and machine, or even between learner and the software being used. Another is that to understand what children are learning through using a computer we may need to understand the history of the teaching-and-learning relationship within which that use took place. Finally, an emphasis upon context emphasises the potential role of the physical outputs of the computer, such as the screen display or print-outs, as concrete representations of thought and action that can be used by teachers and learners to help develop the sort of shared understanding that a communicative theory sees as being at the heart of the learning process.

Mercer then goes on to consider the implications of accepting a Vygotskyan stance for the account one might give of the role of the teacher. He sees the teacher as a potentially crucial support to learners, although not, of course, one that is always successful. The teacher's task is to provide that level of support that will enable the learner to internalise the external knowledge that is being presented, and to convert it into a tool to be used to gain increased control of his or her situation. In this sense, the teacher's task is to increase progressively the learner's autonomy, not (as in radically child-centred approaches) to assume its prior existence, or (as in unreflective teacher-directed approaches) to stifle it through excessive levels of social control. On this view, teachers who wish to respect their pupil's freedom do so not by refusing to intervene in the learning process, but by continually trying to reduce their intervention to the minimum that is compatible with promoting the long-term goal of complete autonomy for the pupil.

Central to Mercer's development of Vygotsky's position is a distinction between what one might call adult knowledge and classroom or educational knowledge. The latter is a version of the former, but reinterpreted by teachers and by curriculum resource designers, in ways that it is hoped will make it more accessible to pupils. The problem is that this attempt may inadvertently produce instead a misconception in pupils' minds about what acquiring real knowledge actually involves. This implies that the aim should be to make pedagogy and the technological equipment as transparent as possible, thus enabling pupils to master adult forms of enquiry and learning as directly as they can manage at any given time.

COLLABORATIVE LEARNING WITH COMPUTERS

In Chapter 4 Paul Light discusses another aspect of computer supported learning. If learning is a social activity in Mercer's sense, then it does not, of course, follow automatically that the people involved must be a teacher and a learner. Collaborative learning, in which pupils help each other to learn, offers another possibility. What then might the computer have to offer in those situations?

Light reviews a range of research that indicates that groups working with computers can be assisted in their learning. He considers the possibility that this may be because individuals can often see different aspects of a problem, and so between them come to a more comprehensive view of it. The act of having to verbalise one's ideas for others in a group too may actually help the speaker to crystallise his or her thoughts. He points out that quite what counts as collaboration is not self-evident, and that factors such as levels of provision and the sort of ground rules set for collaborating may have some effect on outcomes.

In considering such possibilities Light refers both to observational studies of broadly the kind recommended by Mercer, and also controlled experiments. The research he draws upon also includes both qualitative and quantitative studies. This raises an interesting problem, for the assumption behind a pragmatic approach of this sort might be taken to be that all these different kinds of research can produce results that can in some sense be aggregated to enable us to reach an overall conclusion. This would stand in strong contrast to Mercer's view that it is really only the qualitative, observationally centred methods that can produce significant understanding. In fact Light's position is not simply that these results can all be aggregated into a single account that is stronger than its individual parts; rather he argues that all of these results should be treated by teachers as indications of possibilities, and as stimuli to re-evaluate their own work. Such re-evaluations could, of course, take the form of conducting the sort of qualitative observation and analysis that Mercer supports. This suggests a distinctive methodological position, different from both the pure action research model, and from the classical quantitative approach in which qualitative observation forms the informal pilot stage from which clear and testable hypotheses are derived for explicit testing using experimental or other structured methods. The model offered is one where the quantitative research uncovers surprising patterns that are themselves the spur to qualitative study directed towards revealing their real significance, if any.

Another theme of the chapter is the importance of computer supported collaborative learning as a way of delivering the learning outcomes emphasised by more traditional views of education but by methods that embody some of the socially oriented process values of groupwork and cooperation emphasised by progressives. Computers, in short, offer a way of making the aspirations of progressive education a practicable reality for far more teachers and pupils than they at present are, and at the same time producing clear learning results. For different reasons this would be a strategy that would help resolve some of the dilemmas and conflicts that face progressive teachers in both the States and Britain today. In particular, it may offer the beginnings of an acceptable way out of what Mercer calls the 'Teacher's Dilemma'; namely how teachers both achieve externally set goals and do so by learner-centred methods.

THE TEACHER'S ROLE: LEADER OR FACILITATOR?

In the early chapters, especially Chapter 3, the role of the teacher in computer supported learning has been mentioned, but only in fairly general terms. In Chapter 5 Eunice Fisher considers the matter in more detail, exploring in effect the Teacher's Dilemma to which we have already referred.

She argues that the arrival of the computer is likely to change the teacher's approach to managing learning, and in particular the degree of control the teacher exercises over lesson content. She points out that the teacher's role is changed when computers are used, and that this often involves a move towards a more facilitative and less controlling style of working. Some of the evidence for this is discussed, ranging from the teacher self-reports that have emerged from the PALM Project, to systematic observations carried out by Rosemary Fraser and her colleagues. She concludes that if it is the case that truly effective learning takes place within a genuine sharing of experience without input from a more knowledgeable source, then teachers can either stand back and leave children to explore situations that allow them some degree of freedom, or seek to cultivate situations in which teacher and pupils are genuinely fellow learners. She points out that while computers are not essential for either of these two roles to be taken up, the computer can help by providing some of the structuring needed, rather than this being done by the teacher. Also, of course, many computer programs present tasks to which the teacher does not know the answer, thus enabling him or her to become a genuine co-learner, at least for some part of the activity. Again, computer networks that link pupils with others outside their school or even their country expose the pupils to the views of others who may be potentially powerful counterweights to the authority of their own teacher's interpretations. For the teacher wishing to promote independence, this situation can be exploited to encourage both individual and collaborative learning.

A question which arises here is whether effective learning really does require avoiding input from a more knowledgeable source. Presumably one form of collaborative learning is really not much different from teacher led problem solving, for an expert pupil may take on the teacher role instead. If this is not the case, where does the knowledge come from from within the pupil group to solve the problem, and how do pupils establish that they have

achieved an adequate solution without some form of reference to someone
or something outside the group? One answer to those questions might be
that this is precisely the contribution of the computer, namely to supply facts
or evidence against which the group can test their assumptions or hypotheses. Indeed that is how simulations, databases and spelling checkers,
for instance, can be, and often are, used. But what then has become of the
group's independence if they take the computer's answer as definitive? Is this
not just replacing one form of dependence by another?

EXTENDING THE THEORY: ACCESS TO LEARNING AS AN ILLUSTRATIVE ISSUE

All the psychological theories of learning discussed so far concern themselves with how learning (and at least by implication, teaching) are best
promoted. This question of the efficiency of learning and teaching is a very
important one, but it is not the only aspect of classroom activities that a
practice focused theory must address. How teachers teach involves
questions that extend beyond simply maximising learning. A full theory of
computer supported teaching and learning would have to include, for
instance, a moral assessment of possible teaching and learning activities and
a philosphical consideration of the conceptions of knowledge that underpin
each approach. Some analysis of the influences beyond the classroom and
their effects upon what takes place would also be needed.

In a single book no such comprehensive treatment is possible. What can
be done is to lay down an illustrative marker for future work by demonstrating the importance of some of these additional factors in understanding
some major classroom problem. The one chosen for discussion is what
influences the distribution of computer supported learning opportunities
within classrooms. If teachers are to make considered decisions on matters
of equitable access, they need first to be aware of how such access is at
present distributed, and what the reasons for, and effects of, that distribution
might be. In Chapter 6 Eunice Fisher addresses these matters.

As she points out, the first (but not the last) obstacle to gaining such
learning is to have limited access to computers at all. She presents evidence
from both Britain and the United States which shows that schools vary
greatly in their pupil-computer ratios. These differences, at least in the
United States, are correlated with school size, the wealth of the locality and
the ratio of black to white pupils. In the UK the picture seems to be fairly
similar, in so far as evidence is available to judge.

However there is also the issue of inequalities of access within schools.
Here there is some evidence that boys get more use of computers than girls,
despite increasing efforts by many teachers to find ways of avoiding this. A
less easily visible factor (in the United States at least) is that when computers
are given to schools where poorer children are in the majority they tend to

be used more for rote drill and practice activities than for cognitive enrichment, presumably because it is assumed that poorer children will be less likely to be able to use more open-ended software.

Gender differences affect not only how much time children may get at the computer; Fisher points out that what boys and girls are likely to gain from the computer depends in part upon the style of working adopted; with girls in particular likely to gain more from collaborative working than from individual use. Children with special needs too may find computers a great help in the classroom, especially where specifically designed hardware and software is available to them. The level of basic skills in computer use is another potential obstacle to learning, but Fisher indicates that this varies greatly from program to program, as they do not all require the same level of competence at the keyboard.

SOFTWARE: AN UNDERESTIMATED VARIABLE?

There is also a more general problem about the contribution of the computer that is not really addressed in Part I. Mercer points out that when pupils use a computer program they are interacting with a hidden teacher, namely the program designer. But not all programs are the same, just as not all teachers are. Indeed, different programs may well be based, as is made clear in Chapter 2, upon quite different conceptions of education and learning. If so, what software is being used must make rather a lot of difference to all these issues about the teacher's role, the possibilities for collaboration and so forth. Yet throughout Part I the effect of 'the computer' on a classroom activity or an experimental situation is, for all practical purposes, treated as being generic, rather than program specific. While the program used cannot dictate the learning and teaching that takes place, it can certainly affect it in various ways. If the teacher-proof program is a chimera, so too is the program-proof computer user, whether the user be pupil or teacher. This raises the important possibility that many of the effects of computer use described in Part I may be effects only obtainable with particular kinds of software. If so, the overall interpretations given in Chapters 3, 4, and 5, aggregating as they do research results based upon the use of a variety of programs, may be less secure and generally applicable than they seem. More radically still, a communicative theory of computer-supported learning may look less than universally applicable when explicitly assessed against a wide range of situations and software. To check these possibilities, therefore, Part II reworks many of the topics explored in Part I, but treats the nature of the software used as a potential major variable.

REFERENCE

Bruner, J. (1986) *Actual Minds, Possible Worlds*, London, Harvard University Press.

Chapter 2

Theories of learning and information technology

Ann Jones and Neil Mercer

INTRODUCTION

In any form of teaching, assumptions are made about the kind of learning that the teacher hopes will take place, and about the process of learning. In other words the teacher has a model of learning, although it may not be explicit: indeed the teacher may not be aware of it herself. What are the assumptions about teaching and learning which lie behind educational programs? What kind of learning is envisaged by the designer of a particular piece of software? In this chapter we shall look at the relationship between theories of learning and educational software. In order to do this we need to look at some of the theories of learning which are relevant: behaviourism, constructivism and 'socio-cultural' theory, derived from the work of Vygotsky.

THE LEGACY OF BEHAVIOURISM AND THE TEACHING MACHINE

The *behaviourist* view of learning focuses on behaviour and its modifications rather than hidden mental processes, and is an approach to studying learning which has been and remains very influential. Researchers who take this approach to learning are all interested in studying behaviour which can be observed and measured: where one set of observable conditions (stimuli) can be related to another set of observable conditions (responses). Behaviourist theories of learning, therefore, do not attempt to account for any mental processes which occur in learning. The emphasis is on what the learner does, the response that he or she is led to give. Any mental processes that go on in between (e.g. thinking or planning) are not considered to be legitimate areas of study because they cannot be directly observed.

In our short consideration of this view of learning, only the work of the American psychologist B. F. Skinner will be considered, as his approach is the most relevant, and he has been the most influential of all behaviourist theorists. Skinner believed that people can learn more effectively if their environment is carefully controlled. He began by studying spontaneous behaviour in animals, such as pecking in pigeons, and was interested in questions such as what makes an animal repeat a particular behaviour? He developed the principles of operant conditioning, the basic law of which states: if the occurrence of an operant is followed by the presentation of a reinforcing stimulus, the strength is increased (Skinner, 1938). Put more simply, this means that if a behaviour is reinforced, it is more likely to happen again. The 'reinforcer' used in animal training is usually food.

According to Skinner's law of operant conditioning, the essential principle is that the correct or desired behaviour is reinforced. No action is taken after incorrect or undesired behaviour, and this behaviour will gradually disappear, or in Skinner's terms, be extinguished. In this way, by reinforcing pigeons with food when they peck at a particular place, or make a particular movement, they can be trained to exhibit quite complex behaviours. This is done by a procedure known as shaping. In this procedure the pigeon is in a piece of apparatus called a 'Skinner box'. The essential components of the box are a small display panel that the animal can be trained to peck at and a food container in which a small pellet of food is delivered. The display panel where the pigeon pecks can be changed: for example different shapes can be randomly displayed. At the beginning of the procedure the pigeon receives food for pecking in the vicinity of the right area. At the next stage the pigeon has to peck at the right spot. Once the pigeon is doing this it can be trained to do other things such as discriminating between a circle and a square.

To do this, different shapes would be displayed in random order, but this time the pigeon would only be reinforced for pecking when a square is being displayed, and eventually it will only peck at the square. So the shaping procedure involves breaking the desired performance into little bits and reinforcing them first in isolation and then together; integrating the whole performance.

A very common example of shaping in everyday life is in obedience training in dogs. To get a dog to come to the owner and sit in front of them the process is usually broken down into a number of stages. The dog is taught to sit by being gently pushed into the sitting position and rewarded with either food or praise. At the next stage he must sit without being touched to get the reinforcement. Then he must stay in the sitting position until he is told he can move. The dog is trained to come to the owner in a similar way and then the two procedures are combined.

Although procedures like this work well for specific behaviours in specific situations, they do not always work so well in other situations, as anyone who has tried these techniques with animals or children will know. Also, more complex behaviour is hard to analyse in this way. There are also often problems in 'extinguishing' desired behaviour, i.e. stopping it. Skinner would argue that this is because the contingencies for reinforcement haven't been designed accurately enough. What this means is that the process of breaking down the behaviour into its components and rewarding each desired component has not been carried out carefully enough. Or perhaps we have failed to see that undesired behaviour is being rewarded in some way that we haven't realised. According to Skinner, with the 'correct' environment, the desired behaviour can be produced. In terms of human learning, the technology that provided such control became possible with the advent of computers and Skinner embodied his principles in the early teaching machines which provided a way of mechanising his operant conditioning techniques. The principle was that the teaching material should be organised to maximise the probability of correct responses which could then be reinforced. There are three basic steps. First of all some material is presented to the student. The student then responds, for example by filling in missing spaces. The program then informs the student whether the response is correct (which it should be if the program is well designed according to Skinner's principles). The program then moves on to the next frame.

Teaching machines had some very ardent supporters, but nevertheless they went out of use fairly rapidly. However, other associated techniques have been developed from this starting point, and are thought to be successful – for example objectives and task analysis in the design of instructional materials owe their origins to Skinner's view that learning could be rigorously analysed. Behaviourist ideas can still be found behind many programs, where the emphasis is on the relationship between a stimuli and a response. Very few of these are truly Skinnerian in that most programs which are behaviourist in origin are branching programs which give information on both correct and incorrect responses, and emphasise the 'individualisation' possible by using such programs.

Consider as an example the program Posneg, which was designed to help students understand how negative numbers work (Laurillard, 1990). One of the options in the program represents positive and negative numbers displayed along a number line, and a puffin which acts as a pointer by hopping along the number line to rest on a particular number (see Figure 2.1 below). This is one particular view of how to add and subtract negative numbers where positive numbers are interpreted as steps forward, a minus operation is turning to face the other way and negative numbers are steps backward. So a sum like $(+ 5) - (-3) = + 8$ can be viewed as a number of stages as the puffin hops in one direction and then turns and hops backwards and ends up pointing to $+ 8$.

Figure 2.1 shows the screen after an incorrect answer has been given to the sum $(+ 6) - (+ 6)$. The program has now given the correct answer, and has also given an explanation of the correct answer which has been built up step by step. The puffin responds to each step by changing direction or moving along the number line as appropriate.

How does such a program fit with operant conditioning principles? The design of Posneg is consistent with operant conditioning principles in some ways and not in others. The puffin hopping along the number-line can be

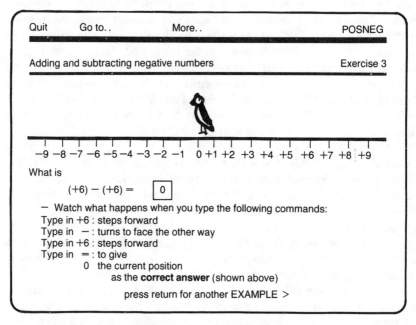

Figure 2.1 Initial screen display for Posneg program

seen as reinforcing correct answers, and so can the comment. The material is presented in small steps (in fact there is little use of new material).

However in other ways it departs quite drastically from Skinnerian principles. Wrong answers receive a detailed explanation, but according to Skinnerian principles no feedback should be given when incorrect responses are made. However the puffin was not intended to be just a reinforcement, but to give a concrete illustration of abstract ideas: a notion which is much closer to the constructivist view of learning (which we will look at next). The point here is that although this program was not written by a behaviourist, we can identify certain elements which can be viewed as behaviourist. Operant conditioning is still very influential in educational psychology generally and especially in dealing with disruptive and hyperactive children and also in forms of behaviour therapy where the objective is to eliminate some behaviours and to encourage others. However, it has been, and still is, widely criticised. One of the main criticisms is that it is based on isolated events which happen to be amenable to being analysed in this way, and works by reinforcing specific fixed behaviours. However, humans are not often in situations which require them to produce specific fixed behaviour: rather we are constantly confronted with novel situations, and we are very good at producing novel responses to them. Language is a good example of this. We don't learn to produce fixed responses; rather, each sentence of any reasonable length that is uttered is completely novel, which suggests that we are learning abstract rules or principles rather than responses. This is even true of animals in Skinnerian situations. If a hungry rat is left to explore a maze with no food or water, it will subsequently run straight to the food box when it is placed in the maze. So it seems as though there is some kind of mental represent- ation of the environment being formed, rather than a simple stimulus response association. In the next section we look at an approach which is interested in such mental representation rather than the behaviour itself.

CONSTRUCTIVISM, PAPERT AND LOGO

One of the best examples of the influence of a particular view of learning on the design of educational software can be seen in the work of Seymour Papert, and this section will look at the work and ideas of Papert and the constructivist approach which inspired him. Papert's book *Mindstorms* published in 1980, which gives an account of his vision of how computers might be used in education, using the Logo language as an example, has been one of the most influential books published in this area in the 1980s. When Papert wrote the book Logo was not a serious possibility for most schools, because it was not available on the computers which schools had in use. Since that time, it has, of course, become one of the most widely known, and used, pieces of educational software. Papert worked with Jean Piaget (1896–1980) in Geneva and some of Piaget's ideas are central to Papert's view of how computers can be used in education.

Piaget's approach has been termed *constructivist* because of the emphasis on the learner's construction of his or her understanding. Whereas in operant conditioning the emphasis is on the learner 'being shaped' by the instructor, (or computer) through selective reinforcement, here the learner is seen as an active participant, who, in the course of learning is structuring his or her experience and knowledge. Following Piaget, Papert views children as 'builders of their own intellectual structures'. Piaget emphasised the way in which knowledge is structured and organised, and the way in which these knowledge structures are changed in order for new information to be added to them, and how the child's perception of his or her experiences is itself modified to fit into these structures.

The idea of knowledge being structured is central to this view of learning. Piaget described knowledge as being structured in the form of schemata; a term previously used by the psychologist Bartlett in the 1930s. A schema can be thought of as a cognitive representation, or concept. It is an *abstract* representation which abstracts the main features of what is being repre- sented. So, for example, when children learn about the idea of what a dog is they develop a dog 'schema' which represents the important properties of a dog: e.g. that it has four legs, fur, a tail and barks. This schema then serves as a kind of prototype against which new animals can be matched. He uses the term *assimilation* to describe how new knowledge is incorporated into existing schemata. Schemata themselves may also change when new or incongruent events or experiences that cannot be assimilated into existing schemata occur. For example, a child's understanding of the category of animals called 'dog' may be based on the assumption that all dogs bark. Upon encountering for the first time a breed of dogs which don't bark, the schema must be changed to handle this new information. Such changes to the schemata are known as *accommodation*. This idea is at the heart of Piaget's account of children's development.

Within Piaget's theory, emphasis is not on the person's behaviour or their response to a situation (as it was in operant conditioning) but on their underlying understanding. Piaget was at least as interested in children's mis-constructions (mistakes and false beliefs) as he was in their correct responses, since these can be very revealing about the processes whereby children construct their understanding. He described a broad sequence of stages through which he saw children's thinking developing, from early 'sensori-motor' beginnings, through concrete reasoning in the early school years to abstract reasoning from adolescence.

According to a constructivist view, then, children learn by relating new experiences to their existing knowledge, which is itself derived from previous experiences. Papert lays out his philosophy of learning in *Mindstorms*. Essentially, he aims to provide a culture which helps to make abstract mathematical concepts simple and concrete so that the child can relate them to his or her existing knowledge. This will allow children either to assimilate Logo experience into their existing schemata, or use that experience to achieve accommodation and so make cognitive progress.

One metaphor which has been a strong influence on Papert's work is how children learn to talk, a process which happens without any formal, organised teaching or learning, and which is fostered by the environment. Papert went on to ask whether children would be more successful in learning mathematics if they could have access to 'Mathland' – 'a context which is to learning Maths what living in France is to learning French'.

Another model in Papert's mind was the way his own concrete experience of gears as a child helped to foster and develop mathematical thinking. From the time he was very young, he had been intensely interested in the gear box of cars, and especially the differential. Once he understood how gears worked, playing with gears became a favourite occupation, and led him into working out exactly how such systems such as the differential gear worked. Later, gears served as a model for abstract mathematical ideas:

I saw multiplication tables as gears, and my first brush with equations in two variables (e.g. $3x + 4y = 10$) immediately evoked the differential. By the time I had made a mental gear model of the relation between x and y, figuring how many teeth each gear needed, the equation had become a comfortable friend.

(Papert, 1980, pp. vi–vii)

The gears were therefore used to think about formal systems: they served as 'objects to think with'.

Papert sees the turtle in Logo as being an equivalent object to think with: something that helps to make the formal concrete. The idea is that through using the turtle in Logo children can explore mathematical shapes, and ideas. The need for the turtle, and Logo itself arises because, in Papert's view, although our culture is very rich in material which helps the child to develop certain aspects of mathematical and logical thinking (counting, conservation, reversibility) it is poor in providing materials to help the child develop other aspects of mathematics such as the ideas involved in geometry.

Logo can be viewed as both a programming language and as a tool for thinking, for problem solving: particularly in mathematics. It is a modular programming language which means that programming projects are subdivided into small pieces and a separate procedure is written for each piece. It is recursive: i.e. a procedure can be written to call itself, and this is one of Papert's 'powerful ideas' which Logo helps children to have access to. It is also extensible, which means that procedures defined by the user look and behave like primitives or built-in procedures. This also gives the user a lot of 'power'.

Logo was designed to provide an interesting entry point to mathematics. This entry point is, of course, turtle geometry.

There has also been considerable interest in Logo as a problem solving tool for language. Logo has a list-processing facility and has been used to develop tool kit programs with which children can explore the structure and meaning of language.

For example, Sharples (1978) developed a series of Poem programs which provided children with the means to generate 'poems'. They began with Poem1 which generates random strings of words. These were then classified according to parts of speech and given as input to Poem2. This program generates word strings to follow a syntactic pattern. Three boys who used the programs produced a number of syntax patterns including one to generate a Christmas poem:

XMAS

The present sparkles
The song shines
Hark xmas
And the heavenly tree flows sweetly near the decoration
Hark the glorious bell

Such computer-based language tools can be used as part of a series of activities in which children can generate and transform text by creating, choosing and comparing language.

Although Papert concentrated on using Logo for developing mathematical thinking, there has been a considerable amount of research on the use of Logo and other languages for developing language skills (e.g. Sharples, 1978) and much of this work stresses the importance of the child having control over such learning. One of Piaget's ideas which is central to Papert's work is the distinction between 'concrete' and 'formal' thinking. As Papert puts it:

> Concrete thinking is already well on its way by the time the child enters the first grade at age 6 and is consolidated in the following several years. Formal thinking does not develop until the child is almost twice as old, that is to say at age 12, give or take a year or two . . . Stated most simply, my conjecture is that the computer can concretize (and personalize) the formal . . . I believe that it can allow us to shift the boundary separating concrete and formal.
>
> (p. 21)

So whereas in operant conditioning teaching is central, here learning is viewed as central and teaching is a vehicle for creating the conditions and contents for children's self-motivated, self-directed learning. In fact, directed learning as suggested by operant conditioning is seen as harmful in that it is not based on understanding.

One issue raised by Papert's approach is that of resources. He does acknowledge that his vision requires a vast number of computers and for children to have a lot of exposure. If one's exposure to France was half an hour's conversation in the bar twice a week, the effect on learning French would be much less dramatic than constant conversation! Papert's view of learning Logo, and through Logo, maths and powerful thinking, has been criticised on a number of grounds. The need for a computer for each child and a very high exposure to Logo is one reason why teachers and researchers have felt it is not a feasible option. Moreover, it may not be desirable for children to spend so much time in 'Mathland'. What about 'Poetryland' or 'Artsland'? If the price for learning maths in this way is complete immersion in 'Mathland', it may be too high a price to pay. Where children have far less exposure to Logo, the evidence is that their learning gains are very modest (Pea and Kurland, 1984). In fact, partly *because* of the unavailability of a large number of machines, and partly because of the culture of primary schools, there has been very little exploration in the UK of individual children learning Logo in the way in which Papert discusses.

A further question concerns the role of the teacher in all this. In fact there is very little emphasis on the role of the teacher or even acknowledgement of the teacher in Papert's writing. The teacher helps create the right environment and gives the children the right tools and stands back. Although Papert does acknowledge the value of crucial interventions in *Mindstorms*, there are very few mentions of the teacher: the emphasis is completely on the learner. Whilst some people have welcomed the emphasis of constructivism on learning as opposed to the emphasis of operant conditioning on teaching, the absence of any real consideration of the teacher's role is problematic for educational settings. There has been little evidence of the 'spontaneous' learning that Papert reports outside Papert's own work, which suggests that the teacher's role is important: in fact there is some support for the argument that children who learn Logo only learn a modest amount and never master concepts such as recursion. Learning does not occur in a social vacuum, so we need to look at the role that the teacher does and can play. One project which has investigated the potential of Logo for teaching mathematics and has taken into account the role of the teacher as well as pupils working collaboratively is the Logo maths project (Hoyles and Sutherland, 1989).

The main focus of this project was to discover whether, and in what circumstances, Logo could facilitate pupils' understanding of mathematics. The researchers found that it was possible for pupils to have more involvement in, and take more control over, their mathematical learning, provided particular conditions were met, which included the opportunity for pupils to work collaboratively with the computer. The particular role taken by the teacher and the nature of the teacher's interventions were also found to be important. These issues of collaborative learning and the teacher's role and interventions will be discussed more fully in Chapters 4 and 5.

COMMUNICATION AND LEARNING

Both the behaviourist and Papert's view of learning embody a strongly *individualistic* conception of learning which has dominated learning theory and educational practice in this field. We will consider later some ways in which computer-related activities may differ from other kinds of classroom work; but as far as it embodies a model of the learner as a solitary striver for understanding, it has a lot in common with most other areas of educational theory and practice.

But you may ask what is meant by an 'individualistic' theory of learning? We mean by this an explanation of how people learn which is predominantly, if not exclusively, formed in terms of individual actions and/or individual thoughts; in behaviourist terms, how an individual's behaviour is modified through the impact of 'the environment'; in Piagetian terms, how an intelligent organism adapts to the complexities of this world. In British education, one can also see the influence of a third individualistic theoretical position – that associated with the notions of inherited intelligence and 'IQ', and which is derived from the work of psychologists like Burt and Eysenck (e.g. Eysenck, 1953). Proponents of this approach argue that the relative success or failure of individuals – or even whole social groups – in performing the learning tasks they encounter in school are largely determined by the inherited structures of individual brains. These three theoretical positions may have little in common beyond their individualistic perspective on learning; but given such diverse support for individualism, it is not surprising that it permeates educational theory and practice. Indeed there are reasons for believing that the very new approach to the study of learning called 'cognitive science' is no less individualistic than these earlier approaches (Newman, Griffin and Cole, 1989).

One might now well say, so what is wrong with an individualistic perspective on learning? Surely learning – effective learning, at least – is usually a solitary exercise? And surely the measure of any learning is what ends up in some individual's head? Is this not as true for learning computer skills, for instance, as for anything else? Learning may seem a solitary endeavour, but in practice nearly all learning (of computer skills or anything else) is in some sense a social experience: some other person – colleague, tutor, manual author – is involved as well as the learner. And success or failure in the various learning tasks can be at least partially attributed to the effectiveness of the teaching you received. The weakness of individualistic models of learning is that they don't take proper account of the social quality of most learning. Their psychological models of the learning process only really deal with the thoughts and activities of one individual.

This kind of social perspective leads to the view that what is going on in successful classrooms is not best characterised as 'learning', but rather as 'teaching-and-learning'. This then suggests that the development of our understanding of the use of computers in education requires a theory and analysis of teaching-and-learning, not just a theory of learning. This applies not only to classroom processes, but also to the design and choice of educational software. For example, in his critique of the educational software program Climate, Self (1985) identifies as one of its major failings the fact that the designers (the 'hidden teachers' behind a program which purports to give students opportunity for autonomous learning!) do not make clear to students some important assumptions about the knowledge built into the program and how the students are meant to use it. Students may thus go astray in activities through no fault of their own. Someone's 'failure to learn' may be better described as someone else's 'failure to teach'.

Outside the peculiar circumstances of the examination room, human problems are commonly solved through collaborative effort. Moreover, much learning, not least in relation to information technology, consists of the sharing of knowledge. When anyone learns word processing, they come to possess knowledge which others (the software designers) created and shared with them. There is now a subset of our cultural resources called 'word-processing skills'. The learner may then go on to use their acquired skills to share other kinds of information, through print-out or, as discussed in Chapter 9, electronic mail. Returning now to the question of measures of learning, perhaps one measure of successful learning is that two or more people manage to share their knowledge and understanding, so that a new cultural resource is created which is greater than the knowledge and understanding that any of the individuals hitherto possessed.

Vygotsky and socio-cultural theory

Anyone looking around for a theoretical framework to accommodate such a communicative, culturally orientated conception of human learning will not, we believe, find much to satisfy them in Piaget or Skinner. They might, however, find much to interest them in the work of the Russian psychologist L. S. Vygotsky. When Vygotsky died in 1934 at the age of 37, his ideas on child development and learning had already had a profound influence on those working with him. However, these ideas were apparently so much at odds with the dominant, officially sanctioned – and individualistic – learning theories of Pavlov that his publications were banned by the Soviet state. His ideas filtered through to the west in only a piecemeal fashion (e.g. the first translation of his book *Thought and Language* appeared in 1962), and they had little impact on a European developmental psychology dominated by Piaget's theories. Recently, however, much more of Vygotsky's work has been translated and his ideas have now begun to be used as the basis for developing new understandings about teaching and learning (see Bruner, 1985; Wertsch, 1985; Edwards and Mercer, 1987; Newman, Griffin and Cole, 1989). The new approach which is being developed from his work is known by various names: 'neo-Vygotskian theory', 'cultural psychology', 'communicative learning theory' have all been used, with 'socio-cultural theory' probably the most common. These are still early days in the neo-Vygotskian era, however, and while the theories of Skinner, Piaget and other individualistic theorists have strongly influenced software design, there is little evidence of socio-cultural theory having yet influenced the educational software design community.

There is no space in this chapter to go into great depth or detail about Vygotsky's work. The relevance of his work to our topic can be summarised by saying that it provides the basis for a 'communicative' perspective on the process of teaching and learning, a way of observing and analysing that process which contrasts with those more 'individualistic' approaches which have informed much of the development of computer-assisted learning. What follows is a brief account of how Vygotsky's approach differs from individualistic approaches in general, and Piaget's (perhaps the most significant influence on theory and practice in British education) in particular. Our intention is to make clear why a 'communicative' approach has particular value and relevance for understanding how teachers and children can work together with computers.

Vygotsky emphasised the social aspects of cognition in two main ways. First, he pointed to the vital role that language plays in cognitive development, problem solving and learning. He proposed that acquiring a language enables a child to think in new ways, so that a new cognitive 'tool' for making sense of the world becomes available. 'Children solve practical tasks with the help of their speech, as well as their eyes and hands' (Vygotsky, 1978, p. 26). Secondly, Vygotsky did not construe the learner as the 'lone organism' of the behavourists or Piagetians, acting on and adapting to some impersonal 'environment'. Instead, 'Human learning presupposes a specific social nature and a process by which children grow into the intellectual life of those around them' (1978, p 89). He also conceptualises children's learning capability in an essentially interactive manner, through his concept of the *zone of proximal development*. This is an area of cognitive activity beyond those tasks which a child can successfully complete individually, but including those tasks which a child can succeed at with some 'cognitive support' from an adult or a more capable peer. It represents an area of growth, and so stresses not only the part which others can play in an individual's development, but also the essentially social nature of cognitive change (see Newman, Griffin and Cole, 1989, for a full discussion of this concept and its application).

Vygotsky thus also emphasised two important cognitive functions of human language. First, it imparts a unique quality to human thought. Secondly, it provides a medium for teaching and learning. Human knowledge and thought are themselves therefore fundamentally cultural, deriving their distinctive properties from the nature of human communication. It is only a short inferential leap from the ideas in the last paragraph to the following conclusion: Vygotsky's theory can accommodate the role of 'teacher' as someone who is an active, communicative participant in learning, and not someone who simply provides rich 'learning environments' for children's own discoveries (*à la* Piaget) or reinforces appropriate behaviour if and when it occurs (in the behaviourist mode).

While, like many valuable insights into human life, Vygotsky's assertion of learning as communicative may seem to have a certain self-evident quality, its acceptance could have significant implications for our conceptions of (1) the role of the *computer* in the learning process, and (2) the role of the *teacher* in relationship to the use of computers in this classroom. To take the first of these, a communicative approach might place less emphasis on the relationship an individual learner has with the computer (with the computer viewed as either an impersonal tool for 'autonomous learning' or as a surrogate, robot teacher) and more on the computer as a medium through which a teacher and learner can communicate. Cole and Griffin (1987) elaborate on this comparison as follows:

Classroom Organization and Computers

To make clear the special relevance of computers for reordering the contexts of education (and thereby, the motivational structure of instruction), we will contrast two metaphors for computer-student interaction. The first assumes that the computer is an agent, operating as a 'partner in dialogue.' This view implies that the student-computer system can be viewed as an analogue to the student-teacher system with the computer replacing the teacher. Within the framework provided by this perspective, it is important to look at the computer's potential for providing structured hints, well-timed feedback, and a wealth of factual knowledge. It is this metaphor that underlies the bulk of research on computers and education at the present time. It leads naturally to dreams of a 'teacher-proof' curriculum.

A second metaphor, the one that will undergird this discussion, is of the computer as a 'medium', not replacing people, but reorganizing interactions among people, creating new environments in which children can be educated and grow by discovering and gaining access to the world around them. This metaphor emphasizes the potential of computers for reorganizing instruction within the classroom and for making possible the extension of education beyond the classroom. It involves teachers in a new system of possibilities and social demands in the education of their students. It often challenges teachers' prior learning, requiring the acquisition of new skills (and extra time on their task of staying abreast of their students). [. . .] successful introducers of computers into classrooms are as much orchestrators of their students' activities as they are occupants of the usual role in a teacher-led group. Certainly other educational innovations (e.g. cooperative grouping strategies, activity-based curricula for science and mathematics) have called for similar role redefinitions for teachers. However, in those other cases role specifications were an overt and articulated element of the innovation; with the introduction of computers into classrooms, the specification of the teacher's role is easy to overlook, but we believe it is essential to arranging for the attainment of learning goals. Effective computer-using teachers are 'Adaptive Experts' (Hatano and Kokima, 1984) at the process of teaching/learning on computers. Through proper combinations of software, hardware, and social support, systems of clear excellence can be obtained for a wide variety of students. But the obstacles to satisfying the hopes for clear success are formidable.

(Cole and Griffin, 1987, pp. 45–7)

Cole and Griffin support their assertion of the importance of teachers as 'orchestrators' of computer-based activities by citing some recent research on patterns of computer use in American classrooms. In this research,

Shavelson *et al.* (1984) observed the activities of 60 primary and secondary teachers who were considered exponents of 'good practice' in computer use, and also interviewed the teachers about their methods. They described 'orchestrating' teachers as those who:

> stressed both cognitive and basic-skill goals, as well as microcomputer use as a goal in and of itself, used a variety of instructional modes to meet these goals (e.g. drill and practice, tutorials, simulations, micro-worlds, games); they integrated the content of microcomputer-based instruction with the on-going curriculum, and coordinated microcomputer activities with other instructional activities; changed their uses based on feedback from students; and, not surprisingly, were evaluated as most successful in their use of microcomputer-based instruction during field visits by our staff.
>
> (Shavelson *et al.*, 1984, p. vii)

Elsewhere, Griffin and Cole (with Newman) offer a more specific comparison between the 'traditional' computer-assisted instruction approach to the organisation of classroom learning and that generated by a Vygotskian framework (which they refer to here as the 'ZPD approach', referring to Vygotsky's concept of the 'zone of proximal development'):

> The two conceptions, the traditional view and the ZPD, result in very different ways of presenting tasks to learners. In the traditional approach there is a tendency to break the work down into pieces that can be learned without reference to the forward direction of the sequence. There is no need or opportunity to understand the goal of the sequence while learning the components. Thus there is a tendency to emphasize rote learning of lower level components. The ZPD approach has an opposite emphasis since the task that is the goal is being accomplished interactively from the beginning . . . There is always an opportunity, therefore, for the child's actions to be made meaningful for the child in terms of the goal of the sequence.
>
> (Newman, Griffin and Cole, 1989, pp. 153–4)

The role of the teacher in the IT classroom will be examined in more detail in Chapters 3, 5 and 6 of this book. The main point we can make here is that socio-cultural theory draws particular attention to the ways in which talk and joint activity are used by teachers and learners to share knowledge. As mentioned earlier, there is still very little in the way of educational software development which shows the influence of this theory. One promising exception is the work of McMahon and O'Neill, described in Chapter 3. Another (of which we have less direct knowledge) is work in the USA by Newman and Goldman (1987), who have created a classroom environment, called 'Earth Lab', in which children can use computers in the same sorts of way that scientific researchers do, to collect data and then collectively analyse it and communicate their findings. One of the aims of their project is to simulate conditions for scientific communication, so that children are able to take on active, dialogic, roles in the process of scientific reasoning. Collaborative structures are built into activities, so that, for example, databases are created by different sets of children in a class providing elements which contribute to the 'jigsaw' picture of the object of enquiry.

Crook (1991) has argued that what he calls 'cultural psychology' offers one of the strongest theoretical bases for the evaluation of computer-based educational activity. He points out that most evaluative studies of computer-based activity are, like most of the practice they seek to evaluate, based uncritically on an individualistic model of learning. In fact, in most British classrooms, joint activity, whereby pupils work in pairs or groups with one computer, is the norm. Socio-cultural theory appears to offer the conceptual framework most capable of dealing with this reality.

CONCLUSION

Constraints of space in this chapter have not allowed us to deal in any depth with the theories we described. However, we hope that we have been able to show that the relationship between educational computing and theories of learning is both interesting and problematic. We also hope we have shown that particular theoretical approaches to learning have different and distinct implications for the ways educational software is designed, for the way classroom activities are organised, and for the ways computer-based learning in the classroom is evaluated.

REFERENCES

Bruner, J. (1985) 'Vygotsky: a historical and conceptual perspective', in Wertsch, J. V. (ed.) *Culture, Communication and Cognition: Vygotskian perspectives*, Cambridge, Cambridge University Press.
Cole, M. and Griffin, P. (eds) (1987) *Contextual Factors in Education: improving science and mathematics education for minorities and women*, Madison, Wisconsin, Center for Education Research.
Colman, A. M. (1988) *Facts, Fallacies and Frauds in Psychology*, London, Hutchinson.
Crook, C. (1991) 'Computers in the zone of proximal development: implications for evaluation', *Educational Computing*, 17(1).
Edwards, D. and Mercer, N. (1987) *Common Knowledge: the development of understanding in the classroom*, London, Methuen.
Eysenck, H. (1953) *Uses and Abuses of Psychology*, Harmondsworth, Penguin.
Hatano, G. and Kokima, R. (1984) 'An expert's skills for using a Japanese word-processor', paper presented at the Joint American/Japanese Consortium on Problems of Cognition and Learning, Tokyo, September.
Hoyles, C. and Sutherland, R. (1989) *Logo Mathematics in the Classroom*, London, Routledge.
Laurillard, D. M. (1990) 'Unit 2: how computers can assist learning', in *EH232 Computers and Learning*, Milton Keynes, Open University.

Newman, D. and Goldman, S. V. (1987) 'Earth Lab: a local network for collaborative classroom science', *Journal of Educational Technology Systems*, 15(3): 237–47.

Newman, D., Griffin, P. and Cole, M. (1989) *The Construction Zone: working for cognitive change in school*, Cambridge, Cambridge University Press.

Papert, S. (1980) *Mindstorms: children, computers and powerful ideas*, Brighton, Harvester Press.

Pea, R. and Kurland, M. (1984) 'The cognitive effects of learning computer programming', *New Ideas in Psychology*, 2: 137–68.

Self, J. M. (1985) *Microcomputers in Education: a critical appraisal of software*, Brighton, Harvester-Wheatsheaf.

Sharples, M. (1978) *Poetry from Logo*, DAI Working Paper no. 30, Department of Artificial Intelligence, University of Edinburgh.

Shavelson, R., Winkler, J. Stasz, C., Feibel, W., Robyn, A. and Shaha, S. (1984) '"Successful" teachers' patterns of micro-computer-based mathematics and science instruction', report to the National Institute of Education, Santa Monica, Calif., Rand Corporation.

Skinner, B. F. (1938) *The Behavior of Organisms: an experimental analysis*, New York, Appleton-Century-Crofts.

Vygotsky, L. S. (1962) *Thought and Language*, Cambridge, Mass., MIT Press.

Vygotsky, L. S. (1978) *Mind in Society*, Cambridge, Mass., Harvard University Press.

Wertsch, J. V. (1985) *Vygotsky and the Social Formation of Mind*, Cambridge, Mass., Harvard University Press.

Chapter 3

Computer-based activities in classroom contexts

Neil Mercer

INTRODUCTION

This chapter offers an analysis of the process of teaching and learning, with special reference to the use of computers in the classroom. It is an analysis which is based on the observational study of the process of teaching and learning carried out by myself and colleagues in recent years (e.g. Mercer and Edwards, 1981; Edwards and Mercer, 1986; Edwards and Maybin, 1987; Edwards and Mercer, 1987; Mercer, Edwards and Maybin, 1988; Edwards and Mercer, 1989; Edwards, 1990; Mercer, 1991, 1992). This research has not been predominantly concerned with IT in the classroom: indeed, until very recently observations of teachers and children using computers have formed only a small part of our data, but we believe our examination of the role of *discourse* in the teaching and learning process has relevance to the whole curriculum and to most, if not all, activities in which teachers and children interact. I will focus here, then, on teacher-child discourse: consideration of discourse between children, as they work and learn together with computers, is left to others (Chapter 4 of this volume; see also Crook, 1987, 1991).

CLASSROOM COMMUNICATION OBSERVED

There are many kinds of observational educational research, and that in which I have been involved should not be taken as typical in its aims or analytic procedures. (See Walford, 1990, for a collection of first-hand accounts of a range of methods for doing educational research, including the methods described here.) Its methods are qualitative, not quantitative. That is, our observations and analysis do not yield numerical data of any kind. Instead, our method is to use the complete corpus of communicative interchanges in the classrooms we observe as data, and to analyse that data to draw conclusions about the nature and quality of the educational process taking place. Although this kind of research is sometimes called 'discourse analysis' it is not particularly concerned with linguistic forms and structures (as are some other kinds of discourse analysis – e.g. Sinclair and Coulthard,

1975; Stubbs, 1981, 1983). This kind of research painstakingly examines the *content* of classroom talk because the researchers believe it is there, in the interactions of the classroom, that education – good or bad, for better or worse – takes place.

Our 'observation' involves more than simply watching the lessons going on. Lessons were videotaped. All the talk in the recorded lessons is transcribed, and then the researchers watch the lessons right through two or more times, making notes on the transcripts about what was happening (action, gestures, equipment being used, etc.) in conjunction with the talk. The researchers also talk to the children and teachers involved in order to learn more about such things as what the teacher hopes to achieve from getting the children to do the activities, and what the children think is the point and purpose of lessons and what they feel they have learnt.

A central aim of this research is to examine how, through talk and joint activity, teachers and children can establish a shared understanding of educational knowledge. It is also concerned with some problematic aspects of that process, such as how misunderstandings arise, and how (if at all) they are resolved; how teachers guide children's talk and activities in directions which lead towards the 'official', established, curriculum-related ways of doing things (e.g. using scientific methods of investigation, employing formal methods for doing calculations) and describing them (e.g. using technical vocabulary, writing up English essays and scientific reports in the conventional manner).

Looking at an extract from some actual classroom talk may help to make the ideas in the last paragraph less abstract. Reproduced below is an extract from a computer graphics lesson. Here, the teacher and Susan (9 years old) are planning a Logo program on paper, before Susan keys it in. Try reading through the transcript just looking at what was said, and ignoring the 'context notes' in the right-hand column. How much sense can you make of what was said and done? Next, read it through again, this time reading the 'context notes' too. Do they help you make more sense of what was happening? How confident do you now feel about making sense of what was going on? Finally, read the account of what was going on, in the paragraph following the sequence. How completely do you now feel you understand what went on?

Sequence 1 Planning a Logo program

T: Now/which angle did you   *T leans forward and Susan*
         have to measure/let's have a   *gives her the paper.*
         look at that one. I notice that
         you've got all lines drawn out
         all over the place haven't you?

Susan: Mm.

T:	You've extended your lines/haven't you?	*T showing paper to whole group of 5 pupils.*
	Did you measure the angles in here?	*T points to one of the drawn hexagon's internal angles.*
Susan:	No.	
T:	No/which angles/you've got/let's see the angles.	*T and Susan examining diagram, pointing to parts of it as they speak.*
	Right one three seven/right one twenty.	
Susan:	One thirty yes.	
T:	One two eight/right one three eight/which angles are those?/Are those the angles/inside the hexagon/or are those the angles outside?	
Susan:	They/they're the bits where you go forward like that./Then you've got your arrow pointing that way./So you straighten it out and you go round and measure it/and go up to that angle.	*Susan pointing at number.*
T:	So which turn have you actually measured there? You've measured/you were pointing that way	
Susan:	Mm.	
T:	and you had wanted to go that way./ yes?	
Susan:	Yes.	
T:	So you've measured that turn/is that right/from there to there?	

(Edwards and Mercer, 1987, p. 66)

In Sequence 1, the teacher and Susan are discussing Susan's planned set of instructions for drawing a regular hexagonal shape (i.e. with six equal sides) on the screen with certain pre-measured angles. Anyone familiar with Logo will recognise instructions such as 'right 120', which tells the computer to turn the cursor (the 'arrow' here; in some versions it is a 'turtle') to the right (clockwise) through an angle of 120 degrees. It can be discerned from Sequence 1 that Susan was working with wrong angles. What she had done was to draw a hexagon, and then (despite what she says to the teacher) used a protractor to measure each of its *internal* angles. However, if she wanted to draw a hexagon by telling the 'arrow' to move through right turns, she should have instead used the *external* angles of 60 degrees (see Figure 3.1 below). To make matters worse, she measured the internal angles inaccurately; instead of calculating them all as being 120 degrees, they were measured as 137, 120, 130, 128, etc. As Figure 3.1 below shows, the correct angles to use should have been the external ones of 60 degrees. The error was never resolved by Susan or the teacher and caused some continuing confusion for the rest of the lesson.

CONTEXT

The discourse in Sequence 1 above is of a kind that Edwards (1990, p. 11) has described as 'heavily contextualized'. This means that, as observers of the talk, we need more information than is given in the actual words spoken for the discourse to be very meaningful. You probably found that the additional information provided in the context notes helped your understanding. But even then you probably didn't feel confident that you understood what was said and done, and – crucially – what it meant to the participants. If you had been there, things would have been clearer, no doubt. But 'being there' would not necessrily be enough, because 'context' isn't those things which can be seen while people are talking; it is all that additional information speakers use to share knowledge and understanding.

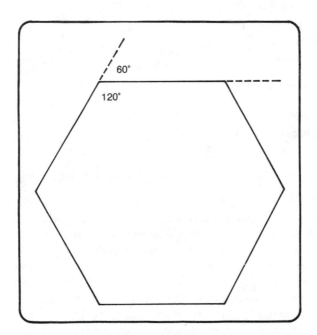

Figure 3.1 Drawing a hexagon: the external angles are 60 degrees

It is a *mental*, not a *physical* phenomenon. It consists of those things which conversationalists *invoke*, explicitly or implicitly, as they talk, and not anything which exists separate or independent from that talk. Things teachers and children do, and talk about, on any such occasion, can be invoked to contextualise later educational discussions and activities. Education is predicated upon the development of such contextual frameworks, and an extension of shared experience and understanding between teachers and children.

We can identify for Sequence 1 two major sorts of context that are necessary for shared understanding. First, there are those aspects of the physical context which are invoked by the words, gestures and directions of gaze of the speakers. These are primarily the piece of paper with its drawings and text, and the joint orientation of Susan and the teacher to various parts of it. Secondly, there is the *implicit* context of relevant shared knowledge which has been established up to this point. This is the second of three lessons on Logo graphics, the pupils having been already taught how to instruct the 'arrow' to turn angles and move in certain directions (forwards and backwards). In the first lesson they defined a hexagon and discovered how to measure its angles with a protractor. Susan knows that she is going to try out her written instructions on the computer itself. The teacher also showed them how to make the 'arrow' turn by measuring the angle between the path the arrow travels if it didn't turn (the dotted line in Figure 3.1) and its new intended direction. It is presumably this procedure that the teacher and Susan are referring to cryptically when they say (*T*) 'You've extended your lines/haven't you?' and (*S*) 'So you straighten it out/and you go round and measure it'. All of the dialogue proceeds against this cumulative, if often imperfect, mental context.

This conception of context could be an important idea for anyone interested in computers and learning in education, because it has three implications:

1 It implies that the process of learning about, or through, computers is not primarily to do with the relationship between a learner/user and the machine – the 'interface' – or even the software being used. It is instead very much to do with the contextual framework within which the learner/user is doing things with the computer. That a contextual framework will have been constructed over time through shared experience and interaction in school, and so may reflect matters such as learners' preconceptions about the aim or purpose of educational activities, and how their behaviour will be perceived and evaluated by others, especially the teacher.
2 It implies that what is learnt by particular children through the use of computers may only be understandable in terms of the history of the teaching-and-learning relationship in which that learning took place. The level of understanding that learners reach, and the extent that they come to possess knowledge as their own (that 'handover' is achieved in

Bruner's (1985) terms), may be enormously dependent on the quality of the communicative relationship between a child and their teacher.

3 It highlights the potential function for the physical outputs of the computer – screen displays, print-outs – as physical representations of decisions, visible products of problem solving and other activity which can be used to develop shared experience between teachers and learners. Print-outs of decision sequences, Logo figures, or word-processed texts can be scrutinised and reflected on by teachers and children together. Of course, this is a function that is not unique to computer output; consecutive drafts of a story may serve this purpose for example, whether they are written in longhand or produced by a word processor. But it is an aspect of computer use – that it can represent processes of thought and action in a physical form that can be shared – that is given little direct consideration in research into the use of computers in teaching and learning.

An imaginative exception to the generalisation above – i.e. some research which does focus on computers as a medium for teachers and children to share thoughts and ideas – is work being carried out in Northern Ireland by McMahon and O'Neill (1989, 1990). This is based on the Apple HyperCard software. HyperCard is a very versatile program of the type now generally called 'hypertext' which can be used to create, categorise and store sets (known as 'stacks') of texts (known as 'cards'). McMahon and O'Neill's research is concerned with the use of computers in language in development activities in both primary and secondary schools.

In one strand of their research, they have generated stacks of cartoon-type pictorial sequences with 'speech bubbles' which can either be filled in by the teacher or left empty for children to complete. 'Thought bubbles' can also be generated, so that children can suggest what they think a character may be thinking while speaking or listening to another character. 'Screen dumps' allow text to be summarised or printed as text in playscript format. In itself this represents a novel and motivating environment for children to explore aspects of language use.

McMahon and O'Neill have given particular attention to the use of their 'Bubble Dialogue' technique for helping children develop writing skills, suggesting that it helps build bridges between oral and literary uses of language:

> By simulating the conversation situation the Bubble Dialogue tool exploits the natural language of children and moves them easily and imperceptibly into the exploration of different aspects of language: from the informal language of the home and the playground to the formal language of the school and on to the increasingly abstract world of written text.
>
> (McMahon and O'Neill, 1990, p. 19)

A further advantage of this kind of use of hypertext facility by teachers is that, by planning and constraining the extent of their own involvement in the production of pictorial sequences and generating texts, children's involvement in the activities can be carefully structured according to their individual needs and rate of progress. So, for example, children can at first be offered ready-made sequences with clear story lines to which they can add text, but later go on to generate completely original pictures, stories and texts.

TEACHER TALK

I now want to go on and consider how teachers engage in the heavily contextualised discourse which is the essence of the process of education. There has been quite a lot of research on teacher-talk, but as a field of research it is very diverse, with a variety of specialists (linguists, psychologists, sociologists, curriculum developers) each using their own research methods and pursuing their own particular interests. For example, linguists have been interested to discover whether there are patterns of discourse common to different teaching situations (e.g. Sinclair and Coulthard, 1975; Stubbs, 1983), while sociologists have often been concerned with how teachers use talk to maintain control of the social microcosm of the classroom (e.g. Hammersley, 1980; Mehan, 1979).

One important way that teachers exercise control over what is legitimate, what 'counts' as educational knowledge is by the way they control classroom talk. In most classrooms, the teacher typically does most of the talking, asks the questions that determine speaker and topic, and defines the points at which each question is satisfactorily answered. They also define what information is to be taken as *shared* by how she invokes and refers to it ('what *we've* been doing'). Teachers likewise mark some past experience and information as particularly *relevant* by invoking it, and by the way they present it in recaps of the past. They mark pupils' contributions as relevant, significant or appropriate by how they respond to them.

Teachers often use questions to discover not the answers themselves, but instead whether or not pupils know those answers. They also ask questions of a special kind which enable them to draw out knowledge from the pupils rather than simply declaim it to the class.

It is thus possible to identify certain features of classroom discourse as reflecting the teacher's role in the process of creating and defining educational knowledge. A list of such features (adapted from Edwards and Mercer, 1987) might be as follows:

Discourse features

1 *Elicitations* of knowledge from learners. These might be straightforward questions or enquiries intended to assess a learner's understanding, or the more complex 'cued elicitations' whereby teachers avoid transmitting information directly and instead coax it from learners.

2 *Markers* of knowledge as joint and significant. These would include 'royal' plurals, saying 'key words' emphatically, repeating statements.

3 *Recaps.* These are of two kinds. First there are *historical recaps by the teacher*; *resumes of relevant or* prior shared events or experiences. Secondly, there are *reconstructive recaps* in which a teacher re-presents something which a learner has just said, or done, in a modified form so that it better fitted to the requirements of educational discourse. One common sort of reconstructive recap is when a teacher, on being offered a description in 'lay' language by a learner restates it in more technical terms. ('Miss I can't get it to make *slanty letters*', 'It won't do *italics*? You have to press ENHANCE').

It is important to note that the identification of these features in teachers' discourse is not, in itself, meant as a criticism of how teachers talk. Although an analysis of teacher-talk may point to some problems in how education is done in the classroom, I am not suggesting that teachers are necessarily wrong to talk in the ways they do. Although 'asking questions to which you already know the answers' is a feature of discourse which might seem odd in most settings outside the classroom, there is nothing wrong with teachers doing this because they need to know what knowledge learners have acquired. Likewise, to restate something in technical terms can be a good way of helping children come to terms with the technical vocabulary they will need to pursue their learning further. What I, my colleagues, and other analysts of the discourse of learning with computers (e.g. Fraser *et al.*, 1988; Emihovich and Miller, 1988) are suggesting, however, is that being aware of such features can help teachers and researchers understand, evaluate, and improve the communicative process of teaching and learning.

A VYGOTSKIAN CONCEPTION OF THE ROLE OF THE TEACHER

Chapter 2 provided a brief, introductory account of the 'socio-cultural' theory of cognitive development developed by L. S. Vygotsky. I want now to return to Vygotskian theory and make a consideration of how the role of the teacher can be construed in relation to computer-assisted learning.

One of the attractions of the Vygotskian approach for me is that it attempts to describe and explain not just 'learning' but the process of 'teaching-and-learning'. As Bruner (1985) puts it, Vygotsky held as basic the belief that social transaction, not solo performance, is the fundamental vehicle of education. In this respect, principally, he differs from the most educationally influential theorist of cognitive development, Jean Piaget. While Piaget saw himself as being concerned with *epistemology*, the development of individual knowledge and intelligence, Vygotsky saw himself as being centrally concerned with *pedagogy*, 'the science of teaching'. This difference is reflected in the different conceptions of the role of the teacher in these two theorists. Piaget saw children's cognitive development as a process of adaptation to the world; he saw children as going through certain stages of mental development that were largely determined by maturation (biological development) and direct personal experience of the world. The role of a good teacher within a Piagetian framework is one who provides children with rich 'learning environments' in which their own discoveries take them further along their own path up the cognitive heights. Piaget said:

> Each time one prematurely teaches a child something he could have discovered for himself, the child is kept from inventing it and consequently from understanding it completely.

> (1970, p. 715)

Piaget's ideas – or at least certain interpretations of them – have shaped what is generally called 'progressive' education in Britain and elsewhere, with its conception of the facilitating teacher who 'leads from behind'. As is indicated earlier in Chapter 2, Piaget's theory also lies at the ideological basis of some important education software, notably Logo (Papert, 1980).

Vygotsky's conception of the role of the teacher is very different. He did not live long enough to fully develop his ideas on pedagogy, but some present-day psychologists inspired by his ideas have attempted to do so because they seemed to offer a way of overcoming some of the limitations of the Piagetian framework. Contrast this statement by Vygotsky with the quotation from Piaget in the last paragraph:

> Human learning presupposes a specific social nature and a process by which children grow into the intellectual life of those around them.
> (Vygotsky, 1978, p. 86, quoted in Bruner, 1985)

Children construct their knowledge and understanding of the world – their own version of the knowledge and understanding of their culture, the 'intellectual life of those around them' – not just through direct personal experience and discovery, but also through the intellectual sharing and support of those around them. The role of 'teacher' is a particular, skilled form of such support. Bruner elaborates on these ideas as follows:

> If the child is enabled to advance by being under the tutelage of an adult or a more competent peer, then the tutor or the aiding peer serves the learner as a vicarious form of consciousness until such a time as the learner is able to master his own action through his own consciousness and control. When the child achieves that conscious control over a new function or conceptual system, it is then that he is able to use it as a tool. Up to that point, the tutor in effect performs the critical function of 'scaffolding' the learning task to make it possible for the child, in Vygotsky's word, to internalize external knowledge and convert it into a tool for conscious control.

> (Bruner, 1985, pp. 24–5)

Bruner has helped shape what is now a distinctive and influential neo-Vygotskian line of research in psychology (see e.g. Wertsch, 1985a, 1985b; Bruner, 1986; Newman, Griffin and Cole, 1989; Wood, 1988; Crook, 1991). One element of this research is the examination of how (and how well) teachers 'scaffold' children's learning through interaction (Mercer, 1991; Maybin, Mercer and Stierer, 1992).

There is more than one level to this examination. At one level, an examination of scaffolding may be largely concerned with what might be called 'presentational' issues – how and when teachers introduce new ideas into discourse, how they contextualise new information in terms of past experience, and so on. This level also deals with teachers' decisions about how to structure and support learning tasks to meet learners' individual needs and rates of progress (note the brief discussion of such matters earlier in relation to McMahon and O'Neill's HyperCard activities).

One kind of problem teachers face at this level is sometimes called 'the teacher's dilemma' (Driver, 1983; Edwards and Mercer, 1987) Edwards mentions it in a book edited by Rogers and Kutnick, but it is worth exploring in more detail here because it concerns both the nature and the extent of a teacher's intervention in the learning process. It is the problem of reconciling an experiental, non-didactic, 'progressive' approach to learning with the requirement that learners follow a given curriculum, and do not waste their time chasing intellectual red herrings or wandering up alleys that the teacher knows full well are blind. An awareness of this dilemma is apparent in the following extract from an article by a teacher on doing Logo work with infants:

Child Autonomy Versus Teacher Direction

The approach adopted in our school, we felt, had to be on the side of child autonomy or the whole purpose and spirit of Seymour Papert's work in inventing the Turtle would be nullified. The children decide what is to be drawn and how to do it and not the teacher. The teacher's role is to be an interested observer and only intervene when necessary. If asked a question, the teacher's response should not be to 'tell the answer' but to guide the children towards their own solution by discussion and questioning. This non-interventionist role is not easy. There is a tremendous temptation to say things like, 'No, that turning number is too big. You will end up facing the wrong way,' or 'If you put in that FORWARD number the Turtle will go off the paper.' These of course are the things the children should discover for themselves and then make the necessary adjustments i.e. solve their own problems.

However, there is definitely a need for the teacher to intervene at times to ensure that when children are on the verge of a discovery the opportunity is not lost for the lack of relevant information. For instance, if a group wanted to draw some circular wheels but drew square ones instead, thinking that 'You can only draw straight lines with Turtle,' I think the teacher would be justified in pointing out that circles could also be drawn, leaving the children to discover how or even assisting in their discovery, again by discussion and appropriate questioning.

(Chattrabhuti, 1986, pp. 24–5)

Of course, this dilemma is not one faced only by primary teachers. In secondary and further education, computers are commonly perceived as offering good opportunities for relatively autonomous learning on the part of students: but it is still a teacher's responsibility to ensure that students' efforts are supported and contextualized. Hijack (DESCIT, 1988) is a lively computer-based simulation activity for students aged 14 upwards, in which two networked computers are used to exchange information between the cabinet ministers of a government and a newsroom of journalists (all roles performed by the students) as a terrorist hijack attempt is under way. The notes supplied for teachers offer the following advice on the teacher's involvement:

The teacher's role

Because this is a simulation, a little role-play from the teacher is appropriate. The most effective role might be that of a senior Civil Servant. Address members of the cabinet as 'Madam' or 'Sir'. It is most important that your presence is unobtrusive. The more 'invisible' you are the better the pupils will react to the situation unfolding in front of them. It would be a disaster for their developing confidence if you were to make direct suggestions or try to take a part in discussion – however badly you were tempted. Keep out, keep neutral as far as you possibly can.

Your role as a Civil Servant will allow you to wander in and out of the Cabinet Room, and visit the Press Room without arousing undue attention.

Just occasionally you will need to contribute – by handing the Home Secretary a piece of paper, or announcing: 'I'm sorry madam, that information is unavailable at present,' or 'I will look into the problem Sir.'

(DESCIT, 1988, p. 14)

There is also, however, a second, deeper level at which the scaffolding process may be evaluated. This level concerns the quality of knowledge which children gain from classroom activities and interactions. The quality of understanding that learners acquire through the use of information technology in the classroom is not, and will never be, determined by the quality of the 'interface' between the learner and the technology. Quality of understanding, the nature of educational knowledge, is determined by a much more complex contextual system which is inseparable from how 'education' is defined in our culture. As I suggested in the earlier part of this chapter (and have demonstrated in more detail elsewhere: see Mercer, 1992), this culturally based contextual system is continually created and re-created in the classroom through interactions between teachers and learners.

At this deeper level of analysis, then, a teacher's scaffolding of a child's learning activities with a computer must be evaluated not only in terms of whether or not children acquire certain procedural rules for operating the computer (e.g. if they remember to teach the 'turtle' a word before using it, or if they remember procedures for redrafting text in word processing) but also in terms of the quality of understanding they gain of the field of knowledge (e.g. geometry for Logo, the creative writing process for word processing) with which they are concerned. Understanding of this kind is much harder to assess. Of course, this is not a problem peculiar to computer-assisted learning. Educational research has not yet provided us with very satisfactory methods for describing and evaluating the effectivness of teachers' intervention in children's cognitive development. My own view is that the neo-Vygotskian 'socio-cultural' perspective provides us with the best basis for the development of such methods. However, the complexity of a tripartite teaching and learning relationship between teacher, learner and computer (perhaps with its own 'hidden teacher' in the software) may add new dimensions which will need special consideration. This, and other aspects of classroom learning, are explored further by Eunice Fisher in Chapter 5.

REFERENCES

Bruner, J. S. (1985) 'Vygotsky: a historical and conceptual perspective', in Wertsch, J. V. (ed.) *Culture, Communication and Cognition: Vygotskian perspectives*, Cambridge, Cambridge University Press.

Bruner, J. S. (1986) *Actual Minds, Possible Worlds*, London, Harvard University Press.

Chattrabhuti, M. (1986) 'Turtle work with infants', *Classroom Action Research Network Special Bulletin*, Cambridge, Cambridge Institute of Education.

Crook, C. (1987) 'Computers in the classroom: defining a social context', in Rutkoussa, J. and Crook, C. (eds) *Computers, Cognition and Development*, London, John Wiley & Sons.

Crook, C. (1991) 'Computers in the zone of proximal development: implications for evaluation', *Computers in Education*, 17: 1.

Derbyshire Educational Support Centre for IT (1988) *Hijack! A Hotline Simulation*, Matlock, Derbyshire Educational Support Centre for IT.

Driver, R. (1983) *The Pupil as Scientist?*, Milton Keynes, Open University Press.

Durkin, K. (ed.) (1986) *Language Development in the School Years*, London, Croom Helm.

Edwards, D. (1990) 'Classroom discourse and classroom knowledge', in Rogers, C. and Kutnick, P. (eds) *Readings in the Social Psychology of the Primary School*, London, Croom Helm.

Edwards, D. and Maybin, J. (1987) 'The development of understanding in the classroom', *Unit 16 of EH207 Communication and Education*, Milton Keynes, Open University Press.

Edwards, D. and Mercer, N. (1986) 'Context and continuity: classroom discourse and the development of shared knowledge', in Durkin, K. (ed.) *Language Development in the School Years*, London, Croom Helm.

Edwards, D. and Mercer, N. (1987) *Common Knowledge: the development of understanding in the classroom*, London, Methuen.

Edwards, D. and Mercer, N. (1989) 'Reconstructing Context: the conventionalization of classroom knowledge', *Discourse Processes*, 1: 91–104.

Emihovich, C. and Miller, G. (1988) 'Talking to the turtle: a discourse analysis of Logo instruction', *Discourse Processes*, 11: 183–201.

Fraser, R., Burkhardt, H., Coupland, J., Phillips, R., Pimm, D. and Ridgway, J. (1988) 'Learning activities and classroom roles with and without the microcomputer', in Jones, A. and Scrimshaw, P. (eds) *Computers in Education 5–13*, Milton Keynes, Open University Press.

Hammersley, M. (1980) 'Classroom ethnography', *Educational Analysis*, 2(2): 47–74.

McMahon, H. and O'Neill, W. (1989) 'Language development and hypermedia', Coleraine, University of Ulster Faculty of Education.

McMahon, H. and O'Neill, W. (1990) *Capturing Dialogue in Learning: Occasional Paper InTER/18/90*, Lancaster, ESRC-InTER Programme.

Maybin, J., Mercer, N. and Stierer, B. (1992) '"Scaffolding" learning in the classroom', in Norman, K. (ed.) *Thinking Voices*, London, NCC/Hodder & Stoughton.

Mehan, H. (1979) *Learning Lessons: social organization in the classroom*, Cambridge, Mass., Harvard University Press.

Mercer, N. (1991) 'Learning through talk', in *P535 Talk and Learning 5–16*, Milton Keynes, Open University Press.

Mercer, N. (1992) 'Culture, context and the construction of knowledge in the classroom', in Light, P. and Butterworth, G. (eds) *Context and Cognition*, Hemel Hempstead, Harvester–Wheatsheaf.

Mercer, N. and Edwards, D. (1981) 'Ground rules for mutual understanding: a social psychological approach to classroom knowledge', in Mercer, N. (ed.) *Language in School and Community*, London, Edward Arnold.

Mercer, N., Edwards, D. and Maybin, J. (1988) 'Putting context into oracy: the development of shared knowledge through classroom discourse', in McLure, M., Phillips, T. and Wilkinson, A. (eds) *Oracy Matters*, Milton Keynes, Open University Press.

Newman, D., Griffin, P. and Cole, M. (1989) *The Construction Zone*, Cambridge, Cambridge University Press.

Papert, S. (1980) *Mindstorms: children, computers and powerful ideas*, New York, Basic Books.

Piaget, J. (1970) 'Piaget's theory', in Mussen, P. H. (ed.) *Carmichael's Manual of Child Psychology*, New York, Wiley.

Sinclair, J. and Coulthard, M. (1975) *Towards an Analysis of Discourse: the English used by Teachers and Pupils*, London, Oxford University Press.

Stubbs, M. (1981) 'Scratching the surface: linguistic data in educational research', in Adelman, C. (ed.) *Uttering, Muttering*, London, Grant McIntyre.

Stubbs, M. (1983) *Discourse Analysis: the sociolinguistic analysis of natural language*, Oxford, Basil Blackwell.

Vygotsky, L. S. (1978) *Mind in Society: the development of higher psychological processes*, London, Harvard University Press.

Walford, G. (1990) (ed.) *Doing Educational Research*, London, Routledge.

Wertsch, J. V. (ed.) (1985a) *Culture, Communication and Cognition: Vygotskian perspectives*, Cambridge, Cambridge University Press.

Wertsch, J. V. (1985b) *Vygotsky and the Social Formation of Mind*, Cambridge, Mass., Harvard University Press.

Wood, J. (1988) *How Children Think and Learn*, Oxford, Basil Blackwell.

Chapter 4

Collaborative learning with computers

Paul Light

COMPUTERS AND THE INDIVIDUALISATION OF LEARNING

It has often been held that one of the main advantages of computers in education is that they make it possible to *individualise* the teaching-learning process, as Chapter 2 illustrates. O'Shea and Self, for example, refer to individualisation and feedback as 'twin gods much worshipped in the computer-assisted learning literature' (1983, p. 70). What does individualisation mean in this context? In its 'strong' form it could refer to a state of affairs in which individual learners each had their own tailor-made curriculum; with content, level and style of learning all being geared to the particular characteristics of the individual. In its weaker, but more usual, form it means that, even if all learners are doing broadly the same thing, they can do it at a pace appropriate to their own level of mastery and rate of progress.

The contrast, then, is with the situation of teaching a large class together, where the pace and level have to be pitched at some kind of 'average', which doesn't necessarily correspond to that of many (or any) of the individuals concerned. From this point of view, the *ideal* class size would be one, and the ideal teacher-child ratio one to one. This can't economically be achieved with 'real' teachers, so the argument goes, but the computer might make it possible.

From a 'behaviourist' point of view, as we saw in Chapter 2, the virtues of individualised tuition can be seen in terms of the possibilities it opens up for generating a gentle 'ladder' of rewarded successes, allowing the child to build up gradually to the desired performance. Within a 'constructivist' framework the individualistic perspective is less explicit, but it is none the less often implicitly present. The dominant image tends to be of the learner as a lone scientist, grappling with problems, testing theories and building models of the world based on experience. Piaget, for example, uses an anecdote about a child (who later became a mathematician) discovering the principles of number conservation while playing alone with pebbles, arranging and rearranging them. If one starts with this perspective on the learning process, it is natural to see the advent of the computer in terms of its potentialities for stimulating and supporting learners in this kind of individual voyage of discovery.

Thus from some points of view the educational ideal might be for all learners to have their own computer, and for them to work on their own projects, at their own level and pace, more or less independently of both teachers and other learners. This potential independence of the machine-based learning process from interaction with other learners has, since the early days of the teaching machine, awoken fears of a dehumanised and dehumanising future for education. As Lepper and Gurtner (1989) remark, the prospect of a classroom in which children spend the day plugged into their own individual desktop computers seems a chilling one to many teachers.

Many of the more negative images of the role of the computer in education associate it with the replacement of warm blooded educational experience, grounded in social interaction, by a cold blooded, techno-logically controlled learning environment. This is in part an ideological matter, of course, reflecting a tension between on the one hand a vision of education (and indeed of society) as a fundamentally cooperative venture and on the other a vision of education and society framed in terms of individual survival in a competitive world. But it is also, in part at least, a psychological matter. To what extent *can* cognitive or intellectual aspects of development be separated from social–emotional aspects? In this chapter we shall be exploring the thesis that learning in any context is as much a social as an individual process. The role of the teacher in the learning process was discussed in Chapter 3. Here we shall be concerned with the claim that what goes on *between learners* can be crucially important to the effectiveness of the learning process. And paradoxically, as we shall see, there is an argument for saying that the advent of the computer could and should lead to greater rather than lesser development of collaborative approaches to learning.

INTERACTION IN LEARNING: OBSERVATION AND DESCRIPTION

The worrying image of the socially isolated and withdrawn learner, usually seen as an adolescent hunched over his or her (typically his) computer for hours at a time, still has considerable currency. However, the reality in most cases seems to be very different, both in and out of school. For example, a group of French sociologists (Boffety *et al.*, 1984) have described the rich social culture of the computer clubs and informal, out-of-school networks of computer enthusiasts which have grown up around one French secondary school of which they made an intensive study. They point out that in many ways these groups and networks resembled very closely those which had grown up in the same school around a shared interest in rock music, or in motor cycles.

Within the school curriculum, the simple fact of scarce resources militates against highly individualised work with computers, especially at primary level. The situation may be subject to rapid change, of course, but in a survey of UK primary schools, Jackson, Fletcher and Messer (1986) obtained clear evidence that the predominant pattern was for children to work in pairs or small groups rather than individually at the computer. Although it might seem at first sight that this is simply a reflection of the normal British primary school practice of working in groups, this is not necessarily the case. As many observational studies have indicated (e.g. Bennett, 1987; Galton, 1989) the children working around a table in a typical primary school are typically not working on *joint* tasks but rather on *parallel* ones. By contrast, when they are sent off to have their turn working at the computer they are often engaged in a truly *joint* learning experience, working together on a shared task. Moreover, it is a learning experience in which the teacher may be relatively little involved. Under these conditions, far from reducing the opportunities for group-based and socially interactive learning, computers may actually be associated with an increase in such opportunities.

In the United States, researchers at Bank Street College, New York, took an early interest in the ways in which the introduction of computers seemed to affect the interactive aspects of children's learning (Sheingold, Hawkins and Char, 1984). Sheingold and her colleagues report that when working with computers, students appeared to be interacting more with each other about learning tasks, and calling on each other more for help. In one classroom observation study, for example, they compared sessions in which children were using computers to learn to program in Logo with other, non-computer-based work. Children were free to interact and work together in both situations, but the researchers observed more interaction in the context of the computer-based than the non-computer-based work. This interaction took varied forms, including systematic collaboration, casual 'dropping in', and soliciting help from a more expert learner.

Researchers in Great Britain interested in the use of Logo in school settings have likewise reported that children working in pairs or small groups with Logo typically show high levels of spontaneous, task-related interaction. As Martin Hughes (1990) notes, the early Logo work, influenced heavily by Papert, was concerned with the effect of working with Logo on individual cognitive skills. However, many anecdotal accounts emerging from individual teachers using Logo in their classrooms attested to striking *social* effects. Intensive case study research, such as that conducted by Celia Hoyles and Rosamund Sutherland (Hoyles and Sutherland, 1986, 1989) also strongly suggests that the introduction of Logo programming can have positive effects on children's *socially interactive* learning. Indeed these researchers argue that the advantage of Logo as an approach to teaching mathematics rests in large part on the way in which it provokes and sustains a high level of *discussion* between learners.

The value of discussion and interaction amongst learners in the context of their learning has been endorsed by a succession of educational reports (e.g. Bullock, 1975; Cockroft, 1982) and is given further official sanction by many of the curriculum documents stemming from the 1988 Education Reform Act. Before we go on to look more specifically at research in the field of collaborative computer use, it is worth devoting a little time in the next section to considering *how* exactly discussion and interaction are supposed to confer benefits on children's learning.

DISCUSSION, INTERACTION AND LEARNING

There is, as we have already noted, a widespread belief amongst teachers and others concerned with education that discussion and interaction are 'a good thing'. The benefits they are supposed to confer may be at a very general level, and may be as much social as intellectual. For example, Crook refers to the belief: 'that cognitive development involves a necessary co-ordination of our thinking with that of others in the interests of various kinds of harmony and in the service of various kinds of joint activity' (1987, p. 31). Producing students who are disposed and able to cooperate with one another is a legitimate goal for education, and some research on collaborative learning has focused on its effects on school children's sociability and cooperativeness. However, in this chapter we are more concerned with any direct effects that a collaborative mode of working might have on levels of achievement or learning outcomes.

One problem which arises straight away is whether one should be concerned with effectiveness in terms of how much the learners manage to achieve when working together, or in terms of the learning outcomes for each of the individuals concerned. For example, the title of the Sheingold *et al.* article referred to earlier, 'I'm the thinkist, you're the typist' refers to one particular pattern of interaction they observed. The authors comment that this distribution of roles may have been quite an effective way of 'getting the job done', but was probably not very productive as a learning experience for some of the individuals concerned.

It is worth pausing a little longer over this issue, though. While it is fairly obvious that we don't want to use group achievements as the sole criterion of the quality of a group learning experience, it is not altogether obvious that we should take the opposite tack and concern ourselves exclusively with what each of the learners can do *on their own* as a consequence of the group experience. In the everyday environment, whether of children or adults, most thinking, reasoning and problem solving does go on in groups of one sort or another. For example, we could go back to the Piagetian conception which we introduced much earlier on, of 'the child as scientist', and remark that the implicit conception of the scientist as someone who *individually* grapples with the secrets of nature hardly squares with the realities of scientific work. In this, as in almost all other work contexts, the ability to function effectively in a team is a key qualification for success.

So different questions could be asked about the efficacy of discussion and interaction in learning, depending on the valuation one places on different kinds and levels of learning outcome. It is perhaps an indication of the strength of the individualistic ethos in our society that even in this area, where we are particularly concerned with social processes in learning, educationalists and researchers have tended to take for granted that we should be concerned mainly or exclusively with *individual* learning outcomes. The question thus becomes: what possible mechanisms or processes might lead to better individual learning outcomes when children work together in pairs or small groups at the computer than when they work on their own?

The effects of having a partner (or partners) can be thought of at a number of levels. We might think, for example, about the possibility that having a partner makes the task more fun, or less threatening. We might suppose that partners could pick up ideas from one another, or help each other to remember things. We might attribute particular significance to the role of argument and disagreement in shaping learning, or more simply suppose that just *talking about* the problem to someone else helps us to think about it more clearly ourselves.

Learners will obviously come to any given task with different backgrounds of knowledge and understanding, and perhaps different levels of familiarity or ability relevant to the particular task at hand. In some cases one learner may offer others a comprehensive model to imitate. In others each may be able to contribute different, perhaps partially overlapping subsets of task-relevant information. Using software which calls for the exploration of a wide range of different possibilities, or which imposes a heavy load on memory, one can see fairly readily that 'two heads might be better than one'.

Research has been undertaken on the way in which conflicts or disagreements between partners in a learning experience might affect learning. Willem Doise and colleagues in Switzerland, for example, have highlighted *socio-cognitive conflict* as a key factor (Doise and Mugny, 1984). Basing their work on some of Piaget's tests of children's logical reasoning for 5–7 year olds, they suggest that individuals typically fail because they 'centre' their attention on one aspect of a problem and fail to notice other, equally relevant factors. By bringing together two or three children, even if they are at more or less the same level of development there is a fair chance that their attention will be captured by different aspects of the situation, so that they will come into conflict with one another. For example, in Piaget's most famous task, where the child has to appreciate that the amount of, say, juice remains the same when the juice is poured into a different shaped container, one child may notice that the 'new' jar is fatter while another may notice only that the level is lower. On their own, they would thus draw opposite, and equally wrong conclusions, but Doise observed that in the course of inter-action the conflict often resulted in both of the children 'decentering' to a higher level, conserving solution which recognised the validity of both of their points of view. In some circumstances at least, then, two wrongs *can* make a right. Whether this kind of 'socio-cognitive conflict' represents an important general mechanism for learning remains an open question.

Some researchers have focused more on the role of talk itself in facilitating the learning process. For example Celia Hoyles (1985; Hoyles, Sutherland and Healy, 1990) uses the term *distancing* to describe the way in which articulating one's thoughts for someone else can help to sort them out for oneself: 'Talking provokes a representation of one's thoughts – a process which inevitably raises them to a more conscious plane of awareness so that they can become the objects of reflection and modification' (Hoyles, Sutherland and Healy, 1990). She also sees talk as having a *monitoring* role, with learners developing shared plans and then monitoring and checking each other's actions, as well as their own, against the plan.

Where have we got to, then? We saw earlier that there is increasing recognition that interaction between learners can confer advantages in the context of computer-based learning. A number of observational studies lent credence to this view. We have also seen a number of plausible ways in which discussion and interaction *could* facilitate individual learning. You may well be able to come up with some others. However, we have not touched on much in the way of *evidence* thus far. Indeed, it could be argued that our account has been unduly partisan, since we have ignored ways in which *individual* computer use might be seen to have advantages. So at this point we need to return to the question of research evidence, specifically concerned with computers and learning, to see just how consistent that evidence is with the story we have been trying to tell.

PEER FACILITATION OF COMPUTER-BASED LEARNING: THE EXPERIMENTAL APPROACH

At the heart of any experimental approach in this, as in any other field is the idea of *comparison*. At its simplest, one might want to compare the progress of learners who work alone at the computer and of those who work together. If large numbers of learners are available, and if it is possible to assign them to different learning situations ('experimental conditions') at random so as to get two equivalent groups, then it may suffice just to set up one condition in which students work in, say, pairs (again, perhaps, pairing them at random) and another condition in which students work alone. The outcome could be assessed by 'post-testing' everyone individually to see what they have learned.

One study which comes close to this 'simplest case' was conducted in Israel by Zemira Mevarech and her colleagues (Mevarech, Silber and Fine,

1987). Five classes of 12 year olds used arithmetic drill-and-practice-type Cal software over a month period. A third of them worked individually from the outset. The others worked in pairs, being encouraged to share the keyboard, to help each other, and to discuss and agree solutions. The main point at issue was whether the children who worked together would in fact learn more than those who worked alone.

The only departure from the design outlined above was that the children were paired up, not at random, but on the basis of having similar scores at pre-test. At the beginning of the study, all the children worked alone at the computer on a sample of all the types of items to be learned. They were then grouped into triplets on the basis of having similar scores. One was selected at random from each trio to go into the individual learning condition while the other two formed a pair. This arrangement ensured that, overall, the initial ability levels of those who worked individually were closely comparable with those who worked in pairs, and also that in the pairs there would be no great disparities in ability.

At the end of four months all children again undertook an individual assessment across all the types of items on which they had been working, and this was repeated again some two months later. Both in the immediate and the delayed post-test the children who had worked in pairs showed significantly greater achievement gains than the children who worked alone. It is also interesting to note that a questionnaire-type measure of the children's *anxiety* about mathematics showed that working in pairs alleviated such anxiety, especially of low ability students, significantly more than did the individual mode of working.

Across a range of studies on this issue, results are by no means entirely consistent. Some studies have found a significant advantage of working in pairs, others have not. However, the third possible outcome, that children would do better when working alone at the computer than when working in pairs, does *not* seem to have been found.

In order to understand why peer facilitation of learning is sometimes found and sometimes isn't, it is necessary to look more closely at the patterns of interaction involved. In some cases it has proved possible to improve conditions for peer facilitation of learning by simple modifications of the software. For example, Light *et al.* (1987) conducted a number of studies using a version of the Towers of Hanoi task. The screen display is shown in Figure 4.1. The aim of the game is to move the three (or more) 'tiles' from one peg to another (say, from peg number 1 to peg number 3). The two key rules are that only one tile may be moved at a time, and that one must never put a larger one on top of a smaller one. With three tiles, as shown, the optimal solution takes seven moves.

The research design involved random assignment of 8 year olds to individual or paired conditions and random assignment to particular pairings, except that children were always paired with another child of the same

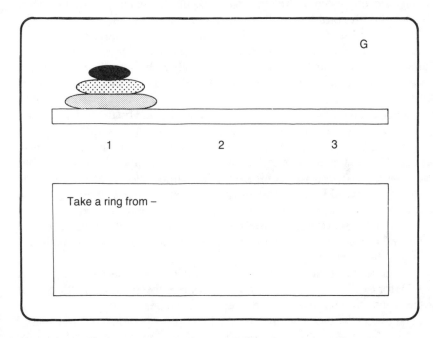

Figure 4.1 The screen presentation for the microcomputer version of the 'Towers of Hanoi' task

gender and from the same school class. The studies, which took place in schools but not as part of regular classes, involved one or sometimes two sessions of practice on the task, followed a week later by an individual post-test for all children, using slight variants on the same task.

The first of these studies showed no significant advantage of working in pairs, which was surprising given earlier findings of peer-facilitation with a non-computer version of the task. Observation suggested that in the computer-based version the students tended to just take turns to make moves, or in other cases one of them dominated the whole task. On the previous non-computer version (Light and Glachan, 1985), we had used handles on each side of each 'tile', and with the students sitting opposite one another, we required them *both* to help make each move. So we decided to try to replicate this in the computer version, introducing a 'dual key' constraint, such that each participant had a different part of the keyboard, and *both* had to key in a given instruction before it would be executed. We compared 20 students who worked alone (for a single session of practice), 20 who worked in pairs without the dual key constraint, and 20 who worked in pairs with this constraint. At the individual post-test a week later, there was no difference in the efficiency of solutions for the first two conditions, but significantly more of the children in the third, 'dual key' condition were able to solve the problem in the optimal number of moves.

This kind of study makes it clear that simply putting learners together in front of a computer will not ensure peer facilitation of their learning. Conditions have to be such that they engage both with the task *and with one another* in the course of their learning. The features of the computer itself will not ensure this. On the whole it seems fair to say that microcomputers have been designed with a single user in mind. The keyboard and the mouse are devices which seem naturally adapted to the single user. On the other hand the VDU screen is a readily shareable resource, at least in a pair or small group. What is written or shown on the screen (or pointed out) has a public and shared character (as compared, for example, to what is written in students' own workbooks). The effects of different types of interface device upon patterns of interaction in learning have been little studied as yet, but research in this area would be well worth pursuing. And of course the nature of the *software* in use has a potentially major effect, as we saw in a small way with the 'dual key' study.

The influence of different types of software has been discussed by Crook (1987), for example. On the basis of classrooom observations he found that some types of CAL software tend to elicit a great deal of simple turn taking. Others, especially those where the problem is readily perceived and shared but the solution is complex, elicited more interaction. The richest forum for discussion was provided by an adventure game. Crook highlights several points as being in need of more research. These include the issue of individual differences in children's ability on the given task, and the possibility that collaborative modes of working might heighten their awareness of relative ability, with deleterious consequences for the less able children. Crook suggests (p. 36) that this may be particularly true where computers provide very clear and direct trial by trial feedback. Again, the information we seem to need more of concerns the ways in which different types of pairings/groupings (e.g. similar vs mixed ability) interact with different types of tasks/software.

One of the candidates which we considered in the previous section, when we were trying to identify possible 'major ingredients' in profitable interchanges around the computer was simply *talk*. It might be just the fact of having to *talk* about what you are doing as you solve a task which makes learning more effective. Some evidence for this comes from a study by Ben Fletcher (1985) using a specially devised problem-solving task, based on a 'spaceship' game, in which children had to find settings of three 'input variables' which would achieve a specified target for a given 'output variable' (such as the number of passengers carried). Fifty-five children aged between 9 and 11 years were the subjects, working in school but out of the classroom. Eleven children worked on their own, silently. Eleven others worked alone but were encouraged to talk aloud about each decision they made and why they made it (the experimenter was present but did not interact). The rest of the children were formed into eleven groups of three, each group containing children matched in ability in terms of reading age. These children were encouraged to talk amongst themselves and reach consensus decisions. On three of the four performance targets the groups *and* the verbalising individuals performed better (in terms of the number of decisions needed to reach the specified targets) than the silent individuals. Fletcher does not want to argue that *all* the advantage of peer interaction in learning stems from verbalisation, but it does seem that it may be an important factor in at least some cases.

'Working together', in the sense that we have used the expression, has referred to situations in which several students work together in a broadly collaborative fashion. There seems to be a broad consensus that *cooperative* learning situations are likely to be more effective than *competitive* ones. One study which has directly addressed this is reported by Johnson, Johnson and Stanne (1986) in the United States. Seventy-five 11–13 year olds worked on a computer-based geography simulation task, involving mapping and navigation. A third of them worked in an individual condition where, subject to sharing time on the available computers, students worked on their own on the task for 45 minutes a day over a 10-day period. Another third of the students worked *competitively*. They were assigned to groups, usually of four, and were instructed to compete to see who was best. Finally, a third of the students worked *cooperatively*. Again they were assigned to groups of four but were instructed to work together as a group. In all conditions, students filled in individual worksheets every day, on which they received feedback and took a final test. In the 'individual' group they were told that they would be graded against an absolute standard of excellence. In the competitive condition they were to be graded by how well they did relative to others in their group. In the cooperative condition they were told that they would be graded by the average of the scores of the group members on the worksheets and final test. Children in the cooperative condition showed significantly higher levels of achievement, both on a day by day basis and in the final test, than either of the other groups. They also, incidentally, showed less dependence on the teacher and more positive attitudes towards working with students of the opposite sex than students in the other conditions. On the basis of this and other similar studies, Johnson, Johnson and Stanne argue that the *cooperative* organisation of groups, tasks and rewards has a central role to play in the peer facilitation of computer-based learning.

One interesting design feature of the study just described is that none of the students were actually working *on their own*. All were working in the context of a class, the difference between conditions being in the 'ground rules' by which they were working and the way in which individual tasks were organised in relation to one another. In most of the experimental studies we have described, which took place outside the classroom, the 'individual' condition literally involved the student working by him- or her-self at the computer with no access to the other students. In classroom terms this is arguably a fairly unrealistic situation.

This point was illustrated, for example, in a study we conducted with 11 and 12 year olds while they began to learn to use the programming language micro-PROLOG (Light, Colbourn and Smith, 1987). The students worked in class groups of eight over a number of sessions. Each group of eight was given access to either two, four or eight microcomputers so that they worked either four, two or one to a machine. We videotaped some of the learning sessions and also tested the students' individual grasp of micro-PROLOG at the end. No overall differences in learning outcome were found between the three conditions. However, when we analysed the videotape it turned out that the amount of task-related *interaction* between students was also very similar across the three conditions. During the learning session, the students were very much left to their own devices, without a lot of teacher input. In these conditions, even when they had a machine to themselves the students tended to engage in a very high level of task-related interaction with their neighbours. The net result was that the amount of interaction was largely unrelated to the number of machines available.

We wouldn't want to claim too much for this one study, but it does serve to highlight the interesting question of how, if at all, changing the level of provision (in terms of the number of computers available), will affect stu-dents' learning. The effects may depend, as much as anything, on any indirect effects that the level of resource may have on the organisation of the learning environment, and thus on the interactional context in which learning takes place.

Studies such as the last two we have mentioned also highlight the prob-lem of knowing what is the appropriate comparison or 'control' condition for research in this field. Should we compare, as many studies have done, the pair or group working at the computer on the one hand and the individual working in isolation at the keyboard on the other? Or is it more appropriate to use as a comparison the individual working on his or her own computer but with free access to fellow students?

Faced with this difficulty, one research option we have is to move away from studies which set up different conditions in order to compare them, towards a more 'correlational' approach. If we want to understand whether a particular type of interaction facilitates learning, we can simply observe students in any situation within which such interaction is *possible*, and see if those who spontaneously engage in a lot of it are in fact those for whom the learning outcome is best. In other words, how well does the quality or quantity of interaction *correlate* with successful learning. An advantage of this approach is that it is much easier to employ it in the context of ongoing 'real' learning situations, rather than specially set up experimental ones.

One example of this approach can be found in the work of Noreen Webb and colleagues (Webb, Ender and Lewis, 1986). They observed a group of 30 11 to 14 year olds following a course in BASIC programming. All the students worked in pairs, but at the end they were given an individual test to assess their competence. During the paired learning sessions careful measures were taken of the children's spontaneous verbal and interactive behaviours. Variables which turned out to be related to individual achievement in programming included giving and receiving explanations, receiving responses to questions, and verbalising aloud when typing at the keyboard: in other words, the students who engaged in the highest levels of these interactive behaviours during learning were the ones who scored best on the programming test at the end of the course.

Webb's categories of verbal interaction are in one sense very *non-*interactive, since they are simply counts of how many of various kinds of utterances each child produced or received. They don't really attempt to get at, for example, the level of disagreement or *conflict* involved in the learning experience. Yet as we saw earlier, it has been argued that 'socio-cognitive conflict' lies at the heart of productive peer interaction. What evidence is there that conflict has an important role to play in the context of computer-based learning?

Some evidence, albeit rather crude, comes from a study by Light and Glachan (1985). Twenty pairs of 8 year olds were observed working in pairs on a computer game based on the popular code-breaking peg-board game Mastermind. The frequency of 'conflicts' was scored from videotapes of the interaction -- a conflict was defined as a situation where one student put forward a proposition for an entry, the other put forward a counter-proposition, and at least one of them explicitly tried to justify their proposition against their partner's (usually by reference to the feedback given by the computer in respect of earlier entries). Note that conflict in this sense implies disagreement about strategy, and argument, but not necessarily mutual hostility! In most cases such 'conflicts' were embodied in very positive and mutually supportive discussions. It turned out that members of those pairs which showed a high level of such conflict during the learning sessions did significantly better on an individual post-test using the same task.

Clearly, this finding is consistent with the idea that such conflict offers a productive learning experience. But alternatively it could simply reflect the fact that more able children tend to engage in more of this kind of conflict. In this study, fortunately, we were able to exclude this alternative explanation because we had included an individual *pre-*test as well as post-test in the design of the study. By looking back to the pre-test data it was possible to show that those students who engaged in more conflict during the learning sessions were neither significantly more nor less able, at least on this particular task, at the outset.

There is thus some support for the idea that conflict plays an important role in productive learning interactions. But neither the socio-cognitive conflict model nor common sense would suggest that the amount of disagreement will always be a good index of effective learning. What the theory predicts is that disagreement will be effective when it serves the purpose of drawing students' attention to aspects of a problem they might otherwise have neglected and when some *resolution* of the conflict is possible which in some way reconciles the various perspectives involved.

Celia Hoyles and her co-workers have approached the task of analysing the constructive role of discourse in a subtler, more qualitative fashion. Their approach has been to work with much smaller numbers of students – just a few pairs – but to follow their interactions around the computer over a long period of time. Their work (e.g. Hoyles and Sutherland, 1989; Hoyles, Sutherland and Healy, 1990) has been conducted in the context of classroom mathematics work in the secondary school. Using audiotapes of interaction in conjunction with a video record of what was going on on the screen, they have attempted to pick out and examine productive interchanges in detail.

As they see it, the collaborative situation facilitates the generation and articulation of hypotheses about patterns and regularities, and the verbal exchanges help to bridge from a particular pattern detected by one of the children to its generalisation in the form appropriate to the computer environment.

Conflict, as they use the term, occurs when there is any kind of mismatch between what a student is trying to bring off and what the partner, or the computer itself, allows or comprehends. Conflict in this sense, they suggest, may be as much or more a feature of the student-computer interaction as it is of the student-student interaction. The nature of this cognitive conflict and the points at which it arises depend very much on the software in use. But the critical role for discussion between learners comes precisely at the point when this conflict arises: at this point the different perceptions of the problem and of the solution have to be negotiated, made explicit and rendered compatible with the mathematical constraints of the task.

This analysis points up the fact that when a pair of students interact with a computer we may see 'two-way' interaction (between the students) or 'three-way' interaction (involving the students and the computer). One might add, of course, the possibility of 'four-way' interactions, bringing the teacher back into account, though we have been studiously ignoring that dimension in this chapter!

In sum, then, as we have seen, the mid- to late 1980s have witnessed the appearance of a considerable body of research on the way in which learner-learner interactions can facilitate computer-based learning. Taken as a whole this research certainly seems to confirm that what goes on between students working together at the computer can and often does form a very important ingredient of the learning situation. In comparing the efficacy of say, pairs as against individuals, though, this kind of research tends to gloss over all kinds of variations amongst students which may be highly relevant. For example, we have not been able to say much about how group size, or the levels and ranges of ability within groups, affect computer-based learning, nor about how individual temperamental differences affect the way students respond to individual versus collaborative ways of working. Nor have we dealt with the issue of *gender* differences, and how these might be affected by different patterns of computer use. Some of these issues will be taken up by Eunice Fisher in Chapter 6, where she considers issues of 'access' in the field of computer-based learning.

CONCLUSIONS: COLLABORATIVE LEARNING AND THE COMPUTER

As well as being limited in its treatment of individual and group differences, this chapter has been limited in terms of the kinds of software and hardware environments and applications we have discussed. We have considered some of the ways in which the computer can support profitable interaction between learners, working together at the machine, but we have not considered interaction *through* the machine, by networking, conferencing or electronic mail, for example (Chapter 9 in Part II takes up some of these possibilities). We have not really considered the extent to which the computer might come to act as a *participant* in an interactive process of learning. Intelligent tutoring systems aim to create a tutorial dialogue between the student and the machine which has many of the features of a 'real' social interaction. Some are aimed at more than one learner at a time, while others are being developed which attempt to simulate an 'interactive partner' within the Intelligent Tutoring System itself (e.g. Chan and Baskin, 1988). Developments in these fields may radically change our conception of the role of interaction in computer-based learning in the future.

We opened this chapter by sketching the argument that computers in education could deliver something that the hard-pressed human teacher was rarely able to deliver, namely 1:1 teaching geared sensitively to the needs of the individual learner. We might end it with almost the opposite scenario. From the Plowden Report right through to the National Curriculum documents, the *potential* of collaborative learning in small groups has been recognised. However, in practice schools have not found it at all easy to tap this potential. For example, in 1980 when Galton and colleagues published the ORACLE study, based on extremely detailed observation of primary classrooms, they reported that despite grouped seating arrangements the children almost always worked separately, on their own individual tasks. This was before computers arrived on the scene.

The studies we have considered in the course of the chapter strongly suggest that the use of computers has the potential to enhance collaborative learning. They also confirm that, in the context of computers, this mode of learning can lead to improved outcomes, even when these are judged at the individual level. It may be, then, that the computer can deliver something which other teaching and learning contexts tend to lack – perhaps by providing just sufficient structure, direction and support to the learning process to enable the collaborative learning process to be effectively sustained.

Before accepting such a conclusion too glibly though, we ought to give some thought to the *kinds* of evidence which we have been drawing on. Experimental research has a natural place in academic disciplines such as psychology, but how useful is this kind of research in the practical domain of education? Often, in order to maximise experimental control of the variables, artificial situations are created by researchers. There is a tension between the goal of maximising the 'power' of the experiment (by keeping it as *simple* as possible) and the goal of making the study *valid* in relation to the real contexts of teaching and learning. Researchers are often accused of giving too much attention to the first of these goals and not enough to the second. The old joke about the man looking under a lamp post for a coin which he dropped somewhere else 'because the light is better here' may be all too applicable.

There is, then, plenty of room for scepticism about the usefulness of research. As Heather Govier (1988) points out, teachers are accustomed to relying on their own judgements as experienced practitioners rather than on experimental research. Perhaps the best way for teachers to treat research in this field is as an indication of *possibilities*, and as a stimulus to evaluate or re-evaluate their own experience. And perhaps the best way for researchers to make progress in this field is by working much more closely than in the past with practising teachers. It is notable that a new large-scale research project on groupwork with computers (Eraut and Hoyles, 1988), which will run well into the 1990s, is firmly wedded to the idea of using teachers as co-researchers and drawing all data from the context of 'real' classroom practice.

If studies such as this kind can claim more validity than shorter-term, more controlled experimental research, it is partly because they recognise that in practice learners are exposed to many more influences than simply those of an immediate learning partner. They are part of a larger group: a school, a college, a class, or whatever. We have concentrated in this chapter on a 'micro-social' domain, concerned with interactions between learners in the immediate learning situation. We have largely neglected questions about the organisation of groupwork in the classroom, and the wider social and cultural context within which learning occurs. Even more significantly, perhaps, we have had little or nothing to say about the role of the *teacher* in all this. Chapter 3 offered one perspective on this, and Eunice Fisher returns to this theme in the chapter which follows.

REFERENCES

Bennett, N. (1987) 'Cooperative learning: children do it in groups – or do they?', *Educational and Child Psychology*, 4: 7–18.

Boffety, B., Descolonges, M., Daphy, E. and Perriault, J. (1984) 'Rock on Informatique?: pratiques technologique d'adolescence et modes de vie', Paris, Institut National Recherches Pedagogique.

Bullock, A. (1975) *A Language for Life*, London, HMSO.

Chan, T.-W. and Baskin, A. (1988) 'Studying with the Prince: the computer as learning companion', paper presented to ITS–88 Conference, Montreal, June.

Cockcroft, W. (1982) *Mathematics Counts*, London, HSMO.

Crook, C. (1987) 'Computers in the Classroom', in Rutkowska, J. C. and Crook, C. (eds) *Computers, Cognition and Development*, New York, John Wiley & Sons Inc.

Doise, W. and Mugny, G. (1984) *The Social Development of the Intellect*, Oxford, Pergamon Press.

Eraut, M. and Hoyles, C. (1988) 'Groupwork with computers', *Journal of Computer Assisted Learning*, 5: 12–24.

Fletcher, B. (1985) 'Group and individual learning of junior school children on a microcomputer-based task', *Educational Review*, 37: 251–61.

Galton, M. (1989) *Teaching in the Primary School*, London, David Fulton Publishers.

Galton, M., Simon, B. and Croll, P. (1980) *Inside the Primary School*, London, Routledge & Kegan Paul.

Govier, H. (1988) *Microcomputers in Primary Education: a survey of recent research*, Economic and Social Research Council Information Technology and Education programme Occasional Paper ITE/28a/88.

Hoyles, C. (1985) 'What is the point of group discussion in mathematics?', *Educational Studies in Mathematics*, 16: 205–14.

Hoyles, C. and Sutherland, R. (1986) 'Using Logo in the mathematics classroom', *Computers and Education*, 10: 61–72.

Hoyles, C. and Sutherland, R. (1989) *Logo Mathematics in the Classroom*, London, Routledge.

Hoyles, C., Sutherland, R. and Healy, I. (1990) 'Children talking in computer environments; new insights on the role of discussion in mathematics learning', in Durkin, K. and Shine, B. (eds) *Language and Mathematical Education*, Milton Keynes, Open University Press.

Hughes, M. (1990) 'Children's computation', in Grieve, R. and Hughes, M. (eds) *Understanding Children*, Oxford, Blackwell.

Jackson, A., Fletcher, B. and Messer, D. (1986) 'A survey of microcomputer use and provision in primary schools', *Journal of Computer Assisted Learning*, 2: 45–55.

Johnson, R., Johnson, D. and Stanne, M. (1986) 'Comparison of computer assisted cooperative, competitive and individualistic learning', *American Educational Research Journal*, 23: 382–92.

Lepper, M. and Gurtner, J. (1989) 'Children and computers: approaching the twenty-first century', *American Psychologist*, 44: 170–8.

Light, P. H., Colbourn, C. J. and Smith, D. (1987) 'Peer interaction and logic programming: a study of the acquisition of micro-prolog', *ESRC Information Technology and Education Programme*, Occasional Paper ITE/17/87.

Light, P.H., Foot, T. Colbourn, C. and McClelland, I. (1987) 'Collaborative interactions at the microcomputer keyboard', *Educational Psychology*, 7(1): 13–21.

Light, P.H. and Glachan, M. (1985) 'Facilitation of individual problem solving through peer interaction', *Educational Psychology*, 5: 217–25.

Mevarech, Z., Silber, O. and Fine, D. (1987) 'Learning with computers in small groups: cognitive and affective outcomes', Second European Conference for Research in Learning and Instruction, Tubingen, W. Germany.

O'Shea, T. and Self, J. (1983) *Learning and Teaching with Computers*, Brighton, Harvester Press.

Sheingold, K., Hawkins, J. and Char, C. (1984) '"I'm the thinkist, you're the typist": the interaction of technology and the social life of classrooms', *Journal of Social Issues*, 40(3): 49–61.

Webb, N., Ender, P. and Lewis, S. (1986) 'Problem solving strategies and group processes in small groups learning computer programming', *American Educational Research Journal*, 23: 247–61.

Chapter 5

The teacher's role

Eunice Fisher

INTRODUCTION

In this chapter, I am concerned to relate the content of previous chapters to the practice of teaching. To do this I shall be examining a variety of examples of learning situations in which IT is being used. All will involve groups of pupils or students and their teachers. I shall be particularly concerned with teacher–pupil and pupil–pupil interaction, and shall ask the following general questions:

- What is the nature of the interaction taking place?
- Is it different from that in other teaching contexts, and if so, how?
- How does this affect the learning which takes place?
- Was IT a necessary component of this learning?

I wish to pick out the following important and relevant points from the preceding chapters:

1 Learning in the classroom is essentially a social activity, not only because it takes place in a shared environment, but also, as Edwards states, it is 'an inculcation of pupils into a predetermined culture of educated knowledge and practice, [rather] than some unfolding development of individual cognitions' (Edwards, 1991, p. 197).

2 Talk is an important feature of classroom learning, and serves the following purposes:

- It encourages pupils to make their thoughts explicit, and in attempting to communicate these thoughts to one another, pupils may move to a clearer understanding, or self-awareness (see Chapter 4).
- It may also provide a window on the pupils' thinking and so enable the teacher to support the learner. Though we must be wary of equating what is said and what is thought, I would argue that any clues, however rough may be useful.
- It may serve to shift the balance of control in the classroom and to increase the pupils' feelings of ownership of their work.

In this chapter we shall consider these points further with specific reference to their relationship to classroom practice.

THE TEACHER AS MANAGER

It is possible that many teachers go through the day largely unaware of the extent of their own power. Indeed, many would argue, I'm sure, that today's classrooms are democratic and that much of the teacher's power has already been eroded or even voluntarily ceded. With regard to *pupil behaviour* this may well be true. Even in the primary sector pupils are now expected to take responsibility for their own actions far more than was the case 50 years ago.

However, teachers (if only as agents for the government through the National Curriculum) still largely determine what is a *suitable topic* for study. What is more, having selected the topic, teachers become very skilled in guiding pupils towards the answers which they have predetermined (see Chapter 3, and Edwards, 1990).

The issues which I now wish to address are:

1   In the face of the encroaching technology, can teachers continue to define lesson content to the same extent?
2   Should they continue to try to do so?
3   Do these potential changes in control of content have wider implications for classroom management?

I'm sure that you will be able to give examples of situations where pupils' independent access to information (independent of the teacher, that is) leads to a different lesson content, or at least to a different relationship between teacher and pupil in defining that content. Of course, these things also happen without computers; pupils may already be free to pursue topics and problems using a variety of instructional resources (e.g. textbooks, maps) which may lead them along particular but individual pathways, and many teachers may actively encourage this. (Though the evidence from classroom discourse studies suggests that even when teachers believe they are leaving lesson content open, they often constrain the definition of topics within a very narrow range – see Chapter 3). In any event, teachers have a *managerial* role and responsibility in their classrooms, which will remain theirs whatever the style in which they chose to carry out that function. Indeed, it is this management function which Galton and his colleagues suggest produces difficulties in introducing the *real* group work – i.e. children sharing ideas, rather than children sitting in groups but working individually, suggested by Plowden. They argue:

> To think out, provide materials for, and set up a series of group tasks having the characteristics just described in the different subject areas which comprise a modern curriculum would in itself clearly be a major

undertaking, even if use is made of relevant curriculum development projects. To *monitor* the subsequent group activities; to be *ready and able to intervene in the work of each group when this is educationally necessary and desirable* ; this also would clearly be a major undertaking for the teacher requiring, as a first condition, a high degree of involvement by the pupils in their task and so a high level of responsible behaviour. For the pupils to gain from such work also certainly requires the development of a number of social as well as cognitive, skills; a degree of tolerance and mutual understanding, the ability to articulate a point of view, to engage in discussion reasoning probing and questioning. Such skills are not in themselves innate, they have to be learnt and so taught.

(Galton, Simon and Croll, 1980, p. 160 (my emphasis))

As you've already seen in Chapter 4, children working with computers, even as young as 7 years, are capable of sustained on-task discourse which suggests the possession of cognitive and social skills not often displayed in other areas of classroom research. However, there is evidence (Olson, 1988) to suggest that pupils put their own meaning on the feedback they receive. It would seem, therefore, that whilst high-level cognitive group work with a computer is a realisable goal, there is still a need for periodic intervention from the teacher if only to informally assess the pupils' progress and sometimes to redirect inappropriate interpretations.

In the next section I shall go on to examine how computers have been used by some teachers and the extent to which they may be said to have attained this goal.

ROLE CHANGING WITH THE COMPUTER

Set out below are some comments made by teachers on the ways in which they felt some aspect of their practice, or of what happened in their classroom had been affected by the computer. The first is from Philip Stevenson, commenting on one of his lessons:

They had obviously been going well and we wanted to keep that programme and the structure. Unfortunately I hadn't come across having to correct a typographical error either, so it was quite a nice shared learning experience, because we, the three of us, just had to try and plough away in the absence of the manual, to clear it. And in fact we did manage it in the end, and it was quite an interesting dialogue.

I think one of the most positive aspects was something, just a small thing that cropped up this morning where I wanted to spend a little longer with the children before they went to the computer, making them think about the criteria that they were going to use before they sorted the shells, because I wanted them to realise that it was going to be a more difficult task than it was with the logiblocks. I'd only been chatting with them for a minute when Graham said quite spontaneously, can't we go over to the computer and do what we did yesterday, because although it went wrong, I knew how to do it properly the second time. So he obviously felt in a much better learning position himself if he was working at the computer rather than table top first, which I had expected them to do certainly for a little while [. . .] and that's precisely what they did and it turns out that he was right, that was exactly the cycle of events.

(Philip Stevenson – Recording made for
Open University course EH232, 1989)

This teacher sees his role (once the introductory preliminaries have been dealt with) as a supporter/facilitator in what the children are trying to do, but he also stresses the importance of being able to stand back, allowing the pupils to develop their own ideas. In the excerpt above he points out his own need to continue learning.

These examples describe instances where the teacher, for some part of the lesson, abandons the role of leader or controller of knowledge and moves, albeit temporarily, towards one of *co-worker* or *facilitator*. As Galton, Simon and Croll (1980) rightly suggest, teachers have a managerial function which includes pre-planning, setting up and monitoring what goes on in the classroom. The style in which they choose to operate that function will depend on many factors, including their own personal preference. The example given above of facilitative style could, of course, be seen in wide variety of educational settings with or without the computers present. However, the issue I wish to raise is whether for most teachers there is a *proportional shift* towards a less didactic and more open style when computers are used.

So far I have also paid scant attention to differences in style depending on lesson content, and the extent to which certain content areas are generally seen by those teaching as requiring a particular, structured approach if effective learning is to ensue. However, I wish to suggest that arguments as to the need for structure are largely subjective. As Somekh (1989) suggests:

In Britain, as probably in the US, teachers are strongly conditioned to believe that their classrooms should be well-ordered, and that the difficulty of learning tasks should be matched to the pupils' ability. These two factors tend to interrelate because disorder is seen as a visible signal of pupils' lack of engagement with the task. Therefore, in analysing data relating to learning, a large number of teachers have focused in particular on instances of uncertainty or hiatus, and have reached a rapid conclusion that the task should have been 'more structured.' [. . .] To what extent should the teacher structure a pupil's learning? To what extent should the computer software structure the pupil's learning? Even at an [. . .] early stage it is important that structure is not assumed to be uncontentious. It can be argued, for example, that any group which is engaged in problem-solving will need to go through a period of uncertainty and trial and error which will give the *appearance* of being directionless. Providing such a group with more structure will only serve to cut short its thinking and destroy the opportunity for its autonomy from the teacher.

(Somekh, 1989, p. 13)

Somekh is raising this issue as a result of her work with the PALM (Pupil Autonomy in Learning with Microcomputers) Project, a teachers' action research project, based in East Anglia. PALM has set out to examine curriculum development in the field of computers in education. Because of the style of the project, based as it is on teachers not only carrying out research in their own classrooms, but also in collaboratively developing their own research issues, PALM's emphasis on autonomy and the emphasis given to that by the teacher researchers is indicative of their approach. As Somekh writes: 'Since PALM is moving towards a major focus on autonomy in learning, the question of structure is of fundamental importance' (1989, p. 13). She also comments that 'The shift of control over learning away from the teacher towards the pupil, and the crucial role teachers play in this process, are fundamental to our understanding of autonomy in learning' (1989, p. 5).

This view accords with comments from the teachers involved in PALM. For example, a teacher of first year juniors, using Folio word processing and Logo, comments:

I feel that autonomy can only be achieved after some degree of directed teacher input into the learning situation. Children need to taste the success that will encourage them to better things, and a teacher can guide them towards that feeling, and show she experiences it also. Once the children have got to grips with the nuts and bolts of a computer program they are in control of it, and it is then that a versatile program can be used to its best effect i.e. the children guiding it, not it guiding the children. They are in effect becoming self-directive.

To achieve this the computer needs to be very much a part of the whole environment in the classroom. It must make very regular appearances (ideally it should never be absent!) and be as familiar a resource as books and pencils.

Computer work should be very much a part of the ongoing topic in class, and this is where I have found an open-ended computer program such as a word processing package, information retrieval software or Logo program is invaluable in that the children can tailor the content to the current need. This must be even more appropriate now that the National Curriculum makes its dictates upon us.

(Hill, 1990, pp. 28–9)

In another (secondary) school where the English teacher used a computer simulation exercise to promote oral activity with a high ability group, she comments:

> Overall, the adults' role during the negotiations were definitely those of facilitator and supervisor, that of a policeman seeing that the interactions did not get physical when heated (they didn't, but several pupils com- mented that they got very cross with each other!) There was no teaching done in the way of imparting information or demonstrating skills. This the children did for themselves through the situation that had been set up. The computer and the materials thus allowed them to be as autonomous and active as it is probably possible for them to be in a classroom situation.
>
> (Baron, 1990, pp. 9–10)

In a secondary school where the Head of Special Needs used a variety of software for several areas in the curriculum, including English, he comments:

> To my surprise my input amounted to about 20 per cent of all the talk going on. Quite an amount when I'm supposed to be taking a back seat and encouraging autonomy. Most of my contributions are in the form of instructions or questions. Was there any autonomous activity going on at all!
>
> I decided to take a closer look at the exact nature of my instructions and questions to see if they shed any light on the dictatorial or other nature of my contributions. To my intense relief it seemed that my instructions were largely of an enabling nature. For example, my first instruction is tech- nical, explaining how to start the program. This instruction is also tied to a question, asking the children to come up with what they thought would be a reasonable number to input. 'Right, you type in the number you want. Now what number do you think you need to go there?'
>
> (Franklin, 1990, p. 12)

These teachers' views suggest a *gradual development* of pupil autonomy whilst at the same time emphasising the imporance of an appropriate teacher strategy which offers support as and when it is needed.

This shift of the locus of control is an important one, and one that has been examined by other researchers. For example, Rosemary Fraser and her colleagues carried out detailed observations of 174 mathematics lessons taught to 17 classes of 12–14 year old pupils in the autumn term of 1981, 'by their teachers, whose individual styles and approaches together covered a wide range'. (Fraser *et al.*, 1988, p. 205). Microcomputers were used in parts of these lessons. One of the aims of this research was to:

> show how the presence of a microcomputer, suitably programmed for use as a teaching aid, introduces a powerful new factor which, in taking on some of the roles enables the teacher naturally to assume others that are normally difficult to adopt or to sustain – particularly those associated with these missing, more 'open' classroom activities. This work has impli- cations beyond the classroom which are discussed elsewhere.

Although the microcomputer plays a central role in this work, perhaps the most important results, in particular the classification of roles and activities [. . .] relate to the teaching and learning processes themselves which are re-examined in responding to this new stimulus.

(reported in Fraser *et al.*, 1988, p. 205)

A feature of this work was that the researchers developed a structured event-by-event system of analysis, *Systematic Classroom Analysis* (SCAN), which adopts a *micro* perspective (as opposed to the more *macro* approach used by PALM above) to examine the teachers' roles. Based on their analysis, reported in detail in Fraser *et al.*, 1988, the researchers suggest that the computer:

is regarded by the pupils as an independent 'personality' and that, suitably programmed, it can temporarily take over some of the roles usually assumed by the teacher in such a way that the teacher adopts other roles, rarely found in the classroom, that are essential to the promotion of higher level learning activities.

(Fraser *et al.*, 1988, p. 203)

These roles to which Fraser and her colleagues refer are some of the *management* roles normally performed by the teacher, such as *task setting* or *explaining*. This, they argue, frees the teacher to adopt alternative roles, such as *counsellor*, *fellow-pupil* or *resource*.

Although this study was carried out on a series of mathematics lessons, its findings were, of course, based largely on the *language exchanges* which took place around the computer between pupils and their teachers. What is of particular interest for our purposes is whether these shifts in role can be demonstrated *across* the *curriculum*, and the extent to which they are accompanied by a demonstrable *enrichment* of the pupils' work. For this reason I shall examine a few more enquiries into these same issues.

Support for the need to make *non-intervention* deliberate comes from comments from teachers quoted elsewhere in this book. For example, see Chattrabhuti (Chapter 3), Stevenson (this chapter). The teacher, having set up work for the pupils, needs to be able to stand back and adopt the role of an interested observer, only intervening when guidance is necessary. The computer then takes over as the mutual focal point for teacher and pupils alike. For example, another teacher, using electronic mail for developing a serial story in English classes with 14 year olds, says of the computer:

I think it's helped our [i.e. her own and a colleague's] relationship with the students actually because we are not technology experts and so there's been a sense of 'you know we're all in this together'. [. . .] It seems silly to say that an inanimate object can actually make you close to the students, but I think the computer's actually helped because it's provided a focus.

(Interview with two teachers at Belper School, 1990,
Open University course EH232)

However, Hoyles and Sutherland (1989), working with Logo mathematics with 11–14 year old pairs of pupils over a period of three years, state that their subjective view had been that 'we did not intervene very much in the Logo learning and did not unduly influence its development'. They go on to suggest:

> *Subsequent analysis of the data has shown that this was not the case and pupils' progress in certain areas is closely linked to teacher interventions.* Studying the data indicates that we intervened in the learning process of the pupils in the following three ways:
> interventions which kept the control with the pupil;
> interventions in the form of Teacher-directed Tasks;
> interventions in the form of Teaching Episodes.
>
> (Hoyles and Sutherland, 1989, p. 143) [authors' emphasis]

Hoyles and Sutherland developed their three types of categories as a result of an analysis of the linguistic exchanges in the classroom, collected in their transcript data during the first year of research. Table 5.1 sets out the first mode of intervention, that which leaves control with the pupil.

The categories of intervention in Table 5.1 were used as a basis for analysis. The categories in Table 5.1 are self-explanatory. Set out in Table 5.2 are their results on just four pairs of students.

Hoyles and Sutherland suggest that:

1 The data shows an increase in intervention in the category of *reflection* (particularly the looking back process) over the three years for all pairs except Linda and Elaine in year 3.
2 The number of *requested interventions* is more than double in the first year for all pairs, whereas the *non-requested interventions* show a very slight increase over time.
3 The interventions in the category of *motivation* decreased over the three years of the project. (George and Asim, who received a proportionately larger number of motivational interventions during the first year did not, in the view of the authors, collaborate well at first.)
4 Interventions in the category of *direction* remained fairly stable.

I think it is worth noting:

- In 2: the shift from *requested* to *non-requested* interventions. One might expect a decrease in requests as students develop competence. The authors explain the increase in *non-requested* intervention as being due to increases in the *reflection* category. I don't think this claim is fully substantiated on these small numbers, and unfortunately at the time of writing no published results are available on a larger study.
- In 3: it is interesting to note the decrease in *motivation* interventions. Presumably this reflects an increasing pupil autonomy, as the authors themselves suggest.

Table 5.1 Categories of intervention

Motivational
Reinforcement (R), e.g. 'That's good'
Encouragement (E), e.g. 'Try it'

Reflection
Looking forward (F)
(a)   Process (P) Encouraging pupils to reflect on and predict the process.
(b)   Goal (G) Encouraging pupils to reflect on their ultimate goal.
Looking back (LB)
(a)   Process (P) Encouraging pupils to reflect back on problem-solving procedures.
(b)   Goal (G) Encouraging pupils to reflect on their goal.

Directional influencing and/or changing the focus of the pupil's attention.

Nudge (N)	e.g. 'Do you want to clear the screen?' or 'How about doing your square?'	
Method (M)	Encouraging pupils to use suitable methods of problem solving (which are already familiar to them).	
Building (B)	Encouraging pupils to apply a particular piece of previously learned material or knowledge.	
Factual (F)	(a) New (FN)	Supplying a particular piece of new information which is necessary to enable the pupil to continue.
	(b) Recall (FR)	Reminding pupils of a piece of information (referring them to the handbook).
Powerful idea (PI)	Introducing a 'new powerful idea' or concept such as 'procedure' the REPEAT statement or the idea of a variable.	
Mathematical idea (MI)	Introducing a new mathematical idea.	

Source: (Hoyles and Sutherland, 1989, p. 142)

What Hoyles and Sutherland suggest is that there is a development toward *pupil autonomy in learning* over time, but that the teacher's role in this may be a more complex one than simply 'standing back'. What happened in their study was that pupil autonomy was encouraged through an initial non-interventionist policy by the teacher/researcher (i.e. responding to requests but minimal non-requested intervention). Once this autonomous working was established, new (teacher-directed) tasks were introduced aimed at 'stretching' pupils, and it was these that led to an increase in non-requested intervention. Presumably this need for increased intervention would be a temporary one, lasting only until pupils were more familiar with the new demands made on them.

Table 5.2 Percentage of interventions categorised by motivation, reflection and direction (given as percentages of total number of interventions)

		Year 1		Year 2		Year 3	
		Not requested	Requested	Not requested	Requested	Not requested	Requested
Sally and Janet	Motivation	10	1	15	–	8	1
	Reflection	43	–	46	1	48	1
	Direction	31	15	34	4	37	5
	Total	84	16	95	5	93	7
George and Asim	Motivation	14	5	2	3	3	0
	Reflection	34	5	66	2	47	0
	Direction	24	18	18	9	36	14
	Total	72	28	86	14	86	14
Linda and Jude/Elaine	Motivation	13	1	15	2	8	2
	Reflection	36	6	36	1	40	2
	Direction	27	17	38	8	41	7
	Total	76	24	89	11	89	11
Shahidur and Amanda/Ravi	Motivation	–	–	15	5	20	1
	Reflection	–	–	36	6	35	5
	Direction	–	–	34	4	31	8
	Total	–	–	85	15	86	14

Source: (Hoyles and Southerland, 1989, p. 144)

Obviously results are needed on a much larger sample before strong claims can be made for these findings. However, taken together with others reported so far, we are beginning to build up a picture of a changing role for teachers with computers. It seems that this change offers many possibilities of increased motivation of pupils and a more flexible approach to learning, though it is also clear that teachers need to be aware of their own strategies, and should guard against making unwarranted assumptions as to the nature and extent of their interventions in pupil learning.

Another approach to analysing what goes on in the classroom is that developed by Edwards and Mercer (1987) and discussed in Chapter 3. Like the other analyses included here, this approach relies on an analysis of the linguistic exchanges which take place. However, there is a slight difference of emphasis in that Edwards and Mercer do not accept the language at its face value. They take a socio-linguistic approach which looks at the socio-cultural context in which the language is used.

Edwards has argued that:

> teacher-pupil and pupil-pupil talk are both important, but often for different reasons. There are overriding asymmetries between teacher and pupil, both cognitive (in terms of knowledge) and interactive (in terms of power), that impose different discursive patterns and functions. Teachers' expertise lends itself to direct explanation and to assisted learning, of the Vygotskian sort, in which the less competent child is helped ('scaffolded' in Jerome Bruner's terms), towards increased competence.
>
> (Edwards, 1990, p. 201)

However, as you have seen here, it may be that when the computer is also present, it can take on some of the management functions normally carried out by the teacher, leaving the teacher free to act as a facilitator or counsellor. Fraser *et al.*, suggest that, since the teacher has quite genuinely ceded a degree of control, s/he is enabled to take a counselling function. They state:

> the consultative roles epitomise a different relationship between teacher and pupils. They are working together on common problems, the older more experienced giving *general* help.
>
> (Fraser *et al.*, p. 220)

The teacher moves even further towards equality in the *fellow pupil* roles, where 'teacher and class are together facing the same challenge, of learning or problem solving say' (p. 220). Is this really the case?

Edwards and Mercer (1987) are sceptical about classroom conversation because they see it as restricting pupils to *ritual knowledge* rather than encouraging them towards an understanding of principled knowledge. (Their work is discussed in Edwards, 1989, and also in Chapter 3.) Yet Fraser *et al.* are suggesting that, where the computer is allowed to take over the more authoritatian functions of the teacher, this removes the agenda-setting role from the teacher (to the computer) for that particular task, and allows the teacher to engage in a genuine sharing of problems and new knowledge.

Do we have evidence to suggest that Fraser and her colleagues are correct in this assumption? One way to compare the two viewpoints would be to apply the Edwards and Mercer (1987) analysis to the dialogue reported by Fraser *et al*. The analysis was introduced in Chapter 3 and is set out again below.

1 *Elicitations* of knowledge from learners. These might be straightforward questions or enquiries intended to assess a learner's understanding, or the more complex 'cued elicitations' whereby teachers avoid transmitting information directly and instead coax it from learners.
2 *Markers* of knowledge as joint and significant. These would include 'royal' plurals, saying 'key words' emphatically, repeating statements.
3 *Recaps*. These are of two kinds. First, there are *historical recaps* by the teacher; resumes of relevant or prior shared events or experiences. Secondly, there are reconstructive recaps in which a teacher re-presents something which a learner has just said, or done, in a modified form so that it better fitted to the requirements of educational discourse. One common sort of reconstructive recap is when a teacher, on being offered a description in 'lay' language by a learner restates it in more technical terms. ('Miss I can't get it to make slanty letters', 'It won't do italics?')

Now we will apply this analysis to a small section of dialogue taken from a lesson in which the teacher is using the Pirates program, where the aim is to find the buried treasure using co-ordinates as reference points.

T: Can anyone say which is the best way to find the treasure?
(Pause)
What is the best first guess?
Tony?
Ty: (5, 5) Miss.
T: Why?
Ty: Because it's in the middle, so each direction has the same size area.
P: ($4\frac{1}{2}$, $4\frac{1}{2}$) is in the middle, Miss.
T: Yes, but we can only have whole numbers. Are there any others as much in the middle as (5, 5)?
Ps: (4, 4) (Pause) What about (4, 5)?
T: Let's try that. It says 'Go east'. What is the best thing to do next?
An: Does it mean exactly east, Miss?
T: I don't know. What do you think? Does anybody remember what happened before?
Rd: Last time it said go south, it has the same first coordinate in the end.
T: Alright, shall we try that? Where shall we go next?

Sn: (5, 6).

T: It says 'Go east' again. Where next?

Ty: (5, 7).

Gn:N o. (5, 8).

T: Why?

Gn:Well, it could be at (5, 7) (5, 8) or (5, 9). (Pause) If we try (5, 8) we either get it straight away or one step after. If we try (5, 7) it could take two more steps if its at (5, 9).

T: Shall we do that then?

Ps: Yes.

T: (5, 8). That's it.
Let's try a different sort of clue –
'Warm' clues tell you if you are getting closer to the treasure or not.
(Pause)
This is harder so we'll change the grid to (0, 4) in each direction.
Where shall we start?

Ja: (2, 2).

T: (2, 2). It says you are cold. Which way shall we go Paul?

P: It doesn't tell you, Miss.

T: No it doesn't. What shall we try?

P: (3, 3) Miss.

T: Why did you choose that one?

P: (Pause) Don't know, Miss.

T: (3, 3) It says you are getting colder.

(Reported in Fraser et al., 1988)

This is, of course, only one very small section of dialogue in a fairly structured lesson, taken out of context. However, Fraser et al., do find in it evidence of teacher as fellow pupil (in the last three exchanges) and as counsellor ('Can anyone say which they think is the best way to find the treasure. (Pause) What is the best first guess?' and 'No it doesn't. What shall we try?'

Using the system devised by Edwards and Mercer, these would be seen as *cued elicitations, reconstruction* and *joint knowledge markers* (*use of royal plural*). These are all common techniques used by teachers to maintain control of the topic, so that genuine sharing of the direction of the lesson has not occurred. Where pupils are truly being given freedom to explore, we would hope to see evidence of *spontaneous contributions* by them, whether these took the form of statements or questions.

As I've pointed out above, this is but one very small sample of dialogue from a structured lesson. Quite different findings might emerge from other lessons. If you refer back to the comments by Somekh (p. 60) you will see that she points out that structure should not be assumed to be uncontentious. I think the examples we have looked at so far have come from structured lessons. What remains unresolved is the issue as to how much structure is desirable. Both Somekh and Edwards are suggesting that structure can inhibit higher-level learning (what Edwards refers to as *principled knowledge*). This structure could be imposed by the teacher or by her choice of software, or it could occur indirectly through some other agency – for example the National Curriculum.

One further factor which we have not so far examined but which would almost certainly affect the nature of the pupils' contributions is the presence or temporary absence of the teacher. Chapter 4 indicated some of the factors which can affect the nature of the exchanges which take place between pupils, for example, the *size of group* is also an influencing factor. However, even when the teacher is not immediately present, it has been reported that the dialogue generally remains task oriented, and that conceptually complex problems are discussed.

What is more important, you have read in Chapter 4 that learning is generally more effective when pupils work in groups (particularly in pairs). Whilst the evidence suggests that some of this learning improvement is the direct result of needing to articulate a problem to another, and thus *distancing* oneself from it, this does not fully account for the improvements that have been found. As Light suggests in Chapter 4, talk may also have a *monitoring* role, perhaps serving to draw attention to particularly crucial aspects of the task.

If truly effective learning takes place best within a genuine sharing of experience, without the threat (or promise) of input from a more know-ledgeable source, there do seem to be two alternatives for the teacher wishing to 'cash in' on this. First, she can plan to increase the time that she genuinely 'stands back', leaving pupils free to explore within a task *not* so highly structured that all degrees of freedom are lost. Alternatively, she can seek to cultivate situations in which they are *genuine* fellow learners.

One teacher in the Palm Project discusses her attempts at fostering an autonomous attitude to computer work with a class of first year juniors using Folio to produce a story as follows:

The children were eager to begin their story, so I left them to it. It was interesting to see how the ongoing discussion amongst the group changed the storyline as they typed it in. They became very excited by the idea of 'The Stranger' in their story, and it became evident that their initial discussion bore no resemblance to the story they were typing

The Stranger

I went to the shops to buy some sweets at night time. A car parked in a drive way. A man got out of the car. He had a gun in his picket. I saw his shadow following me.

They often re-read their story out loud to give them ideas as to what would happen next. Kieron and Mark came up with most of the ideas for the story, and Theresa was good at spelling difficult words.

[. . .] The children had six separate sessions using Folio to write their story, and there were six printouts, each longer and more refined than the one before. The children's first attempt at editing their piece of writing concerned the actual appearance of the script, this was to them their prime objective. They marked on their printout all the places where they wanted to delete spaces and add spaces. They also added one full stop and changed one capital letter for a lower case one. By the end of their next session they had written considerably more and brought this story to a conclusion.

I felt that I should intervene at this point to show them that editing was not purely a cosmetic affair. I got them to read out their story, and to talk about how we could improve their written language. I wrote their suggestions onto their printout as I thought this would be easier for them to follow when editing at the computer. Firstly we looked for repetition and the children discussed how they could change any repetitive phrases. They changed

I went into the shop. He went into the shop

to

I went into the shop and he followed me,

and

He pulled out his gun. I ran out of the door. I ran to the park. I ran to the wall.

to

He pulled out his gun and I ran out of the door. I rushed to the park. In a flash I was at the wall.

The children used the children's thesaurus *Better Words* to find alternative words from those they had used and this prompted them to come up with other words without looking them up. 'I ran home' became 'I sped home'. 'I saw the police car come around the corner' was now 'I saw the police car skid around the corner'. We tackled spellings next, and found that there were not that many:

frourt	front
off	of
coner	corner
could	called
happed	happened
thacks	thanks
eveything	everything
shoak	shock
towords	towards

sruggle	struggle
cacthing	catching
draem	dream

Lastly we looked at punctuation. This mainly consisted of adding speech marks and differentiating where one person's speech stopped and somebody else's began.

In the last two sessions the children put their changes into effect, saving and printing their new version each time. They were able to do this with no help at all from me and it was evident they enjoyed this 'juggling' with their writing, especially when the end result showed no evidence that major overhauls had taken place.

(Hill, 1990, pp. 7–9)

No doubt it could be argued that this can be achieved without the presence of a computer. However, I would like to remind you that:

1 There is now a considerable body of research which suggests that even when teachers believe they are giving pupils freedom to develop their ideas and to make knowledge 'their own', this is often not the case. Not only do pupils constrain their offerings within what they see as the teacher's requirements, but they are assisted in doing this by teacher's questioning (Chapter 3).
2 Work around the computer offers a special situation in that it can be more or less structured without being inhibited by the teacher. The interaction that takes place with the computer is a genuine dialogue, allowing the pupil to explore new areas which may be unknown to the teacher.

This dialogue can also be extended beyond the classroom. By using computer telecommunications (for example networking or electronic mail systems), pupils and teachers can draw on a wider range of information and expertise and can reach a wider and more varied audience. However, for successful collaboration to develop between classrooms or within classrooms, careful organisation is essential. Availability is not enough to ensure improvements in the quality of instruction and learning. As LCHC comment:

just as within-classroom, small-group activities have proven powerful when they encourage *both* collaboration among students *and* a new role for the teachers, so telecommunications becomes a medium for productive educational activity only when it facilitates joint activity at a distance. In order to do so it must support the role of teacher-as-orchestrator and provide rich opportunities for children to communicate in detail about jointly addressed problems.

(LCHC, 1989, p. 80)

In their own work teachers often have the opportunity of obtaining and analysing longer samples of dialogue from a video, collecting samples from their own classrooms. They can then examine for themselves the extent to which these changes occur, and perhaps identify management and discourse features which promote or limit learning in the classroom.

CONCLUSIONS

This chapter has been mainly concerned with the power relations in the classroom, how these might be affected by the computer and the extent to which teachers might take advantage of the technology available to promote higher-level discussion in the classroom, and through that interaction facilitate high-level learning for all pupils.

We looked at examples of classroom practice, and considered whether it is possible for teachers to adopt a more facilitative approach to teaching, using the computer to carry out the more basic-operational/didactic functions of classroom management. If this is so, the teacher is then released to concentrate more on the educational needs of pupils and can free pupils from the need to operate within the usual classroom discourse frameworks.

The extent to which these changes are possible, or indeed, are desired, will depend on many factors, only some of which will fall within the teacher's control. At a mundane level, the computer hardware and software must be in adequate supply. As you see in the following chapter, in the UK, we have almost reached the stage of sufficient computers for one per classroom across all sectors, but how they are distributed within any one school may still be a limiting factor.

Secondly, we need a political and educational climate which does not insist on a 'bottom-up' approach to learning, that is, one with undue emphasis on the mastery of basic skills (of whatever sort) before more interesting and demanding learning can be attempted. At the time of writing it is still too soon to assess the effects in England and Wales of the National Curriculum and of the concurrent Scottish and Northern Ireland curricular changes on these aspects of classroom practice.

Lastly we need a confident teaching force, happy to take on new initiatives and a redefinition of the teacher's role. The likely level of technological change will, I think, be extensive and demanding, but it could provide highly rewarding for teachers and pupils alike. The new curricula and the focus on assessment at all ages also poses an additional loading, but these new initiatives have at least put the issue of IT very much on the teaching agenda.

REFERENCES

Baron, J. (1990) 'The computer referee: using "conflict and compromise in society"', *Teachers' Voices 5*, National Council for Educational Technology.
Chatterton, J. L. (1988) 'Knowledge control: the effect of CAL in the classroom', *Computer Education*, 12(1): 185–90.

Computers in context

Edwards, D. (1990) 'Classroom discourse and classroom knowledge', in Boyd-Barrett, O. and Scanlon, E. (eds) *Computers and Learning*, Wokingham, Addison-Wesley. Reprinted from Rogers, C. and Kutnik, P. (eds) *Readings in the Social Psychology of the Primary School*, London, Croom Helm.

Edwards, D. and Mercer, N. (1987) *Common Knowledge: the development of understanding in the classroom*, London, Methuen.

Franklin, B. (1990) 'Hang on we're going that way', *Teachers' Voices 6*, National Council for Educational Technology.

Fraser, R., Burkhardt, H., Coupland, J., Phillips, R., Pimm, D. and Ridgway, J. (1988) 'Learning activities and classroom roles with and without the microcomputer', in Jones, A. and Scrimshaw, P. (eds) *Computers in Education 5–13*, Milton Keynes, Open University Press.

Galton, M., Simon, B. and Croll, P. (1980) *Inside the Primary Classroom*, London, Routledge & Kegan Paul.

Hill, J. (1990) 'Children in control', *Teachers' Voices 2*, National Council for Educational Technology. (Copies of case studies in this series are available from Bridget Somekh, CARE, University of East Anglia, Norwich, price £2.00 each plus postage.)

Hoyles, C. and Sutherland, R. (1989) *Logo Mathematics in the Classroom*, London, Routledge.

Laboratory of Comparative Human Cognition (1989) 'Computers and learning: a review of recent research', *Journal of Educational Computing Research*, 4(4).

Olson, J. (1988) *Schoolworlds – Microworlds: computers and the culture of the classroom*, Oxford, Pergamon Press.

Open University (1990) *Computers and Learning* (EH232).

Somekh, B. (1989) 'Teachers becoming researchers: an exploration in dynamic collaboration', a paper presented to the National Educational Computing Conference, Boston, Mass., June.

Chapter 6

Access to learning: problems and policies

Eunice Fisher

INTRODUCTION

With the advent of electronic communication, the amount of information available on record somewhere, and the speed with which it can be accessed have increased phenomenally. Information is an important component of power and those with access to it are therefore empowered. In the classroom, this power through knowledge has traditionally been the privilege of the teacher. However, this situation is changing, and I would argue that one important task which now faces teachers at all levels of education is to help pupils towards a full realisation of what is now on offer and how they might access it. As we know, the content of the information available is likely to change rapidly, so that increasingly it may be the case that there is little point in learning the facts of a topic. What is more important is to learn how to access them efficiently, how to interpret what is found, and to have well-developed strategies for coping with the new problems which are likely to emerge as new knowledge is synthesised. What is the situation at the moment?

OBSTACLES TO EQUAL ACCESS TO LEARNING OUTSIDE THE CLASSROOM

In the primary sector computers are most often used within the general classroom and so are available to the class teacher for use across the curriculum as she sees fit. Generally these are used by more than one pupil at a time – a fact which probably arose originally through a severe shortage of machines, but which is now entwined with a philosophy of group learning which you have already encountered in Chapter 4 and which I will discuss further below. In the secondary sector and beyond computers are more likely to be housed in a special computer room and their use may therefore be limited to discrete timetabled blocks of time. However, this locational concentration means that there may be sufficient for 1:1 usage for any one class, and the learning process which is involved may therefore be of a very different, more solitary nature. These differences may in turn have differential effects on children from different social classes or ethnic groups, at different stages of skill development, depending on their gender and on their preferred learning style. You have already encountered some discussion of these issues in Chapter 4. According to the researchers at the Laboratory of Comparative Human Cognition (LCHC), the present position in the United States is that the net effect of the microprocessor 'revolution' in primary education has been to reinforce and exacerbate previously existing inequalities of educational achievement.

> the manner in which computers are being employed in American classrooms is making the position of minorities worse with respect to the Anglo male norms which are used in such comparisons. In particular, more computers are being placed in the hands of middle- and upper-class children than poor.
>
> (LCHC, 1989, p. 74)

In 1988 the Office of Technology Assessment produced a major review of the role of new technologies in teaching and learning in the US (OTA, 1988). This included a summary of the information available on differences in access to computers for different categories of schools and pupils, and supports the claims of LCHC.

One thing that it revealed was that there were very substantial differences in the access that pupils can get to computers in different states. In Louisiana and Mississippi there are on average 45 pupils or more per computer. In New York, Minnesota, Wyoming and Nevada, by contrast, there is at least one computer per 24 pupils.

There are also very significant differences between schools on a national level. In elementary schools in 1988 around a third of schools had a pupil-computer ratio of 29:1 or better, while about a tenth of schools had a ratio of 120:1, or worse. The discrepancies were less in senior high schools, but even there about half the schools had a ratio of 29:1 or better, while about 15 per cent had a ratio of 60:1 or worse (OTA, p. 34). These divergences correlate in part with school size; smaller schools tend to have a better pupil-computer ratio than larger ones. As ethnic minority pupils are more likely to attend the large schools that are a feature of urban areas, this works against them.

So too does the fact that it has been the richer schools that have acquired computers more quickly than poorer ones. However, even after allowing for the correlations with school size and location, there is some evidence that elementary schools with predominantly black pupils are less likely to have computers than those with mainly white pupils.

The situation in the UK is not dissimilar, where the available information allows direct comparisons to be drawn, despite considerable improvements over the last three or four years. For example, a Survey of Information Technology in Schools conducted by the Department of Education and

Science (1991), reports that computer-pupil ratios varied between 1:211 in the 'worst' primary school and 1:5 in the 'best'. In secondary schools the discrepancy between 'best' and 'worst' was rather less marked, and was reported as 1:57 and 1:3 respectively. As in the United States, wide discrepancies can also be found within one education authority. For instance, one local education authority reports primary ratios between 1:142 and 1:6, and secondary ratios between 1:33 and 1:12 (Counsell, 1990). It is difficult to think of any other kind of basic educational resource where such wide variations between the best and worst equipped schools would be likely to occur.

In part, differences in provision within an LEA are a matter of schools giving different priorities to IT within their budgets. However, differences in attitudes within schools are only part of the story.

The DES national surveys (1989 and 1991) suggest that differences in per capita expenditure on IT equipment are related in part to the relative prosperity of the schools' catchment areas, though there has been a marked increase in per capita expenditure in the years 1989–90 (Table 6.1).

It is very probable that the presence of computers in homes (and the power of those purchased) is broadly correlated with family income. Primary schools therefore are tending to increase differences of overall access for pupils to computers. A major cause of this divergence is that parents in relatively prosperous areas contribute far more to the school to buy IT equipment (see Table 6.2).

To the extent that Parent Teacher Associations (PTAs) are providing funding, it seems likely that the introduction of local management of schools will have increased differences in IT provision between them (Table 6.2i). Numbers of computers may be taken as a highly visible index of modernity by many parents, increasing pressure upon heads and governors to increase their numbers. Yet school budgets contain only a small proportion of genuinely discretionary funding, because by far the greatest part of their

Table 6.1 Average expenditure per pupil on IT equipment in different categories of school, by type of catchment area

| | Primary | | Secondary | |
| | £ | £ | £ | £ |
	1987–8	1989–90	1987–8	1989–90
Relatively prosperous	3.45	6.05	6.89	12.01
Neither prosperous nor economically disadvantaged	2.75	5.32	6.79	29.14
Economically disadvantaged	2.10	5.44	5.59	15.12

Source: (Tables 19 and 5, DES, 1989 and 1991)

Table 6.2 Sources of funding for information technology equipment

		% met by:		

6.2i

Primary schools	Capitation allowance	Other LEA/central government	PTA	Other
Relatively prosperous	21	23	40	16
Neither prosperous nor economically disadvantaged	27	30	37	6
Economically disadvantaged	38	39	12	11
Overall average	28	30	32	10

6.2ii

Secondary schools	Capitation allowance	Other LEA/central	TVEI	PTA	Other
Relatively prosperous	27	22	33	8	10
Neither prosperous nor economically disadvantaged	29	20	28	9	14
Economically disadvantaged	31	20	41	2	6
Overall average	29	21	31	7	12

Source: (Table 6, DES, 1991)

money goes on staffing and other relatively fixed costs such as heating and lighting. The level of PTA contributions can therefore have a dispropor-tionately high impact on such things as numbers of computers provided, if the parents are willing and able to increase their contributions. Furthermore funding through commercial sponsorship is, if anything, more likely to be successfully obtained by schools where parents have personal contacts with local business decision makers or, indeed, include such decision makers amongst their members. Such contacts are not distributed randomly between schools.

The spending in secondary schools also showed a marked increase over the last two years (Table 6.1), but the pattern of spending is more complex. Whereas the 1987–8 figures, like those for the primary schools, showed that spending was aligned to the affluence of the schools' catchment areas, the latest figures show the *lowest* figures for the most prosperous areas. Further-more, the expenditure per pupil in the 'neither prosperous nor economically disadvantaged' category is almost double that in the 'disadvantaged' areas and more than double that in the 'prosperous' areas.

There is no explanation of these figures in the DES survey, and it is not easy to see why they should be as they are. Table 6.2ii indicates the percent-age of the expenditure that the various funding agencies contribute. PTA support, as might be expected, is much lower in the 'disadvantaged' areas, and their spending on IT from capitation as well as the contributions they receive from TVEI represents a slightly larger proportion of their total than is the case for the other catchment areas. Since the proportions from all the sources are roughly the same between the 'prosperous' and the 'neither prosperous nor economically disadvantaged', the absolute differences are even more puzzling.

OBSTACLES TO EQUAL ACCESS TO LEARNING WITHIN THE CLASSROOM

LCHC make two other points, namely:

1 when computers are placed in schools for poor children they are used for rote drill and practice instead of the cognitive enrichment that they provide for middle- and upper-class students;
2 female students have less involvement than male students with computers in schools, irrespective of ethnicity.

If supported by the evidence, the first of these points is invidious since it is both less obvious and less excusable. They argue (pp. 74–5) that a view of education as a 'bottom-up' process, together with the belief that ethnic minorities and the poor lack basic skills, combine to support a commitment to rote drill and practice for disadvantaged pupils. However, there is reason to hope that there has been less discrimination of this type in the UK. In the recent past our schools have not been oriented towards teaching-to-tests as have schools in the US. At the time of writing it is still too early to tell to what extent the National Curriculum in England and Wales, or the plans for the new curricula for Scotland and Northern Ireland, will encourage similar bottom-up and rote-learning approaches there, but I would hope that our own educational ethos which has, for the most part, actively discouraged teaching-to-test, will survive. Certainly, on our recent visits to schools, my colleagues and I have found plenty of examples of pupils drawn from the poorer social backgrounds, working on a wide variety of computer work.

Lastly LCHC claim a gender bias which favours males. There is also evidence for this in UK schools, as shown in the work of Celia Hoyles and her colleagues. As Hoyles writes:

While girls and boys might show a similar appreciation of the significance computers might have for their personal futures, boys tend to be more positively disposed than girls towards computers, are more likely than girls to take optional computer courses in school, to report more frequent home use of computers, and tend to dominate the limited computer resources that are available in school. It is also the case that even when girls are able to obtain access to the machines in school, only a restricted set of activities (which exclude programming for example) are often deemed to be appropriate for them. Finally, few girls take up any employment using computers skills (other than data processing or word processing).

(Hoyles, 1988, p. 1)

LCHC point out that there is some evidence that attitudes are beginning to change in the US. A study by Siann *et al.* (1988) suggests this may also be true in the UK. They administered questionnaires to 928 Scottish Higher Education students, which required the students to rate male or female computer scientists by means of 16 attributes. The results indicated that the females were more positively rated than the males on eight of the attributes, regardless of the gender of the rater. However, Cockburn (1987) reports a male bias in terms of both opportunity and curriculum content in Youth Training Schemes and other government training initiatives, with women relegated to 'office technology', i.e. word processing.

Taken together, these results could be interpreted to mean a greater shift in attitudes in HE rather than FE, or they could indicate a greater shift 'north of the border'! It should be borne in mind, however, that the Scottish study was based on the attitudes of the students, whilst the Cockburn study looked mainly at the provision and the providers. This does suggest that the gender bias may be stronger in older rather than very young adults. In fact Cockburn reports that the only female in her study who had opted for a major subject *other than* office technology was a young Asian woman of Indian Moslem background who had been encouraged by her accounts manager father to follow in his footsteps. This 'chatty' and confident young woman survived in the otherwise all-male environment by becoming 'one of the boys'. Another less fortunate young woman who believed she had told the training officer at her initial interview that she wished to go into the programming section was actually reserved a place in office technology because the (male) training officer thought that was what she had asked for! According to Hoyles (1988), this lack of provision for girls in computing at FE correlates with statistics which suggest that not only are girls less likely than boys to pursue computer-related courses at school and university, but that this imbalance is worsening.

This is not to suggest that gender bias should now be seen as entirely a fault of teachers. Indeed it has been frequently reported that both boys and girls see computers as a male preserve, and a recent study suggests that this may still be the case even at primary school age (Hoyles, Sutherland and Healy, 1990). On the other hand, it would seem that there is a need for increasing the awareness of the problems faced by girls and young women in gaining access to computers, and a need to educate those in charge of provision so that they can optimise the chances of female as well as male pupils and students.

One way of doing this might well be to build on the linguistic and communicative skills of girls, and to recognise the importance of these abilities in computer work. In the next section I examine in more detail the ways in which these female 'strengths' may be of benefit in computer work.

GENDER AND COMPUTERS

An interest in gender differences in educational computing use dates back at least to the early 1980s, when computers began to appear in the school classroom.

Collaborative working

A number of early studies which involved close observation of various kinds of software being introduced experimentally into classrooms looked at the issue of gender differences. Hawkins (1984), for example described one American study which focused on individual programming work using Logo with 8–12 year olds and found clear evidence of greater enthusiasm, and higher levels of dedication and eventual achievement amongst boys than amongst girls. However, she also reports another study involving the introduction of word processing, which found no such differences. Hawkins suggests that this may have been because the word-processing software elicited a much more collaborative mode of working, though I would suggest that it might also arise from girls' preference for language over mathematics. I shall return to this issue later. This suggestion, that girls respond more favourably to a collaborative mode of working than boys, is of obvious interest to us. Evidence consistent with this comes from another early American study by Cynthia Char and colleagues (Char et al., 1983) which compared three pieces of software being tested in elementary school classrooms. One produced greater interest and superior performance from boys than girls, but the other two did not. Of the latter two, one explicitly called for a collaborative mode of working while the other tended in practice to be organised that way by teachers concerned.

In her more recent review Celia Hoyles (1988) also argues that the issue of gender differences in computer use is inextricably tied up with the issue of individual versus collaborative modes of working. Where computers are associated with individual or perhaps competitive modes of working, she argues, girls tend to find them alienating. Where they are associated with collaborative modes of working, girls are likely to be just as enthusiastic and achieve just as highly as boys.

On the basis of observational evidence from her own Logo Maths Project, Hoyles suggests that for many boys, discussion with peers seems like just a time consuming diversion, but girls tend to value the mutual help and sharing of ideas which interaction with a partner allows:

> Boys not only tend to monopolise computer hardware but also find it difficult to share interactions at the keyboard and see arguments with peers as time consuming and diversionary. Girls, on the other hand, tend to appreciate the opportunity available in computer-based group work for mutual help and the sharing of ideas.
>
> (Hoyles, Sutherland and Healy, 1990, p. 4)

Boys seemed more concerned to establish their autonomy and impose their problem representation and solution. They used few verbal supports to their partner's contribution and appeared to be trying hard to convince each other, which led to a competitive style of speech. Hoyles and Sutherland conclude:

> It might be easy to interpret from the boys' language that they do not collaborate or listen to each other's suggestions as their final actions often appear to be based on 'who was the strongest or most persistent'. In fact we have found frequent cases when ideas from a partner were taken up later – but *not* acknowledged!
>
> (Hoyles and Sutherland, 1989, p. 175)

Nielsen and Roepstorf (1985) reported a similar situation amongst Danish 15 year olds. They say:

> The differences are striking in the examples. The girls tend to orient themselves towards each other. The human relation seems equally – or more important – than the object they are working with. They seem to operate within a we-circle, and the cooperation is predominantly collective. [. . .] The boys also cooperate, but the dominant tendency is towards an individual performance, often with what we have termed an element of competition.
>
> (Nielsen and Roepstorf, 1985, p. 65)

A similar picture emerges from classroom accounts gathered in the course of an ILEA project (Burke *et al.*, 1988), lending support to the view that a collaborative mode of working is crucial to girls' effective use of computers.

Tasks and working styles

However, the issue is undoubtedly more complex than this. Sutherland and Hoyles (1988), again drawing on the Logo Maths Project, distinguish qualitatively different programming *styles*. Their observations suggest that, when working in pairs, boys tend to choose well defined programming goals whereas girls tend to work with much more loosely defined goals. As they point out, which of these styles is judged the more effective will depend very much on what outcome measures are used.

Amongst the experimental 'groups versus individuals' studies reviewed in

Chapter 4, few seem to have discovered any differential effects between male and female students. One exception is a study by Martin Hughes and colleagues (Hughes, Brackenbridge, Bibby and Greenhaugh, 1988). A group of 60 7 year olds were divided up into girl-girl, girl-boy and boy-boy pairs, matching as far as possible for age and ability. After an initial practice session, the children worked in pairs using Logo commands in 'direct drive' to navigate a 'turtle' around an obstacle course. On a final session, all children worked on the same task, but this time on their own.

When the children tackled the task in pairs, all ten of the boy-boy pairs were successful, as were nine of the boy-girl pairs. However, only two of the girl-girl pairs completed the task. Likewise on the final individual session, girls from the girl-girl pairs took nearly twice as long to complete the task as the boys. But the girls from the boy-girl pairs did just as well as the boys on the final session.

This is a 'one off' finding, and needs to be treated with caution. It may well be that the particular task chosen (akin to driving a remote controlled car, albeit via a keyboard) was more stereotypically a boys' than a girls' task. Perhaps the fact that this was a timed test, where speed was of the essence, might be important too. Perhaps the competitive flavour of timed tasks was also 'off-putting' to the girl-girl pairs. But then the finding that the girls did just as well as the boys in the mixed-sex condition needs explaining. The researchers' videotapes showed very little evidence of the boys either telling or showing the girls what to do. Studies like this are perhaps more valuable for highlighting issues than for resolving them. The particular pattern of findings may turn out not to be replicable, or to be specific to a particular type of task, or a particular age group. But the issue it raises, of how learning interactions and outcomes are patterned for single and mixed gender groups is one which clearly deserves more detailed attention.

Girls and language

Anderson (1987), in a large study involving more than 6,000 high school students in Minnesota, USA, found that females performed better than males in some areas of programming. His findings suggest that females are better at problem solving where the problems are expressed verbally rather than mathematically.

This finding accords with a commonly found female preference for language over mathematics, whatever the origin of that preference might be, and underlines the need to be aware of the difference between conceptual difficulties and those arising from more superficial aspects of a problem such as the language in which it is posed.

LEARNING-DISABLED STUDENTS

In the UK there have been many examples of the use of computers in schools and colleges to extend the learning potential of learning-disabled students. Some of this use has undoubtedly concentrated on basic skills (for example, teaching word-processing skills to those unable to write manually by virtue of specific disability, mental or physical). However, there have also been many attempts to develop disabled learners beyond their apparent limitations by making use of the special capabilities of the computer to reduce the learning load and facilitate the learner's access to higher-order processes. For example, in one school I visited the teacher showed me some long and interesting stories produced on the computer by a 10 year old boy with serious reading and writing difficulties. The child had never previously produced more than a line or two of almost illegible written text. Here is a copy of a story he produced on the computer and edited himself with a dictionary.

The adventure of the ozone layer

This is how it happened. I was bored on a wet day. It was in the morning, on a Sunday. I was just looking out of the window and then I said excitedly 'I forgot to go to the professor today.' So I jumped up and got my coat and mum said, as I rushed past the kitchen, 'Where are you going'.

I said 'out to play with my friends'.

My mum sighed. I ran across the road then darted through an alleyway, jumped a fence, ran across a field and crossed over another fence. I then came to this big hut and went in. I jumped and gasped at the same time. There was Professor climbing out of a spaceship. He looked at me and said 'well what do you think?'. I just stood there with my mouth open and he said, 'This is the experiment I've been waiting for all my life and I can not wait any longer'. I looked at it for a long time. Then the professor said go inside, so I did. It was brilliant I could not belive my eyes. The professor ran out to get something and I was still in there when he came back. But when he was running back he triggered a switch that was the on button. I was just walking out when suddenly the door slammed right in my face. The professor said, 'Oh no, we're taking off. I was trying to get out but the professor wanted to go to the ozone layer. So he typed in the ozone layer to the computer. We're taking off. We crashed through the roof. We were travelling very fast. Then it got hotter and hotter and hotter. Suddenly we stopped hard. THUMP! 'Where are we' I asked. 'At the ozone layer' said the professor proudly. He pressed a switch and called, 'Open door' and it did. We were sweating buckets.

What are all those holes professor?', 'What are they there for?' He scratched his head and said, 'We dump too much rubbish on the Earth. You must not throw rubbish on the ground or spray chemicals into the air.

See what you and your friends have done.' 'Now I see,' I said. 'That is what happens when you dump too much rubbish and chemical sprays.'

'Shall we go and have a look around.' said the professor. 'Yes,' I said. So we did, we got round in a day. I looked at my watch and it said 12:00 am. 'CRIKEY' I said, 'we have to go professor' He sighed and said, 'All right.'

So we got in the spaceship and went home. I ran as fast as I could and jumped the fence and ran across the field and jumped another fence and darted through the alleyway. Then I ran across the road. I was home. I was very relieved to be back home. I jumped in bed and fell fast asleep.

by Ian

Computers have also been profitably used by learners with physical disabilities. For example, those unable to hold a pen may none the less be able to use a standard keyboard, a modified keyboard or a mouse. Blind students may also be helped by using conventional keyboards, but with aural indications (e.g. 'speaking' computers) to give them access to what they have produced.

ETHNIC MINORITIES AND BILINGUALS

As suggested in the previous section, those pupils from backgrounds other than white middle-class may find themselves disadvantaged for a variety of reasons with regard to access to computers. These disadvantages may arise from the following.

Differences in cultural attitudes

Differences arising from contrasting social mores may result in different attitudes to working, or in preferred problem-solving styles. Attitudes to computers and experience at home with computers may also be very different. In practice, it may be impossible to separate differences due to cultural ethos from those of language (see below), gender or poverty, and I know of no study which sets out to isolate cultural attitudes with regard to computers. However, since we know that attitudes to computing do affect learning with computers (Hoyles, 1988), that computer use can increase student interest in other academic subjects (Krendl and Lieberman, 1988) and since we also know that attitudes to learning and styles of approach are also influenced by the socio-cultural context within which they occur (Vygotsky, 1962; Bruner, 1985) we should bear in mind that culturally related attitudes may be factors interacting with others of cultural origin.

Language differences

Bilinguals working in their second language may experience difficulties with computer software or hardware caused by:

1 Their level of competence in English and the demands of the task.
2 The suitability and availability of the support available from the teacher, fellow pupils, computer hardware and software.

Difficulties arising from poor English skills may be tackled in a variety of ways, and an imaginative approach can overcome feelings of isolation and disadvantage. For example, both Folio (a word processing package) and My World (Framework) both have activities which use Punjabi, and My World will shortly offer Urdu, as well as Welsh, French and German. Programs such as these could be helpful to those with limited English, but perhaps more importantly, can offer activities in which 'minority' children may excel, and in which they may perhaps tutor their English monolingual classmates.

There are also ways in which ESL pupils can work with English-language software, yet still use their preferred language to advantage. As Fadil found (private communication), 9-year-old children working collaboratively with Logo show an increase in both the quality and quantity of their work-related talk when they switch from English to their home language. She also notes that 'The changes in power relations and modifications to the teacher's role noted elsewhere in IT classrooms were increased in this situation, which accentuated the change in teacher's role from controller to expert consultant.' Fadil's work so far has been limited to a small pilot study, but it seems likely that a monolingual teacher's role *must* change in such situations. The issue then becomes *how best* this might be dealt with so that learners can capitalize on their linguistic expertise, but still have the guidance of the teacher where appropriate. Fadil claims that Logo is an ideal medium for this purpose in that the processes and results of the children's work are systematically set out for the teacher, even though the supporting oral discussion is not. However, since the Logo work requires such a limited English input, it alleviates much of the disadvantage which ESL pupils might experience with a more linguistically demanding program.

One further point of interest is the boost in morale which could be given to ESL learners when using software in their home language. AS LCHC suggest:

> At first glance it might seem that networking which involves communication in more than one language would be a detriment to the construction of joint activity, except where language learning was the specific object of study. Experience has proven otherwise. In an early experiment on the organization of joint computer-mediated activity using telecommunications in San Diego, Diaz (1988) found that students of Hispanic origin became excited and involved when they encountered material coming over the network in Spanish as well as English. These occasions provided a rare circumstance in

which knowledge of Spanish was treated as a social advantage instead of a stigma, a finding also reported by Riel (1986). Diaz reports that the students' language arts skills increased in both Spanish and English.

(LCHC, 1989, p. 81)

BASIC SKILLS AND WAYS OF WORKING

Whilst there is little doubt that some basic *keyboard* skills are essential if progress towards computing competency is to be made, the way these are acquired is more problematic. As suggested in the previous section, a view of education as a bottom-up process is likely to lead to a preference for an early emphasis on rote drill, and this emphasis may be unevenly distributed across social groups. The limiting factor then becomes the point at which pupils are enabled to branch out and use the computing skills they have acquired for tasks which involve higher learning processes, even though the computer/keyboard competencies required may be minimal. Thus basic skills in computer use should not be confused with basic skills in, say, writing or mathematics. What we can envisage is a matrix in which the horizontal and vertical interact:

		Computer demands	
		low	high
Subject	low		
demands	high		

Where computer skills are not advanced but progress within the topic being studied is advanced, it is nonetheless possible for pupils to use the computer profitably. For example, there are many programs set up for use in primary schools, where the program includes instructions to depress only one or two keys for each response, yet where the problem solving skills required may be complex. For example, Granny's Garden, which involves reading and following directions from the screen, as well as quite complex problem solving skills, only requires a few keys to be pressed for any one 'turn'. In fact, most CAL programs that employ multi-choice questions require only a single key press. Others involving answers in numbers or words require more than one key press, but do not require advanced keyboard skills. It is even possible to avoid the keyboard altogether with some software, and use a 'mouse' or 'concept' keyboard. On the other hand, once children become reasonably competent at 'typing' on the keyboard, they can use word processing in software for writing, editing and communicating with an audience even though their literacy skills are poor.

Since the computer temporarily removes the stress on legible hand-writing, it is often found that children are motivated to produce far more computer 'writing' than they would be prepared to do by hand. What is more, the editing facility enables them to produce finished work which is devoid of mistakes and corrections, even though their usual level of competence in manually produced text would prevent this.

However, as we have seen above, there are variations in preferred styles of working which are affected by factors such as gender and other socio-cultural factors. It is therefore important for teachers to be aware of these potential differences in preference and to attempt to help all learners to gain optimal access and experience from the computer. At the time of writing there is an emphasis in our schools on the use of language across the curriculum and on the development of oral communicative skills for which it seems that computers, appropriately used, are extremely useful. Dudley-Marling and Searle (1989) conclude:

> The greatest potential for microcomputers in language learning may be as a medium for increasing student opportunities for using language by bringing students and teachers together around a shared activity.
>
> (Dudley-Marling and Searle, 1989, p. 41)

This sharing is undoubtedly important, but there is also a great deal to be gained through composing and editing on the computer. Researchers (for example Haas, 1989, and Robinson-Staveley and Cooper, 1990), as well as many teachers (see this and the preceding chapter) consistently report an increase in the *quantity* of work produced on the computer as compared with pen and paper. Changes in *quality* seem to be more complex. Whereas Robinson-Staveley and Cooper (above) report improved quality in terms of content and fewer errors. Haas (above) suggests a more complex interaction. Letters composed directly on to the computer in her study were of poorer quality in terms of content (though not in terms of 'mechanics'). However, when revising with the computer writers re-read their texts more. In Haas' study participants were not allowed to print out their letters for the purpose of correcting and editing. As she reports, this may well have affected their 'text sense'. From my own experience I would suggest that this is a serious factor and one which illustrates the importance of encouraging a flexible approach to composing and editing with computers so as to encourage preferred modes of working. This topic is discussed more fully in Chapter 8.

Clearly the issues of basic skills and preferred methods of working are likely to interact in highly individual and complex ways. At the very least, lack of basic computing skills should not be used as an argument for denying access to pupils in school. Failure to develop such skills within the school environment has increasingly serious implications for adult life, and no child should be denied the opportunity and advantages that IT can bring to their development across the curriculum. Rather, we would ask what are the *minimum* skills required to tackle the particular task in question, which would also be sufficient to avoid frustration through lack of skill competence.

CONCLUSIONS

This chapter discussed the difficulties of access, and we saw that these are in part associated with gender, ethnicity and social class. Closely bound with the issue of physical access to the computer in the classroom and to appropriate software are also those of access to computer skills and to appropriate curricular and classroom organisation.

REFERENCES

Anderson, R. E. (1987) 'Females surpass males in computer problem solving: findings from the Minnesota Computer Literacy Assessment', *Journal of Educational Computing Research*, 3(1).

Bruner, J. (1985) 'On teaching thinking: an afterthought' in Chipman, S. F., Sega, J. W. and Glaser, R. (eds) *Thinking and Learning Skills, Vol. 2, Research and Open Questions*, Hillsdale, NJ: Lawrence Erlbaum Associates Inc.

Char, C., Hawkings, J., Wooten, J., Sheingold, K. and Roberts, T. (1983) 'Classroom case studies of software, video and print materials', Report to the US Department of Education, New York, Bank St College of Education.

Cockburn, C. (1987) 'Computers: hands on, hands off', in Cockburn, C. (ed.) *Two-Track Training: sex inequalities and the YTS*, Basingstoke, Macmillan, pp. 149–68.

Counsell, P. (1990) 'Hardware – are you on target?', *Hexagon: Oxfordshire Computer Education Newsletter* 12.

Department of Education and Science (1989 and 1991) *A Survey of Information Technology in Schools*, London, Government Statistical Service.

Dudley-Marling, C. and Searle, D. (1989) 'Computers and language learning: misguided assumptions', *British Journal of Educational Technology*, 20(1).

Haas, C. (1989) 'Does the medium make a difference? Two studies of writing with pen and paper and with computers, *Human–computer Interaction*, 4.

Hawkins, J. (1984) *Computers and girls: rethinking the issues*, Bank Street Technical Report, 24.

Hoyles, C. (ed.) (1988) *Girls and Computers*, Bedford Way Papers 34, London, Institute of Education, University of London.

Hoyles, C. and Sutherland, R. (1989) *Logo Mathematics in the Classroom*, London, Routledge.

Hoyles, C., Sutherland, R. and Healey, J. (1990) 'Children talking in computers environments: new insights on the role of discussion in mathematics teaching', in Durkin, K. and Shine, B. (eds) *Language and Mathematical Education*, Milton Keynes, Open University Press.

Hughes, M., Brackenbridge, A., Bibby, A. and Greenhaugh, P. (1988) 'Girls, boys and turtles: gender effects in young children learning with logo', in Hoyles, C. (ed.) *Girls and Computers*, Institute of Education, Bedford Way Papers 34.

Krendl, K. A. and Lieberman, D. A. (1988) 'Computers and learning: a review of recent research', *Journal of Educational Computing Research*, 4(4).

Laboratory of Comparative Human Cognition (1989) 'Kids and computers: a positive vision of the future', *Harvard Educational Review*, 59(1).

Nielsen, J. and Roepstorf, L. (1985) 'Girls and computers', paper prepared for GASAT III Conference, Kingston, UK, April.

Office of Technology Assessment (1988) *Power On! New Tools for Teaching and Learning*, Washington, US Government Printing Office.

Robinson-Staveley, K. and Cooper, J. (1990) 'The use of computers for writing: effects on an English composition class', *Journal of Educational Computing Research*, 6(1).

Siann, G., Durndill, A., McLeod, H. and Glissou, P. (1988) 'Stereotyping in relation to the gender gap in participation in computing', *Educational Research*, 30(2).

Sutherland, R. and Hoyles, C. (1988) 'Gender perspectives on Logo Programming in the Mathematics Curriculum', in Hoyles, C. (ed.) *Girls and Computers*, Bedford Way Papers 34, London, London Institute of Education.

Vygotsky, L. S. (1962) *Thought and Language*, Cambridge, MIT Press.

Part II

Computers and language development

Chapter 7

Software: an underestimated variable?

Peter Scrimshaw

In Part I we looked at a number of different aspects of the role of the computer in classrooms, but throughout the computer was treated as a monolithic entity. Yet it is clear that the provision of different software changes the potential uses of computers quite dramatically. In Part 2 therefore we will look at some of the main kinds of software available for promoting language development, and see in what ways the differences between them might affect classroom activities. For each kind of program considered we can ask four questions:

1 What are the distinctive features of this sort of software?
2 What forms of cooperation does it encourage between learners?
3 How can the teacher contribute to its effective use by learners?
4 How useful is a communicative theory of learning in understanding how this software is used in classrooms?

Each of the remaining chapters in Part II looks at a specific kind of software, and considers some aspects of these questions. In part the differences of emphasis from chapter to chapter reflect our own interests and the amount and kind of material available, but we have also tried to avoid undue repetition by using each chapter to look in depth at particular aspects of computers in classrooms, passing more lightly over issues dealt with elsewhere in the book.

Word processing packages are probably the most common form of software in schools. In Chapter 8 we look in particular at how these packages can be used to encourage different kinds of cooperative working. Word processors tend to be used only as electronic typewriters, but it is clear that the more advanced packages now becoming available allow the teacher to use them to support all stages of writing from planning through to printing out the final version. There is also some evidence that word processing does affect both the quantity and quality of writing that is produced, in part by changing the methods of composition that learners use. But without some assistance, these improvements tend to remain at the level of the surface detail of the writing. This assistance may come from the teacher or from other learners, yet even if we consider only cooperation between learners, this can take different forms and provide different opportunities for learning. A key element is how the group shares out tasks between them, and how skilled they are at managing their own collective learning; as one researcher notes, arranging text is easier than arranging collaboration. Where learners are cooperating together, teachers' contributions are if anything, more rather than less complex. They need to try out ideas and observe their effects, instruct learners in the basics of computer use and in the more obscure aspects of the word processing package being used, and to help the group develop and sustain a successful way of working together.

In Chapter 9 Bernadette Robinson discusses the new possibilities opened up when a computer is linked to others, allowing the user access to other learners and to new databases of information outside the classroom. She sees them as providing new opportunities for social transaction, either through electronic mail ('e-mail') systems, that allow the exchange of messages between individuals, or through conferencing systems, in which a whole group is given open access to all the messages that each wishes to send. This provides, so to speak, the equivalent of the face-to-face meeting, in which what is said by each is heard by all. It thus provides a new forum of collaborative learning, giving members access to the views of others that they would be unable to meet face to face. The educational implications of this for the physically disadvantaged or those living in remote locations are clear.

As Robinson shows, there is a wide range of ways to take advantage of this sort of electronic network. She discusses, for example, an e-mail project in which secondary pupils provided the start of an adventure on the network for a group of primary pupils, and then responded to them in role as the adventure evolved. This led not only to the composition of the text, but also a great deal of discussion and problem solving by both groups. At the same time it illustrates neatly the way in which the teacher's role is also changed, with the older pupils in effect taking over part of the responsibility for the younger children's learning. It also provides some parallels to the word processing case, for when a group is sitting round the keyboard preparing their message they are in effect engaged in cooperative word processing. Yet introducing a collaborative enterprise of this sort changed rather than eliminated the teacher's contribution; as Robinson notes, the e-mail messages were seen as real and authoritative, while one result of letting the secondary pupils lead the process of story development was that the teachers became enablers of the pupils' activities.

Robinson then turns to computer conferencing. She points out that there is already evidence that this is not simply a new form of written communication or a new form of 'spoken' communication, but a novel hybrid containing features of both, and still visibly evolving its own conventions. This is not just a different method of developing conventional writing competences, but one that in part redefines the nature of both writing and speech. The invention of the typewriter and word processor made hand-writing just one way of writing rather than an integral part of what we take writing to be. Similarly, computer conferencing may significantly alter the notion of a conversation because it strips out all the non-verbal cues (and many of the verbal ones too) from the talk, without turning it simply into conventional writing.

Computer conferences require a moderator, who ensures that everyone keeps to the rules, handles the mechanics of connecting new members to the conference, and so on. Here too we can perhaps see a potential new role for teachers, which has some points of contact with their usual methods of supporting a group dialogue, but also raise new issues of teacher control and learner freedom.

Robinson sees computer conferencing as potentially providing some elements of scaffolding for learning, because it allows knowledge to be constructed from wider sources and stores the interaction for later reflection, thus helping to build a very explicit shared context. On the other hand, the sheer amount of information retained, without the automatic screening that eliminates much of what is heard in discussion, may overwhelm the learner. Robinson suggests that it is here that an informed tutor or peer may be needed to help the learner identify critical structures in the material. Again, the very informality of conferencing dialogues, compared to other forms of written communication, may make it harder to stay task focused. Never-theless, Robinson concludes that, despite the considerable technical and practical difficulties it presents, communicating through computers can make a number of substantial contributions to classroom learning.

In Chapter 10 we move away from open ended software such as word processors and computer conferencing, to consider text disclosure pack-ages. These are used to develop pupil's text comprehension abilities. A text is entered by the teacher and then largely made invisible, leaving just a few letters and the punctuation marks visible. The pupils then try to recreate the text by guessing what letters are to be found at each point in the text. As the text emerges, so they have an increasingly rich context for such guesses, and can begin to hypothesise as to what the text is about, and what particular sentences and phrases might be. These programs are generally used by groups, and allow the teacher a considerable degree of freedom in the way that they are used.

Such programs are clearly ones to which a communicative theory of learning should have some relevance. In this chapter we look at a number of teachers' accounts of their experiences with such programs and at some research studies on them. None of these publications were written explicitly within the framework of a communicative theory, but they do collectively pick out the issues to do with these programs that teachers are most inter-ested in. So by using concepts from a communicative theory to organise this information we should be able to see how far such a theory really does help to make explicit the educationally important aspects of such programs and their use. In particular, the relevance of the concepts of educational tasks, zones of proximal development and scaffolding is explored.

In educational contexts the notion of a task is very often problematical. Pupil and teacher may have different understandings of what the task is. Indeed, where the aim is to increase understanding, pupils will not, by definition, initially have a full grasp of the task, as to achieve that grasp is part of what needs to be learned. In the teachers' accounts of their use of text disclosure programs it is possible to see a range of notions of the task involved, that makes up a developmental sequence. The teacher's role as scaffolder is to help pupils achieve the task in the most simple sense, and then to move them on to a more complex formulation of the task and repeat the sequence. For each reconceptualisation the teacher will need rather different classroom strategies. In choosing these, one aim will be to keep in step with the pupil's growing understanding of what can be learned from the program; i.e. to ensure that each new demand falls within each pupil's zone of proximal development.

What emerges from considering the concepts of task, scaffolding and the zone of proximal development in the context of using these programs? One conclusion is that these concepts are indeed helpful as a way of identifying what to look for in the teacher accounts and the other kinds of research evidence we have. By implication, therefore, they should be even more useful to a teacher systematically observing classroom activities with these concepts in mind from the outset. On the other hand, these concepts gain at least as much from being considered in this concrete context as they contribute. They are, in themselves, general and hard to translate into specific advice for the practitioner. If, however, they are seen in the framework of the actual choices that teachers and learners have as they use these programs, a much more informative picture emerges.

In Chapter 11 Diana Laurillard looks critically at the question of the extent to which claims made in this book for a communicative approach to first language learning can be extended to cover second language learning too. She first reviews the available methods of promoting second language learning, and recognises that a communicative approach is widely used in Britain. She argues that the success of this way of teaching is far from established, and that there are good reasons to doubt its effectiveness, at least as the sole approach to be used. She emphasises the value of a knowledge of generative grammatical rules for second language learners, and the need to provide opportunities for both learner-controlled exploration and teacher-controlled demonstration. She argues that Vygotsky's work does not provide support for a second language teaching strategy based purely on a communicative theory. If language usage and learning are context dependent, then we need to consider whether the context is the same for second language learning as it is for a first language. She argues that they are not, and that a Vygotskian approach to second language learning would see it as involving learning consciously and deliberately, rather in the way that children learn scientific concepts, rather than the spontaneous and informal mode of learning through which a first language is acquired.

Laurillard then discusses a psycho-linguistic perspective, which suggests a number of problems that the spontaneous second language learner faces, and suggests that these too indicate that a more structured and explicit approach will be needed. This approach she then specifies in general terms. She concludes that the communicative approach, which relies principally upon induction for learning linguistic forms in the target language creates too great a cognitive load for learners. What is needed is a communicative methodology that is supplemented by the explicit teaching of the underlying grammatical rules.

So can we look to computers to support this grammatical learning? Laurillard sees many of today's programs as clearly inadequate in terms of the analysis of the problem that she has already presented. She concludes the chapter with a detailed analysis of a program designed to teach some underlying grammatical rules in a way that meets the requirements she has identified. This program is tightly structured and designed eventually to make the choice of a correct grammatical form automatic for the learner. It offers, therefore, a highly organised form of scaffolding for the learning of an important but specific kind of linguistic knowledge. In both these respects it stands in strong contrast to the way in which a word processing or computer conferencing system assists the learner.

For all the kinds of software considered so far it is possible to ask how open ended they are; indeed they form a rough spectrum from open ended to closed. In Chapter 12 we consider hypertext systems. These can be seen as a specialised type of programming language which can be used to create pieces of text, pictures and, in more advanced versions known as hyper-media systems, moving pictures, sound sequences and runnable computer programs. All of these elements can then be linked together in a network of connections, so that at any one point in the network users can choose which piece of information to go to next. Hypertexts can be designed to be as open or closed as the designer wishes; users may be tightly constrained within networks with few links (and so few user choices) at each point, or very open with plenty of alternative routes through the network on offer. On a more radical level, there is also the choice between allowing users to read a fixed hypertext created by someone else, to write their own from scratch, or, as an intermediate position, to be given a modifiable hypertext from which to start, which they then extend or rewrite.

Within the read-only category we can distinguish factual hypertexts and fictional ones, with adventure games as the best known example of the latter. As with a conventional text, read-only hypertexts can be designed for the reader to handle alone, or with the help of others. At the other end of the spectrum a hypertext system can be given to learners as a writing aid; a sort of non-linear word processing and information handling device. One approach is simply to let writers put together whatever information they wish, linking up items as they go on the basis of an intuitive sense of the relationships. Another is to see the system as an aid to good writing, and to build in procedures that require the writer to work within a particular model of planning by, for instance, providing an initially open structure and then directing them towards a more hierarchical pattern of writing.

Most hypertexts can be used by individuals or groups at a single computer, but they can also be put on to computer networks for shared use by people in different locations. In this variant, the hypertext system becomes a particular and very flexible variant upon the sort of systems discussed by Robinson in Chapter 9. Indeed we can envisage such systems that include read-only hypertexts for reference (i.e. a sort of networked database), an electronic mail and conferencing system for collaborative discussion of what is in the shared database, and a hypertext writing system for each individual's own evolving notes and ideas. But we can also put computer programs on such a system, such as the text disclosure packages and second language learning programs discussed in Chapters 10 and 11. Hypertext systems, therefore, emerge as a form of integrating system that can in principle be used by an individual learner to bring together and coordinate the contributions of otherwise inaccessible learners, teachers, reference sources and computer aided learning packages. It would thus provide what has been called the virtual classroom; a classroom that has no single physical location, and one in which all the sources of advice and information are sucked into the computer and optimally structured for learners' use before being made available to them. Such systems are technically possible already, and will get steadily more easy to use and more sophisticated in what they can offer. However, face-to-face teaching and collaboration will remain essential, not least because not everything worth learning can be transmitted electronically.

What the possibility of the virtual classroom emphasises is the way in which the introduction of computers does not eliminate the need to make fundamental educational choices. A theme that emerges in all the chapters in Part II is that of the tension between teacher and learner control over what is learned, and how this tension is to be productively resolved. Computer programs may appear to be a third independent influence upon learning, but in practice their effects are always mediated and altered by the particular social context of activity within which they operate. Exactly the same kinds of educational issues are therefore likely to appear in the virtual classroom as in the conventional one, albeit in interestingly different forms.

In the final chapter we both look to the future and summarise some of the main themes of the book, by considering what aspects of classroom life need to be researched if we are to make better use of computers, what research methodologies are most appropriate for improving our understanding of their role, and how a communicative theory needs to be developed further to provide the conceptual framework that this research needs.

Chapter 8

Cooperative writing with computers

Peter Scrimshaw

Introduction

Word processors are one of the most popular kinds of computer package for use in schools, and discussions of their use figure prominently in publications for teachers on IT and language, such as the NATE book on the subject (NATE, 1990), as well as in more general introductions to the place of IT in schools (e.g. Straker, 1989). There is broad agreement that word processors are very useful, and that they can and should be used co-operatively. As Eunice Fisher points out in Chapter 6 this is in part no doubt a practical matter; there are too few computers in most schools to make extensive individual use possible. However, there are, as we have seen from Chapters 3 and 4, good reasons to favour cooperative use anyway. Several questions arise at once. In the case of word processing in particular, what does such cooperation involve? What facilities does a word processor offer, and how do they map onto the demands of writing? Is there any evidence that using word processors makes any difference to how and what children are likely to write? Finally, what demands does this method of working make of the teacher? This chapter aims to address these questions.

WRITING WITH WORD PROCESSORS

The writing process has several elements; these can be variously labelled and subdivided. The NATE English and New Technologies Committee (1990) suggest the following stages, each with its predominant concerns:

- Planning (purpose, audience, communication, collaboration, etc.)
- Drafting (mode, tenor, style, register, etc.)
- Creating (aesthetic, transactional, expressive)
- Re-drafting (critical assessment of own and other's work)
- Editing (attention to spelling, re-casting of awkward sentences)
- Publishing (neat copy, layout, headings, print style, etc.)

This list helps to identify elements in the writing process and the relationships between them, but does not imply that these stages are sequential. The cycle of planning, drafting and re-drafting may need to be gone through more than once, while the boundaries between stages are not always clear-cut. Nevertheless, such a list identifies the terrain that children have to cover, individually or jointly, when creating a text. So how far can word processors help with such a task?

Word processing packages, or at least the more complex ones, can contribute something at every stage of writing. While the word processors available in schools are sometimes rather limited, more sophisticated packages are appearing all the time, as the more powerful computers come down in price. These packages allow children, either individually or in groups, to employ the word processor flexibly at every stage of writing, so that the facilities it offers can be mixed and matched to suit the educational requirements of the situation.

When starting to compose a text the child can simplify the mechanics of planning with programs called outliners or ideas processors. These are often built into the word processing package itself, and provide a quick method of sketching out and rapidly reordering headings, subheadings, notes on topics and other details. Often the resulting outline can be used directly as the basis for the main text. Such a program can fulfil many of the functions of a rough plan on paper. While the actual keying in of the outline could be an individual task, the brainstorming, discussion and ideas for sequencing that it involves are carried out as well, or better, by a group.

At the drafting and creating stage a word processor acts as something close to a conventional typewriter, but where redrafting is needed it has considerable advantages over the typewriter. The main one is that phrases, sentences or whole blocks of text can be moved, copied or deleted from the draft. An illustration of the value of this is provided by Jill Sawford's case study of drafting (1989). These capabilities allow structural changes to be made quickly, and they can be easily reversed if they are not acceptable. Children can also print out alternative versions of their text for comparison and discussion.

Detailed textual editing is also very much simplified, as letters and words can be entered, changed or deleted in the same way. Children can use built-in dictionaries or spellcheckers to monitor the text; these pick out any words that the dictionary does not contain, including spelling errors. Some programs can suggest correct spellings too, while many allow the users to add their own customised list of additional words that the checker will in future accept as correct. In some cases a thesaurus is also provided.

At a more advanced level, a type of program that is becoming more widely available for use at the re-drafting stage is the style checker. This looks through a text for grammatical or stylistic features that its designers consider unsuitable, e.g. overused words, or clumsy constructions. The pupil (or the teacher) may also be able to choose the style of writing (say, 'literary' or 'business') against which a particular text should be checked. To the extent that these style (and spelling) checkers are automatic, they can be used equally well by a group or an individual.

When the publishing stage is reached, another range of facilities comes into play. These allow the writer to choose from a variety of typefaces and sizes of print, and sometimes from a range of print colours too, if a colour printer is available. Simple page layout features can also be altered as required, and sometimes graphics can be added. One particularly important provision is that of non-English characters. Some packages allow the user to choose between, for instance, English, French and German character sets. There are also word processing packages available allowing children to write in Urdu, Bengali or Arabic. The importance of this for enabling bilingual children to extend their literacy skills is obvious, as one National Oracy Project Coordinator has pointed out (Kemeny, 1990).

Word processors are now very widely used in schools, and there are an increasing number of reports by teachers of the ways in which they are being used. In the UK the PALM Project, for instance, has been investigating the ways in which information technology can be used by teachers to promote their pupils' autonomy in learning. Several of the teachers involved have published their reflections on the very different ways in which word processing packages have affected their work, and what their pupils gained from their use (Webb, S. (n.d.), Fuller, D. (1990), Mills, M. (1990)).

WHAT DIFFERENCE DOES A WORD PROCESSOR MAKE?

A helpful article by Marilyn Cochrane-Smith (1991) summarises much of the published American research (both classroom and laboratory based) on word processing and writing. Let us first consider the findings in situations where, generally speaking, there was no direct teacher intervention. She reports that both the quantity and quality of texts are affected by replacing pencil and paper by a word processor. One result is that texts tend to be longer, and students spend more time over them. They often also produce neater, more error-free texts; however word processing of itself does not generally improve the overall quality of students' writing.

The source of these effects may be that word processors change how students actually compose texts. The effects include increases in the number of changes made to the text compared with pencil and paper methods, although such changes are more likely to be surface level alterations and correction, rather than modifications to the substantive meaning of the text. Where the computer provides some form of prompting this can result in students producing longer and more error-free texts. This is particularly helpful to those with less well developed writing and revising skills.

On the other hand, writers with greater writing and revising skills initially are able to use word processors more effectively than those who are less skilled. This may be in part because when using word processors students tend to think of the capabilities of the word processor in terms set by their own conception of composing and revising. This enables those with more sophisticated conceptions of the writing task to see more potential in the word processor than others.

However in studies where instructional intervention took place, the picture was rather different. Cochrane-Smith reports that when students are prompted by tutors to see their writing as a meaning-making activity the use of word processors may make it easier for them to experiment and take risks with their writing. In short, word processors without teacher support are helpful to at least some students in improving the surface details of their writing, but for any more fundamental improvement they need the advice and encouragement of a more experienced writer than themselves, in order to fully grasp the potential of the word processor as a writing aid. While the word processor may help writers to pursue what they see as their writing task more efficiently, it does not challenge any shortcomings or oversimplifications in their conception of the task itself. For instance, children who think of a story as a linear sequence of loosely connected events may be able to write such stories at greater length and with less spelling errors using a word processor, but they will still produce the same kind of story unless the teacher or another child challenges this approach.

This leads to another central point. As Cochrane-Smith emphasises, computer use is a social practice, not something that is simply determined by the nature of the hardware and software involved. The American research she reviewed suggests that within the classroom this has three main effects.

The first is that how individual teachers interpret word processing will affect what can be done with it by students in their classrooms. Furthermore, teachers' conceptions develop over time, as they gain experience with the software. Secondly, how teachers organise the classroom for learning and how they structure the writing curriculum will also affect the role created for the word processor. Finally, the more public nature of computer based writing often prompts teachers and students to construct new social arrangements, especially ones involving collaboration and coached writing situations. This in turn may alter the conceptions of writing of both teacher and students. As Cochrane-Smith puts it:

> the way word processing (or other computer technology) is deployed in the individual classroom is dependent on the learning organisation of the classroom which, in reciprocal fashion, may also be shaped and changed by the capacities of computer technology to accommodate new patterns of social organisation and interaction.
>
> (p. 122)

But a central thesis of this book is that working together is potentially the best way to learn, so how can word processing help support that approach in particular?

HOW CAN COMPUTERS HELP CHILDREN WRITE COOPERATIVELY?

In planning for cooperative working, it is important to be clear about the particular kinds of working styles the teacher wants them to adopt during the activity, and how the computer may help with these.

Cooperative working picks out a diverse range of pupil's activities, which vary greatly. The distinctions between them are reasonably clear, but there is no settled terminology for describing them. I will take cooperative working to cover any teacher-independent activity involving more than one child. Within this general heading we can usefully identify four important variants, distinguished by the way in which the group divides up both the tasks that make up the activity and responsibility for scaffolding learning.

One strategy is to arrange a division of labour. Here the pair (to take the simplest case) share out the tasks between them each taking responsibility for particular tasks within the overall activity, which they then *do* individually. Although both learners are doing some part of the overall activity they have little need to discuss what they are doing, as each of the tasks involved is seen as the exclusive property of one or the other. A second strategy we may call serial working. Here each task is done by both learners, but always individually, the two exchanging roles after a certain point. Again there may be little need for discussion of the tasks, although this depends on the rate at which the changeovers occur. Pupils using either division of labour or serial working strategies may have little opportunity for, and see little need for, scaffolding, as each learner is at any given time absorbed in a different set of problems from the other.

The third strategy is peer tutoring. This involves a more skilled child acting as tutor to another. Unlike the division of labour or serial working strategies, this requires that they both deal together with each task as it arises, but with one of them scaffolding the attempts of the other to deal with it. Responsibility for defining each task falls to the tutoring member of the pair, who is, by definition, the one who knows what the pair should be doing. Finally, in collaborative working both learners jointly take part in each task whenever it arises. The defining of each task (and how best to complete it) has to be jointly negotiated, and there is no fixed allocation of scaffolding roles between the pair. Each takes the lead as and when they feel able to do so, resolving any differences of view by appeal to the likely results rather than to their relative positions.

In practice, elements of all four approaches can appear in real situations, but the balance between them is what gives different kinds of group work much of their distinctive character, as well as greatly influencing the learning opportunities that arise.

It follows therefore that just putting a group at the word processor will not be sufficient, as they may adopt division of labour or serial working as their main strategies. The weakness of these methods of working is that they discourage discussion of the task, because by definition the children using those approaches are actually concerned with different tasks from each other at any one time, making discussion unnecessary, unless there is some problem encountered, in which case they have to move into either peer tutoring or collaboration to solve it. Yet we have argued in earlier chapters that discussion is a very important aspect of the learning experience. Both peer tutoring and collaborative working give children responsibility for the learning of their peers. Helping another thus arises throughout, rather than occurring only when there is some obvious collapse of their attempts to work individually. How then can word processing be handled so as to support either collaborative working or peer tutoring approaches?

PEER TUTORING AND WORD PROCESSING

Peer tutoring has been defined above as a situation where a more skilled child acts as tutor to another. Yet the reality is hardly likely to be as neat as this definition suggests. Given that there are a variety of tasks to cover, these may be handled in different ways, some by peer tutoring, others collaboratively and so forth. Even where the teacher plans a definite division of roles, these may fray round the edges in practice, as the children interpret the work in their own way.

Both of these points are illustrated in Heap's (1989) study of word processing in a Canadian classroom. Working from observation and some 13 hours of videotaped sessions, he analysed carefully the ways in which tasks were shared within a number of different groups, working in what was envisaged as a form of peer tutoring.

In this classroom the teacher's method of using the word processor was to simplify the task of writing with a computer for the children by dividing off the task of writing a story from that of learning the more technical aspects of word processor use. A child would therefore be designated by the teacher to write a story on the computer, but would be allowed to choose a helper or, in some cases, two. The helper was meant to act as a technical adviser, having the main responsibility for arranging text on the video monitor through using the keyboard, while the writer's main task was to compose the story itself. In the event this neat division of labour was not sustained, as all the helpers Heap observed actually assisted in all parts of the writing. From our point of view the main interest of this study is what happened to the discussion between the children as the text was being produced.

Heap distinguishes between three tasks that the use of the word processor required of the children. One was composing; i.e. deciding what would go into the story. The second was inputting the text through the use of the display keys, i.e. those that placed a letter or number on the screen display. The third was the operation of arranging this text through the use of the executive keys, such as those which started a new line, deleted a letter or entered a space between words.

Composing was 'officially' the right and responsibility of the writer; in reality the helpers always contributed, but their offerings consisted mostly of suggesting words that could be used in the writer's story; it was for the writer to make the final decision.

Inputting the text was seen by the children as something over which the writer had control, but this entitlement could be transferred at will to the helper, especially where the helper appeared to know the keyboard better than the writer. The writer tended to take on the use of the display keys, with the helper given the main responsibility for the executive keys, such as delete or space.

When it came to the arranging of the text, Heap's observations suggested that the pattern of responsibility was different again. Both writer and helper assumed that they had the right to arrange the text, and so sometimes competed for the use of the executive keys. This was in part affected by the physical layout of the workplace. In a description of the form that this competition sometimes took, Heap illuminates many of the central issues about the relationship between collaboration and word processing:

> Such disputes sometimes arose because of there being three chairs but only two students . . . Confusion arose if the writer took the left chair and tried to 'drive' from it, with the helper too well positioned for the writer successfully to resist invasions of display-key terrain. Or trouble arose if the helper sat on the left side chair. Use of the delete key required the helper to cross the display-key terrain. This in itself became a problem only when the writer was engaged in inputting.
>
> As the above makes evident, access to and use of the keyboard was at times a contentious issue. The writer faced the most trouble when there were two helpers, one on each side. In such terrain disputes, which were mainly inputting and punctuation disputes, a writer occasionally grabbed a helper's hand. The helper's hand would be lifted from a key, shoved away, held immobile, or, more rarely, sometimes directed to a specific key.
>
> What these struggles reveal is the importance to students of control over the text production process. The practices of composing, inputting, and arranging presuppose solutions to the problem of who will control what happens next. The problem of control is entwined with the problem of communicating what they are doing and what needs to be done. The problem of control is endemic to collaboration. It is easier to arrange text than it is to arrange collaboration.

(p. 285)

This also brings out the way in which quite small changes in seating arrangements or keyboard layout may affect working patterns significantly; a point that has been further documented in another Canadian study by John Brine (1991).

COLLABORATIVE WRITING WITH WORD PROCESSORS

One account of collaborative writing with a word processor is given by Gareth Davies, a British teacher researcher, working in his own classroom, (Davies, 1989). He began from a wish to encourage the 10- and 11-year-old children in his class to develop their writing from their own needs, rather than from his instigation. He saw the key to this as being to emphasise the enjoyment of writing and to give them a wider audience than himself. One way of doing this was to set pairs of children to write a story collaboratively, initially with paper and pencil. He comments:

> the collaborative writing had gone a long way, but not all the way towards meeting my initial optimistic expectations . . . This was particularly apparent when I came to consider the question of ownership of the writing. In many groups neither child felt that he or she really owned it. In others, one child felt that it was exclusively hers. In such cases the partners felt left out and were even more disgruntled that where their ideas had been incorporated they had been appropriated by the more dominant writer.
>
> (pp. 100–1)

Davies noted that ownership of the writing depended largely upon who was actually transcribing. He also observed some changes in the quality of writing produced in those areas (plot, structure and characterisation, for instance) where the enthusiasm generated in the initial discussion was a factor. With other aspects, such as spelling and syntax, there was less apparent improvement.

He then arranged for pairs to work together using the word processor. He noticed a distinct change in patterns of working:

> Irrespective of who was controlling the keyboard it simply did not happen that one child took over control of the story and the composition process. Quite often the task of composition was as equally shared as the mechanical task of keying in the words. Each child in turn would have responsibility for composing a sentence, a few lines or a paragraph. [however] It was common for one partner to take over and finish a sentence begun by the other, to suggest alternatives and additions, and to draw attention to inconsistencies with what had already been written.
>
> (p. 102)

In this classroom at least, the introduction of the word processor into the group's activities produced a shift from division of labour to a mixture of serial and collaborative working. There was, however, little impact on the quality of the writing itself, although the visual presentation improved and the children's pride in their work increased. In the light of the earlier discussion, it could be that this was because there was rather more serial than collaborative working. If so, this would not be likely to lead to much investigation of the alternatives that might exist to suggested words or phrases. Without such discussion it is hard to see how an improved quality of text would be achieved.

THE TEACHER'S CONTRIBUTION

The specific studies by Davies and Heap bring out in particular contexts the general point that Cochrane-Smith also emphasises: computer use is a social practice in which the ways in which the actors interpret and approach their tasks are as influential as the characteristics of the hardware and software itself. One important and encouraging consequence of this is that the teacher, far from being superseded by the computer, emerges as a key contributor to the situation. As the Heap study illustrates, even when children are working independently the teacher's way of framing and organising the situation affects how they operate. Similarly the Davies study, as well as those of the PALM teachers mentioned earlier, illustrate how reflective teachers can try out ideas in their classrooms, observe the effects carefully and then revise their strategies to explore the possibilities for greater understanding that computers offer for themselves and the children.

The teacher's contribution to cooperative work at the word processor is therefore both essential and complex. One task is to observe and analyse what is going on; what this chapter brings out is that it is the fine detail of classroom practices and assumptions that affect what happens. While summaries of research are very helpful in suggesting things for teachers to look out for in their classrooms they by no means guarantee that they will find them, or that if they do that they take the form that the research describes.

Another of the teacher's responsibilities is nothing to do with computers at all; it is to select and present the writing tasks that will stretch children's present competences further. In particular this will often involve helping children to understand at progressively more complex levels, what is involved in the strategic planning of different kinds of texts. No amount of hardware will make up for any deficiencies here, because as we have seen, the word processor can only be used to help children realise the plans that they are trying to formulate; it cannot improve the plan for them. For this the teacher, other children and non computer based curriculum materials have to provide the help.

A further set of tasks is progressively to introduce children to the facilities of the word processor that they have, and to insure, by instruction if necessary, that they are able to make effective technical use of them (and of the computer too, if they are not fully confident with it). First, they need to understand how to work the computer system on a purely mechanical level. Teachers are often anxious about their own understanding, making it easy to take children's claims to competence at face value, especially when the teacher wants to encourage and use the self-confidence that children so often reveal. But this is no reason for not noting very carefully exactly what different children can and cannot do, and taking steps to fill the gaps that emerge.

Much of what children eventually need to know cannot be learned efficiently through discovery, because computers do not show clearly enough on their surface what their underlying design and structure is. The computer I am using at present is supposed to be highly user-friendly. But it still has keys reading 'tab', 'caps lock', 'cntrl', 'delete', 'return', 'shift' and 'clear'. The meaning of these labels is not self-evident. Nor is the fact that these keys can often be used in combination to produce effects that bear no relationship at all to their labels, although it is something that any child will discover as soon as he or she inadvertently touches the wrong two keys at once. To make good use of this computer, arguably needs some straight instruction or closely guided 'discovery'.

All this gives a distinctly 'teacher-led' picture, and for these kinds of learning I believe this is appropriate. But it still does nothing to begin to shift the burden of learning on to the children themselves, through collaboration and peer tutoring. Yet this is essential if all the opportunities for learning in a classroom are to be taken up. In large classes the demands upon teachers are always going to outrun their time, unless some of that time is regularly devoted to helping children learn how to help each other. The teacher therefore has to require, facilitate and monitor the children's increasing use of collaborative or peer tutoring methods of working in preference to others.

To summarise, the teacher needs to help groups deal with the computer, with the overall strategic planning of their texts, and the organisation of their own methods of cooperative working. If there is little in the writing task, the computer system or word processing packages to move groups towards collaborative working, the teacher has to supply that direction and support in some way.

It follows that there is no general answer to the question of how much scaffolding teachers should provide for children's activities, except that it should be as little as possible, but as much as necessary. What this implies will vary greatly from situation to situation. Helping to promote strategic planning, and collaborative working require a different kind of teaching style from that needed to assist children in grasping the specifics of the computer's operation. This gives teachers a difficult problem, because it probably requires them to shift quickly between quite directive and much more open-ended ways of working with a group, within a single encounter. Getting children to understand why that is necessary may not be easy, but one measure of the teacher's success is that children do come to understand the rationale for these changes, and begin to try to implement them in their own work together.

REFERENCES

Anon (1990) 'Creating a context for multilingual work', in Kemeny, H. (ed.) (1990) 'Talking IT through', National Oracy Project and NCET, Coventry.

Brine, J. (1991) 'The implicit power of educational technology: word processing and collaborative publishing at the primary level', in Goodson and Mangan (1991).

Cochrane-Smith, M. (1991) 'Word processing and writing in elementary classrooms: a critical review of related literature', *Review of Educational Research*, 61(1).

Davies, G. (1989) 'Writing without a pencil', in Styles, M. (1989).

Emihovich, C. (ed.) (1989) *Locating Learning: Ethnographic Perspectives on Classroom and Research*, Norwood NJ, Ablex Publishing Corporation.

Fuller, D. (1990) 'Committed to excellence: a study of child learning using "desktop publishing" programs', *Teachers' Voices 14*, PALM Project, Norwich, National Council for Educational Technology.

Goodson, I. F. and Mangan, J. M. (eds) (1991) 'Computers, classrooms and culture: studies in the use of computers for classroom learning' RUCCUS Occasional Papers, vol. 2, RUCCUS, University of Western Ontario, London, Ontario.

Heap, J. L. (1989) 'Collaborative practices during word processing in a first grade classroom', in Emihovich, C. (1989).

Mills, M. (1990) 'Desk top groupies: group work with year 4 and 5 pupils', *Teachers' Voices 12*, PALM Project, Norwich, NCET.

NATE English and New Technologies Committee (1990) *IT's English: Accessing English with Computers* (2nd edn) Exeter, National Association for the Teaching of English.

Sawford, J. (1989) 'Case Study 8: the process of drafting', in Sawford, J. (1989) *Promoting Language Development Through IT*, Coventry, MESU.

Straker, A. (1989) *Children Using Computers*, Oxford, Blackwell Education.

Styles, M. (ed.) (1989) 'Collaboration and writing', Milton Keynes, Open University Press.

Webb, S. (n.d.) 'Like a jigsaw puzzle: helping each other put in the pieces', *Teachers' Voices 9*, PALM Project, Norwich, NCET.

Chapter 9

Communicating through computers in the classroom

Bernadette Robinson

INTRODUCTION

People communicating with each other using computers to do so is a relatively recent phenomenon. At the school level it is still a new and little used facility though interest and experiment in it are growing. This form of electronic communication is frequently described as having unrealised potential for education but seems a difficult one to implement. Nonetheless, the capability of the medium for providing interaction through communication networks offers new possibilities for the construction of shared knowledge through joint teaching-learning activities. Computer-supported workgroups are rapidly developing in other fields.

As Brand (1987) describes it, a computer without a telephone line attached to it is 'a poor lonely thing'. Linking a computer into a telecommunications system provides a means for people to exchange written messages across distance, to get information from remote databases or to join in the shared construction of one. New educational networks or groups can be created over local, national or international networks. Local Area Networks (LANS) can link individual terminals by cable within a campus or building; Wide Area Networks (WANS) can connect together individuals or schools over large distances, nationally and internationally, through public and private telecommunications systems. The technology needed for electronic communication is a telephone line linked to a central or host computer, a microcomputer with a modem (a signal converting device) to link it to the telephone, and the appropriate software for word processing and communications.

Some evidence has been offered by Paul Light in Chapter 4 that the use of the computer can lead to greater development of collaboration through encouraging increased verbalisation and peer interaction. It was seen as providing the means of structure and support to sustain this (the importance of structure in collaborative learning is highlighted in a review of research by Topping, 1992). Examination was made of ways in which talk and joint activity are used by learners and teachers to share knowledge, and the role that computers in classrooms can play in this. Underpinning this view of learning as a communicative process is Vygotsky's argument (1978, 1986) for social transaction, not solo performance, as the fundamental vehicle of education. Computer networks provide new opportunities for social transaction; they can create new kinds of groups (new in size, configuration and dispersal) and can remove constraints of time and distance on their interaction. They offer a 'medium for reorganising interactions' (Cole and Griffin, 1987) among learners and teachers and for creating new learning structures and 'zones' both within and beyond classrooms. One example of this is seen in an Australian experiment which used computer conferencing to expand the scientific community for learners beyond individual schools, and to create a learning environment which modelled the kind of collaborative investigation that 'real' scientists do (Rowbottom and Muhlebach, 1989). So communication through computers (or as it is commonly termed, computer mediated communication: CMC) provides the technical means of supporting collaborative learning and the sharing of knowledge beyond the confines of a particular place. But how well does the capability translate into practice? Is it possible for learners to generate dialogue and discourse using the medium? Does it support collaborative learning? What is it used for?

USES OF COMPUTERS FOR COMMUNICATION IN TEACHING AND LEARNING

The number of projects using computers for communication in teaching and learning has increased rapidly over the last five years, most particularly in North America, more recently in the UK and Europe. It has largely been used in three ways:

1 To provide access to databases.
2 To transmit messages electronically (e-mail) between individuals or bulletin boards. Messages, which can vary in length from a few words to many pages of text, are routed to the addressee's mailbox (a computer file) and stored until the addressee logs on to the system. Some group communication is also possible through the use of circulation lists and shared bulletin boards.
3 For computer conferencing or group 'discussion' through written exchanges by means of different conferencing systems (such as EIES, Caucus, CoSy, Participate, EKKO and others).

These facilities have been used to provide, for example:

1 An 'electronic university campus', such as Connected Education, USA. This uses the EIES conferencing system based in the central computer of the New Jersey Institute of Technology to offer courses to students in several countries (Smith, 1987).

2   A means of generating collaborative science investigations through a LAN within a New York city school (Newman, 1987; Newman and Goldman, 1987).
3   International pen-pal communication; Computer Pals of Australia promotes 'writing for a real reason'.
4   An Electronic Academical Network in Virginia which links all its 2,000 schools, initially for administration but also intended for teaching (Bull *et al.*, 1991).
5   A means of tutorial support for home-based students on Open University courses in the UK (Mason, 1991a).
6   On-line electronic journals.
7   Access to remote library catalogues and databases.

There are many more examples to choose from. What they have in common is the way in which computer communication creates new access, groupings and structures for teaching and learning. It also offers a means of delivering learning material through down-loading files from databases. The role that computer communication plays in the educational process takes a variety of forms: it covers the spectrum from being a small element of a project to being the main means of conducting it with participants, either home-based or school-based.

In the UK, the level of awareness about the communicative potential of computers in education is generally low at present though there are a number of experimental projects. Most use has been in adult education and training. For example, the English National Board for Nursing, Midwifery and Health Visiting uses it for nurse educators learning to use computers as part of their work; course modules are sent to individual learners and assignments returned via the network, which also provides a means of contact between learners and tutors (Procter, 1988). The most extensive educational use in the UK has been for tutorial discussion in distance learning with Open University students (Mason, 1991a), though new projects in higher education are appearing in increasing numbers.

In schools the main use of computers has been, until recently, for the retrieval of information from databases and the contribution of data to them. For example, the NED Project (National Environmental Data Base) has involved about fifty schools in collecting data on acid rain and water pollution by experiment and questionnaire, which is entered by the schools into the computer database. The pooled data is then used to encourage students to generate hypotheses which cannot be tested using their own data alone (NCET, 1989). The next most used facility is e-mail. Computer conferencing is so far used very little in schools. However, interest in using computers as a communication medium is growing. The Microelectronics Education Support Unit (MESU) has been instrumental in this through the support of ten individual projects in the UK (1988–90). These have included the use of e-mail for the construction of a collaborative epistolary novel by six schools, a cross-curricular adventure story project involving secondary and junior schools, language learning exchanges between French, German and UK schools, and pen-pal links between London and New York schools (NCET, 1990).

The role that communication through computers can play in classrooms and some of the issues involved may be illustrated by closer examination of one of these applications.

A CASE STUDY OF ELECTRONIC MAIL

The following case study describes the 'Live Adventuring' projects in Derbyshire (UK). It shows how a limited use of e-mail messaging sustained a long period of cross-curricular work and identifies some of the issues involved in integrating into classroom work computers used for communication purposes.

The roots of this project lay in the previous work primary school teachers and children had done with adventure games on disk (such as 'Granny's Garden' and 'Flowers of Crystal'), using them as stimulus material for activities involving problem-solving, talk and writing. While this was found to be enjoyable and productive, their potential was limited, mainly because of their predictability. When modems became available in Derbyshire schools new possibilities were created. The boundaries of the activity changed and new 'zones' of interaction made possible. To begin with, adults outside the primary schools took the lead in creating a story, delivered and responded to in interactive message form by e-mail. In a later phase secondary school students became involved and took over this role.

The communications network used was Campus 2000, an educational network using the public telephone system (British Telecom). The costs were an annual subscription and an additional charge for local telephone calls during use. Each user received a mailbox address on the computer; a school as well as an individual could register. Each school involved in the Live Adventuring project had one telephone line with a modem linked to a microcomputer.

The kinds of exchanges that took place are best illustrated by some extracts. These are taken from the Live Adventure 'The Jewel of Dawn'. This involved two schools: a group of 9- to 10-year-old children at St Giles Primary School, Killamarsh, and some 14 year olds at Tupton Hall Secondary School. It began with this message sent by e-mail from the secondary school children to the primary school; the latter did not know where the messages came from.

November 4th

SOS SOS SOS SOS SOS SOS SOS SOS SOS SOS SOS SOS

Yesterday we were walking in this valley near Lathkill Dale. It started to rain so we sheltered in a cave. We decided (well Mickey did really) to explore. Chrissie insisted that we let someone know where we were going. That's what this message is about.

Anyone picking up this message please answer, so that we know you're there!

What we want you to do is keep looking for messages. Please answer soon if you get this message. If you do we'll let you know how far we've got!

Chrissie, Steve, Micky, EMMA, outside the cave in our secret valley.

Hope we hear from you soon.

SOS SOS SOS SOS SOS SOS SOS SOS SOS SOS SOS SOS

November 4th

Hello, Chrissie, Steve, Micky and Emma.

We have received your S.O.S. message. Your message has reached St. Giles Primary School in Killamarsh, near Sheffield.

Are you in any danger? Have you any supplies? Food? Drink? Warm clothes? Torch? Where are you going to sleep?

We are worried about letting your parents know where you are. Shall we let them know?

We are looking forward to receiving another message from you. From the 'Terrific Ten' Rachael, Charlotte, Hannah, Tracey M., Tracey S., Deborah, Paul C., Paul B., James and Richard.

November 5th

Dear Terrific Ten . . .

And so the jointly constructed story gathered momentum and continued in the form of relatively short daily e-mail messages. All of this was facilitated by the planning and support of the teachers. For the primary school group it generated a large amount of cross-curricular work, including mathematics, built into the story by the secondary school children, with their teacher acting as 'consultant'. For example: [from the secondary school children, leading the story]

Can you think of a way to tell the height of a tree without climbing it first? We don't want to climb all that dangerous way only to find that our rope is too short to let the [giant] berry down safely to the ground (if it drops it will squash and be useless). Our rope is 100 metres. If the tree is less than that we will climb it.

Byeee!

Chrissie.

[from the primary school children]

December 6th

Dear Gang,

We hope you are good at maths because we think we've solved the problem of finding out the height of the tree. We don't think you will have a protractor on you, but if you've got a piece of paper which has a right angle corner, fold the corner in half to make an angle of 45 degrees, then hold the piece of paper parallel to the ground with the 45 degree angle towards the top of the tree. You will need to walk backwards (watch where you are walking) from the bottom of the tree until your 45 degree angle is in line with the top of the tree. When it is in line you will need to measure from where you are to the bottom of the tree.

You've got a 100 metres of rope, so we are sure you will be able to work out the rough distance. You can now make a scale drawing which will be like a triangle. The base of the triangle is the scale distance from the bottom of the tree to where you are standing. The 'tree' is at right angles to the base of the triangle, the third side of the triangle is at 45 degrees from the base line. Where the 'tree' line and the angle line meet, you can now roughly work out the height of the tree and whether you've got enough rope to climb it.

BYE FOR NOW! FROM TRACEY S AND CHARLOTTE AND THE REST OF THE TERRIFIC TEN!

As this illustrates, problems were set and solved as the story progressed. Clearly the solution offered above involved a good deal of working off-line in a practical way before the message was constructed, reviewed, debated and redrafted by the group and sent.

THE OUTCOMES

As well as maths and science work, much creative writing and artwork was generated in all classrooms as well as thoughtful character development of the 'lost' five children by the secondary school group. This 'Adventure' continued for over six months which indicated the motivating power of the e-mail messages (providing they were responded to) and the underlying organisation of the learning activities. The simple messaging facility of e-mail in these projects supported and generated a variety of collaborative group work, between groups separated by distance and within groups working together in classrooms. The teachers described the outcomes as follows:

The task of writing a story that evolves in an unpredictable way requires a whole range of writing skills. Some are the basic skills of accuracy and clarity of expression; but in addition, to make a story like this really work well, imaginative description, realism, use of varying styles and registers:

all of these will be needed . . . From my point of view, as teacher, perhaps the most impressive thing to observe was the sheer quantity and quality of the talk. As each scene was planned there were fierce, well-argued disagreements; there was some superb speculative talk; there was intense discussion of the likely reaction to a particular twist in the tale, whether it was too disturbing or too weak. One factor emerged: we were all equals before the task. My ideas were as often shot down for being ridiculous as hailed as the thoughts of a genius.

(Chris Warren, secondary teacher, p. 22, DESCIT, 1989)

Over the weeks a high standard of work has been achieved: map reading; code breaking; scientific experimenting; problem solving; logistics; the trans-lation of practical ideas into written language. The adventure has stimulated a great deal of team work, creative thought, discussion and written work.'

(Simon Bull, primary teacher, p. 15, DESCIT, 1989)

a lot of talking and listening in a variety of different situations. This varied between small group discussions, teacher and group discussions and a whole class discussion. The project allowed children to develop and refine their oracy in a meaningful context. This could not have been done as easily with other projects and the sense of audience e-mail produces is a powerful element in developing these skills.

(NCET, 1990, p. 20)

MANAGING THE LEARNING

The use of e-mail stimulated much collaborative classroom work beyond the writing and reading of a story, collaborative in Davidson's (1990) sense of 'structuring positive interdependence'. Its impact on the classroom organi-sation and curriculum of the junior school children and the demands it made on the teachers were considerable. But it also highlighted issues in the management of learning, not just for the teachers. One of the 'Adventures' involved a secondary school class of 15- to 16-year-old pupils leading the story for four primary schools. The story was started in a similar way to that above, but the secondary school class had a more complex management task, responding to messages from four different schools and keeping track of the story line for each. This required project management skills of a high order together with stamina. At the end of it there was agreement that managing the interaction with four primary schools was too heavy a burden within the constraints of the secondary school timetable. The coordination of messages was sometimes a problem (mistakes in sending out messages before the previous one had been responded to) and occasional time-lags caused a hiatus or some confusion. A good deal of written and verbal communication was generated within the secondary school classroom simply because it was essential for each small group with its special responsibilities to know the current state of the story overall and to communicate their own intentions and ideas. For all the schools involved, it formed a significant part of their classroom work, and for some of the primary ones it led the whole of it. The secondary school used the project as part of their assessed course work for the General Certificate of Secondary Education (GCSE).

The teachers' role as managers of learning was clearly a key one. It was also taxing, involving challenges to their existing practice, new social demands and relationships and the acquisition of new skills (most were new to using computers). Despite the fact that the sending and receiving of e-mail messages itself occupied only a very small amount of on-line time, it was a powerful catalyst in changing what happened in the classrooms. The e-mail messages were perceived as real and authoritative. Since the story was led by secondary school pupils, one result was to move the teachers into the kind of role that Cole and Griffin (1987) describe as 'orchestrators' of the learners' activities. As one of the teachers concluded:

> electronic mail on its own offers very little. As with so much in computing it is up to the teacher to take hold of the technology and made it work for the children in the school.

> (DESCIT, 1988, p. 3)

This 'taking hold' refers to providing real educational purpose (other than getting the technology to work) and managing the learning environment by identifying and agreeing goals with the other teachers involved, planning, negotiating with each other and with the classroom groups, reviewing progress throughout, organising resources to support the small group or class activities and integrating the project work into the rest of school life. It also meant, in this case, allowing ownership and direction to lie with the learners: the content and pace were not under the teachers' control. This raised several problems. Because the adventure was an interactive and evolving one, with the learners taking charge of it in many ways, its demands were unpredictable. The concerns expressed by the teachers centred on:

1 Issues of control; the unpredictability stimulated and motivated (as one teacher said, 'it's like being on a roller coaster'), but it could also mean missed opportunities for teaching.
2 Competing priorities in the curriculum: how much time should an e-mail adventure of this kind absorb? Should some subject work, such as mathematics, carry on alongside it? How could it fit with demands of the National Curriculum?
3 External examination pressures for the secondary school: were the two demands compatible?
4 Integrating computer communications into classroom life; how far could school timetables be changed to accommodate this kind of activity? How far should work be reorganised to capitalise on it?

5 Teacher collaboration and resource issues; the teachers needed to meet regularly to review and plan: this involved time, travel and extra resources.
6 Change in teacher's role: should this be carried over into other teaching? What conflicts did it create with other staff?

The use of computer communications in this way raised a number of fundamental issues to do with teaching and learning.

WHAT CONCLUSIONS CAN BE DRAWN FROM THIS CASE STUDY?

In this case the use of the computer for communication purposes generated much productive discussion (seen in the videotape made as part of an Open University course) and groupwork which was evident in the displays of work produced. To draw conclusions about the precise nature of the collaborative learning that took place we would need more information on the interactions within the groups: those between the groups in different schools are recorded in the story print-out (a weighty volume but representing only a small proportion of the total interactions), those within groups is not. To understand the processes of collaboration, we would need to examine the form of involvement of individuals and the nature and extent of their activity (Pozzi, Hoyles and Healy, 1992).

What can be concluded is that the use of e-mail in this case was a powerful motivator, a finding confirmed in other projects (for example, Freyd *et al.* (1992) project linking young learners with a staff member at Philadelphia zoo). The same kinds of exchanges could have been conducted by facsimile (fax) messages; whether the motivation stimulated would have been greater or less with handwritten messages is an unexplored question, though an interesting one as the use of fax communication in schools grows. The experience of these e-mail 'Adventures' also demonstrated the importance of planning so that teachers could work out and agree, in advance, shared objectives, curriculum needs, a match with events in individual schools (for example, to accommodate a school visit to London and a study of the Fire of London), an appropriate story line (one school had a high ethnic minority population) and ground rules. The technology was explicitly treated as a tool for conducting these particular curricular activities rather than as an end in itself. This appears to be one reason why the activity generated so much classroom work over a sustained period. Other projects have achieved varying degrees of sustainability and outcome. Many have 'fizzled out' quite quickly, despite enthusiastic teachers.

The case study above illustrates just one way in which communication through computers can contribute to and change the activities of classrooms. Electronic mail can be used in a variety of ways to enable schools and learners to interact with each other. In this particular case the amount of e-mail was relatively small, though its impact on the classrooms was considerable. At the other end of the spectrum is the use of computer conferencing as the classroom (an electronic one). In contrast to the use of e-mail above, collaborative work and discussion in the electronic classroom is largely conducted by means of the medium, though other forms of interaction may support it (letters, telephone calls, fax exchanges, audio-tape messages and even face-to-face meetings). Most of the current developments in 'electronic' classrooms involve individual distance learners, usually adults, each with their own computer and communications facility. This creates what Hiltz (1986) termed the 'virtual' classroom ('imaginary' or 'hypothetical' as opposed to 'real', though it can carry out the functions of a 'real' one).

> A virtual school thus does not exist as a physical building. Nevertheless, it may be thought of as real, since it can assume all the responsibilities of an ordinary (physical) school. Most tasks will be handled by people, as in a physical school. Many of these tasks involve interpersonal communication. A virtual school should therefore possess a maximum of facilities for this. . . . A virtual school may be regarded as an information system, that is, a system for generating information. This entails the gathering, processing, storing, transmission and presentation of information. . . . Computer conferencing would be the main communication medium in a virtual school.
>
> (Paulsen, 1987–8)

Can communication by computer in this way be effective? What influence does the medium have on language and communication? Does it support teaching and learning exchanges?

THE NATURE OF COMPUTER-MEDIATED COMMUNICATION

Computer conferencing allows many people to join in a written 'conversation'. Because it is asynchronous, that is, individuals can read and add to the conversation at any time whenever they log on to the conferencing system, the structure of the discourse is not linear in the way that face-to-face conversation is. The group size can vary from a handful of people to hundreds, depending on how it is set up. So, as well as learning to use the technology, individuals need to adapt their habitual ways of communicating.

New kinds of conversational structures occur which can lead to uncertainty. As Kiesler, Siegel and McGuire (1984) suggest, an 'etiquette of electronic communication' is as yet lacking, so participants are not quite sure what the ground rules are. Some electronic groups create their own protocol in the course of sharing exchanges and build up the kind of contextualised discourse described by Edwards (1991). Conventions are created which typically compensate for missing customary cues, for example, the use of asterisks or upper-case to denote special emphasis, or the use of <joke> or (ha!ha!) or:-) to denote intended humour (the last one is a sideways smile!). The 'conversational' exchanges have to be conducted through written text without the usual visual or voice cues that form part of other kinds of discourse. If we take the two main characteristics of CMC (the lack of face-to-face cues and the asynchronous nature of the exchanges) and examine the effects on discussion through the medium of computers, we find the distinctive features and their attendant advantages and disadvantages outlined in Table 9.1.

The written discourse of communication through computers is different to the more familiar forms of letter or memorandum or essay. Some view e-mail as closer to the written form of communication, with conferencing closer to the spoken. However, e-mail often seems to be very similar to conversation

Table 9.1 Features of communication through computers

	Potential advantages	*Potential disadvantages*
Lack of face-to-face cues	• anonymity • reduction in status	• reduced feedback • impersonal cues • jokes and feelings difficult to convey
	• task-focused (less interpersonal distraction)	• more attenuated interaction
	• reduced pressure on individuals to contribute	• reduced pressure on individuals to contribute
	• increased importance of logical argument	• need for skilled moderator to control, orchestrate (or censor?)
	• contributions not restricted by turn-taking	• increased emotion or aggression in messages ('flaming')
	• less domination by an individual	
Time-lag between responses (asynchronicity)	• opportunity to reflect before responding	• loss of impetus to reply
	• opportunity to reformulate and correct messages before sending	• slowness in decision-making • reduction of language exchanges for social purposes only
	• convenience	
	• access to discussion with others	• difficulty of reaching consensus

Source: (Adapted from Baron, 1984)

with its short utterances and informal colloquial style (producing what Daiute, 1985, p. 291) calls 'talky writing') and in my experience of using e-mail in a work environment, is well suited to quick exchanges. But trying to allow for this in the conventional classroom is difficult: because of issues of access to the equipment and other classroom constraints such as time-tabling, its immediacy is difficult to accommodate. At present there is little research evidence available on the nature of computer discourse. What is clear is that the structure of group conversations in conferencing is different from equivalent forms using other media, and is also shaped by the design of the particular software conferencing system as well as the medium.

The structure of 'conversations' varies according to the conferencing system used. On some systems, all the messages relating to the original one are in one column and viewed in linear form. Other conferencing systems, like CoSy, have a branching structure which enables user to branch away from the original message in order to respond to one of the numbered responses. One system, Participate, has a branching structure where sub-topics can be moved from one place to another, or copied to several places. While this provides flexibility, it can also be confusing since a particular line of discussion can get misplaced and it requires users to remember where they have moved messages to. Increased flexibility carries a cost.

Even with a small group, the interaction can contain several simul-taneous strands. Riedl (1989) says of his experience with a small group of seven graduate students:

> multiple topic, multi-level series of interchanges tends to make the dis-cussion much richer than that found in a traditional class setting. It can also be more difficult to follow unless students take the time to print out messages and read them carefully before reacting to any of the topics. Such multi-level discussion does put significant demands upon students and requires regular participation if the student is going to benefit from the experience.

(pp. 217–18)

He points to the advantages for the tutor who because the discussion is 'recorded' on screen or in print, 'can analyse student contributions for their quality and for any misconceptions' or can 'observe student contributions without the need to control the discussion' (ibid., p. 219). With a larger group, the work involved and the complexity of this task increase. This places heavy demands on the tutor or conference moderator whose role is to facilitate or mediate the discussion. The moderator's role involves setting up the conference, laying out the ground rules, negotiating goals and procedures, setting up branch topics, intervening in the discussion to review, redirect or defuse heated exchanges, and editing. In playing this role, the moderator also has extra powers within the group, for example, as the only person with the power to delete a contribution.

SCAFFOLDING IN CMC

How then does communication through computers fit with communicative theories of teaching and learning? Do the written exchanges in computer conferencing support scaffolding? Scaffolding by others (teachers or peers) is a process which enables learners to solve problems interactively while they are in the process of learning to solve them for themselves. The internalised knowledge of the individual is constructed from the interactive processes through which the problem was worked on. Communicating through computers can support this in two ways. First, it allows knowledge to be constructed from wider sources; joint activity with more people from more places is possible. The construction of a different kind of knowledge picture is possible with more widely shared input of information. There is no time-limited 'speaking space' restriction which excludes contributions. Secondly, because the interaction is stored, it is less ephemeral and rapid than spoken exchanges. The interactive processes can be captured in a concrete record of the dialogue and discourse (the screen displays, stored files and print-out copies of items or sequences of exchanges). These provide the focus for reflection and review and can then themselves become the focus of further joint activity. This can be valuable for both learners and teachers. In the teaching-learning interaction, teachers often do not have a clear understanding of exactly how learners are approaching a task. The record of discussion can make this more explicit, as Riedl (1989) describes. It enables shared analysis of it and can provide the specific basis of discussion between teacher and learner in a way that conversation recalled from memory cannot. It can also build a shared context.

On the other hand, one can speculate that the structure of computer conferencing discourse both helps and hinders the scaffolding process. Help is provided by the breadth of input available to the learner: a broad picture of a topic under discussion can be gained because contributions can come from many sources. But at the same time, the contribution of many items may leave a particular learner's needs overlooked. Or sifting through many contributions may dissipate the force of the relevant ones which a learner would need to integrate in order to scaffold a particular piece of learning effectively. It is claimed that this difficulty can be overcome because the computer software permits the recording of exchanges and their re-ordering in different ways:

> a number of different themes may be pursued in the same chronological sequence. The reading of messages in the order in which they are posted does not therefore usually produce a structured discussion. But conference discussion, because it is recorded in electronic form, is in effect stored in a kind of database. The discussion on a conference can be re-examined and re-read in a variety of ways taking advantage of the computer's ability to search for key words, to present messages in sequence according to subject

matter, and so on. The input of conferencing is not necessarily structured, but the output can be structured by the user.

(Thomas, 1989, p. 13)

Thomas thus argues that computer conferencing is capable of supporting 'purposive structured discussion' by this means. While this search and re-ordering strategy offers a way of sifting and integrating relevant items, it may not be sufficient to scaffold understanding effectively in all instances (I'm making the assumption here that scaffolding can be either an incidental or conscious process). It suggests that the user already knows enough to know what needs to be done and is able to structure the selection necessary; this may not always be the case. 'Key words' or themes may not always be enough to assist the scaffolding of a concept. If you don't know what you don't know, you can't organise the structure to help you know what you don't know! The intervention of a more informed tutor or peer may at times be needed to identify critical combinations or structures. This is likely to be more necessary for younger learners who will have fewer skills and strategies than adults to draw on to scaffold their own learning. There is also the likelihood that not every individual's problems will have a solution articulated by others. Fafchamps *et al.* (1989) categorise messages in CMC as islands, dialogues and webs (islands are messages that do not get a response, dialogues involve two participants in turn-taking, and webs involve several responses to one or more messages).

Another feature of discussion in computer conferencing is the amount of 'informal talk' that appears. While some participants report that this gets in the way of more focused teaching-learning exchanges, others (for example, Graddol, 1991) argue that is, in fact, a highly structured equivalent to verbal activity which performs a valuable social maintenance task similar to that in face to face interaction. Graddol sees it as providing a valuable context for learning. This, it may be argued, is one kind of context building activity which supports other, more task-focused exchanges. It is also likely to be an activity directed at 'humanising the medium' (its equivalent can be found in audio-conferencing or group telephone discussion, Rutter and Robinson, 1981). But it remains the case that some participants report it as interfering with communication of a more task-focused kind rather than assisting it. It may also reflect that computer conferences are serving the multiple needs of participants (the need for social contact as well as task-orientation exchanges). However, despite the complexity of conferencing discussion, there is some evidence that the medium supports productive learning exchanges between tutors and learners, and learners and learners. Open University adult students participating in tutorial discussion by computer conference were able to pose questions for discussion, present arguments, introduce new material, summarise other relevant material, present opposing points of view, apply their own experience to issues under dis-cussion, and summarise previous material (Mason, 1991b).

FACTORS IN SUCCESS AND FAILURE

Not all projects using computer communications for educational purposes are successful. This is true of information technology projects in general. The reasons for failure or rejection are not necessarily technical, though problems relating to the user-friendliness of the system often contribute. It is unusual for hardware or software designers to take the user as their starting point in the design process. Data about the success or failure rates of IT projects is difficult to obtain. Evidence available from a North American survey suggests that 20 per cent of new projects achieve their intended benefits, 40 per cent fail and 40 per cent have only a marginal impact (Mowshowitz, 1976). Although no similar survey exists for the UK, Eason (1988) concludes that the studies available point in the same direction. One major reason why projects fail is that they are 'technology-led' rather than 'needs-led'. Another reason may be perceived cost, particularly at the school level. However, organisational and social factors are sometimes an under-estimated component in determining the success or failure of projects using communication through computers. We still know little about the human dynamics of organising network activities. Negotiation, planning and the time involved in introducing new ways of teaching and learning are often reported in projects (with hindsight) as underestimated. Commitment to shared curriculum objectives is also an important and sometimes under-estimated factor in sustaining collaborative work and in maintaining the continuing participation of partners (NCET, 1990, p. 14).

Like other interactive media, there appear to be three discernible stages in achieving effective learning and teaching through it (Robinson, 1984). First, problems of the technology have to be overcome: that is, getting it to work and learning to use it, despite often cumbersome and unfriendly procedures and software. Secondly, the user has to learn how to communicate by means of it, adapting their social and linguistic behaviour to the medium in order to engage with other people. Thirdly, learners and teachers have to use their new skills for teaching and learning tasks and purposes, often involving the development of new structures. In schools this can markedly alter classroom routines. Many projects fail to reach the third phase because the first two are too difficult or time consuming. Sometimes the third stage is reached, but not sustained; this is likely to be because it lacks a real educational purpose or the users do not perceive the need for it. Other alternatives may be available. For example, the use of fax exchanges may serve the same purposes more easily. Limitations of computer communication in graphics facilities prevent its full use for mathematics and science or for subjects with a high visual content; schools are increasingly using fax communication to compensate for this.

In terms of the individual's experience, Boshier (1990, p. 62) suggests that new users of computers for communication pass through the following stages:

anticipation/apprehension (before the first sign on), exhilaration (when the first message is sent or received), frustration (when the first reinforcement is followed by errors and problems), consolidation (as skills are sharpened), adventure (with skills in place the user starts sending overseas and graphic messages), routinisation (as use deepens the gee-whiz quality of the technology diminishes).

It is at this last point that, in my view, the purpose of use becomes a deciding factor in its continuation. Access to computers also plays a key role in attaining the stage of 'routinisation', the point at which a culture of usage within a school or organisation begins to develop. In many school settings this would be difficult to reach, partly because of limited access to computers, more because of access to a telephone line. While recognising the issues of cost involved, it remains a fact that teachers and classrooms seldom have easy access to telecommunications:

> regarding the availability of equipment to teachers, it has turned out that the last 200 feet, the distance from the school office to the teacher's classroom, is the most difficult to traverse electronically. Classroom teachers remain the only professionals in the world without convenient and easy access to telephones.
>
> (Wolpert and Lowney, 1991, p. 24)

As Somekh (1989) describes, issues of control and power are linked to issues of access in using computers for communication purposes in schools. However, despite the difficulties of turning the capability into practice, communication through computers can:

- be integrated into classroom activities in different ways, albeit not easily;
- provide a means of teaching and learning, either as a small or large element;
- stimulate and sustain collaborative learning in more than one way;
- reorganise interactions between learners and teachers;
- record and store message exchanges for further use and analysis;
- store pooled data, combining many small contributions to form a larger different database for learners to use;
- link groups that would otherwise be unconnected, creating new groupings.

CONCLUSIONS

Projects and trials by schools using computers for communication purposes are increasing and, with them, better understanding of the medium's benefits and limitations. Those involved in projects which survive to the point where evaluations can be made continue to reaffirm its potential for teaching and learning. They also identify more clearly the factors contributing to its success or failure.

Computers can provide a means of communication which allows

knowledge to be constructed from a wider range of sources, and which can support interaction taking place either within classrooms or through the medium. The integration of computer communication into classroom activities is not easy, often resulting in it playing an 'add-on' marginal role rather than a central one although, as the earlier case study illustrated, this need not necessarily be so. One of the problems (as in other fields) has been in setting up projects whose goal is more than just getting the technology to work or for its 'novelty' value. A major contributor to success lies in using computer communications as a tool for a 'real' purpose, that is, for curriculum projects which have their own goals. This finding is not new, but it seems to be a message which is constantly re-discovered, both in the literature and by practitioners. In reviewing their experience of the Global Telecommunications Network, linking schools in the UK with schools in New York, USA, through computers, the leaders involved concluded:

> in future we aim to work on collaborative international educational projects but not telecommunications projects, i.e. projects which aim to develop and enhance learning and may use telecommunications for that end, when such technology seems most appropriate.

(NCET, 1990, pp. 12–17)

What is also clear from experience so far is that technological problems (though persistent) are not always the ones which cause projects using computers for communication to fail. Organisational ones are often an important factor. But perhaps most of all, is the recognition the technology does not provide solutions to fundamental problems of teaching and learning. In talking about the advantages of a networked campus, Gardner (1988) concludes that: 'there is no evidence that it automatically effects sustained improvements in the quality of teaching, learning and scholarship' (p. 5).

To be effective, communication through computers needs to be for worthwhile educational activities which it is not possible to do equally well by alternative, more convenient means. However, this leads us to a more fundamental question: is the use of computer communication in classrooms a new way of meeting old goals in education, or a new way of creating new goals?

REFERENCES

Baron, N. S. (1984) 'Computer mediated communication as a force in language change', *Visible Language*, 18(2).

Boshier, R. (1990) 'Socio-psychological factors in electronic networking', *International Journal of Lifelong Education*, 9(1).

Brand, S. (1987) *The media lab: inventing the future at MIT*, New York, Viking Press.

Bull, G., Hill, I., Guyre, K. and Sigmon, T. (1991) 'Building an electronic academical village: Virginia's Public Education Network.' *Educational Technology*, 21(4).

Cole, M. and Griffin, P. (eds) (1987) *Contextual Factors in Education: improving science and mathematical education for minorities and women*, Madison, Wisconsin Centre for Education Research.

Daiute, C. (1985) *Writing and Computers*, Addison-Wesley.

Davidson, N. (1990) 'Co-operative learning research in mathematics', paper presented at the IASCE 5th International Convention on Cooperative Learning, Maryland, USA, July.

Descit (1988) *Live Adventuring*, Matlock, Derbyshire Educational Support Centre for Information Technology.

Descit (1989) *The Jewel of Dawn: the transcript of the SOS Adventure*, Matlock, Derbyshire Educational Support Centre for Information Technology.

Eason, K. (1988) *Information Technology and Organisational Change*, London, Taylor and Francis.

Edwards, D. (1990) 'Classroom discourse and classroom knowledge', in Rogers, C. and Kutnick, P. (eds) *Readings in the Social Psychology of the Primary School*, London, Croom Helm.

Fafchamps, D., Reynolds, D. and Kuchinsky, A. (1989) 'The dynamics of small group decision making over the E-mail channel', in Bowers, J. and Benford, S. (eds) *Proceedings of the First European Conference on Computer-Supported Cooperative Work*, 13–15 September, EC–CSCW.

Freyd, P., Massey, C. and Roth, Z. (1992) 'How do the animals cry? Children's question asking in a science unit on classification', paper presented at the Annual meeting of the American Educational Research Association, San Francisco, USA, April.

Gardner, N. (1988) 'Bringing the electronic campus to reality: opportunities and challenges in teaching', in Brindley, L. J. (ed.) *The Electronic Campus: an information strategy*, British Library.

Graddol, D. (1991) 'Some CMC discourse properties and their educational significance', in Boyd-Barrett, O. and Scanlon, E. (1991) *Computers and Learning*, Addison-Wesley in association with the Open University.

Hiltz, S. R. (1986) *The Virtual Classroom: building the foundations*, Newark, NJ, New Jersey Institute of Technology.

Kaye, A. (1988) 'On line services for schools: an appraisal', in Jones, A. and Scrimshaw, P. (eds) *Computers in Education: 5–13*, Milton Keynes, Open University Press.

Kiesler, S., Siegel, J. and McGuire, T. W. (1984) 'Social psychological aspects of computer-mediated communication', *The American Psychologist*, 39(10).

Mason, R. (1991a) 'Refining the use of computer conferencing in distance education', in Boyd-Barrett, O. and Scanlon, E. (1991) *Computers and Learning*, Addison-Wesley in association with The Open University.

Mason, R. (1991b) 'Analysing computer conferencing interactions', *Computers in Adult Education and Training*, 2(3).

Mowshowitz, A. (1976) *The Conquest of Will: information processing in human affairs*, Reading, Addison-Wesley.

National Council for Educational Technology (NCET) (1989) Communique, *NCET Newsletter*, July 1989.

National Council for Educational Technology (NCET) (1990) Communique, *NCET Newsletter*, July 1990.

Newman, D. (1987) 'Local and long distance computer networking for science classrooms', *Educational Technology*, 27(6).

Newman, D. and Goldman, S. V. (1987) 'Earth Lab: a local network for collaborative classroom science', *Journal of Educational Technology Systems*, 15(3).

Paulsen, M. F. (1987–8) 'In search of a virtual school', *T.H.E. Journal*, Dec.–Jan. Reprinted in Paulsen, M. F. and Rekkedal, T. (eds) *The Electronic College*, NKI Forlaget, Norway, 1990.

Pozzi, S., Hoyles, C. and Healy, L. (1992) 'Towards a methodology for analysing collaboration and learning in computer-based groupwork', *Computers and Education*, 18: 1–3.

Procter, P. (1988) 'Framework for computer-assisted learning: implementations for nursing, midwifery and health visiting in England', in Mathias, H., Rushby, N. and Budgett, R. (eds) *Designing New Systems and Technologies for Learning. Aspects of Educational Technology*, 21, London, Kogan Page.

Riedl, R. (1989) 'Patterns in computer mediated discussions', in Mason, R. and Kaye, A. (eds) *Mindweave*, Oxford, Pergamon Press.

Robinson, B. (1984) 'Telephone teaching', in Bates, A. W. (ed.) *The Role of Technology in Distance Education*, London, Croom Helm.

Robottom, I. and Muhleback, R. (1989) 'Expanding the scientific community in schools: a computer conference in science education', *The Australian Science Teachers' Journal*, 35(1): 39–47.

Rutter, D. R. and Robinson, B. (1981) 'An experimental analysis of teaching by telephone: theoretical and practical implications for social psychology', in Stephenson, G. M. and Davis, J. (eds), *Progress in Applied Social Psychology*, Chichester, John Wiley.

Smith, B. (1987) 'The electronic university', *New Jersey Monthly*, January.

Somekh, B. (1989) 'The human interface: hidden issues in CMC affecting use in schools', in Mason, R. and Kaye, A. (eds) *Mindweave*, Oxford, Pergamon Press.

Thomas, R. (1989) 'Implications for conventional institutions of Open University experiences in use of computer conferencing', *International Journal of Computers in Adult Education and Training*, 1(3).

Topping, K. (1992) 'Co-operative learning and peer tutoring: an overview', *The Psychologist*, 5(4), April.

Vygotsky, L. S. (1978) *Mind in Society: the development of higher psychological processes*, Cambridge, Harvard University Press.

Vygotsky, L. S. (1986) *Thought and Language*, Cambridge, Mass., MIT Press.

Wolpert, E. M. and Lowney, F. A. (1991) 'Building an electronic community', *Educational Technology*, 31(4).

Chapter 10

Text completion programs

Peter Scrimshaw

INTRODUCTION

If educational theories are designed to illuminate practice, we should be able to use teachers' accounts of their experience, to provide a standpoint from which to begin to judge the general adequacy of such theories. An educational theory which offers no way of conceptualising distinctions or processes that practitioners think crucial is to that extent inadequate. So too is a theory that simply maps unresistingly upon teacher perceptions, suggesting no new perspectives on practice, and offering no critical standpoint from which current classroom strategies can be judged. The test of theory here is that practitioners see its concepts and descriptions as intelligible, relevant and comprehensive, and its explanations and hypotheses as thought provoking and relevant to the future decisions they must make. These requirements are additional to such internal criteria for judging any theory such as consistency, economy, elegance, conformity to available data and explanatory power.

This chapter addresses two questions:

- How can concepts drawn from communicative theories of learning enhance our understanding of the educational value of text completion programs?
- How must such concepts (and the theories they underpin) be revised in the light of accounts of the classroom use of these programs?

First we consider one of the commonest programs in this family, describe how it is used and secondly discuss the experiences of practitioners and researchers with the program, but reinterpreting these accounts in terms drawn from communicative theories of learning.

WHAT ARE TEXT COMPLETION PROGRAMS?

Text completion programs are designed to develop various language skills, and involve learners in reconstructing an initially invisible text, previously entered by the teacher. Developing Tray is the most widely available example in Britain of such a text completion (or text disclosure) program. It can now be found in a variety of forms, but the common features are all we need to consider, so I will use Tray as a generic name for all the variants. The name comes from the photographer's developing tray, in which a hidden picture gradually emerges as the developer works on it (see Figure 10.1). Users reveal the text by predicting the position of a letter or sequence of letters, or by 'buying' a letter, a procedure which shows them all the occurrences of that letter in the text.

Tray has a scoring system which effectively rewards learners for predicting rather than buying, and for predicting long strings of letters rather than shorter ones, the current score being shown on screen throughout. A memo facility allows the students to pause and record their hypotheses about the subject of the passage. These memos can be called up later for group discussion with or without the teacher.

From a purely technical point of view, Tray is a relatively user friendly program, and at least some of its value is quickly understood by teachers. It can handle any short piece of continuous text but those most commonly used are pieces of imaginative writing by professional authors or children. The program has a special place in the development of educational computing, and is often mentioned alongside word processors, databases and other generic packages as a standard requirement in teacher texts on educational computing (for example see Mann, 1989; Keith and Glover, 1987; Straker, 1989; Chandler and Marcus, 1985). It was developed on a cheap micro by a class teacher, Bob Moy, to meet the educational needs that he recognised. It was progressively taken up at local and national level (see, for instance, Straker and Schenk, 1984; Sawford, 1989; Stephens, 1985). Its development epitomises one ideal of educational computing design and development: the teacher generated innovation supported but not distorted by pressures from the education system or the world of commerce. On the other hand its design was by no means a purely pragmatic matter. Moy has a definite theoretical position on text comprehension (Moy and Raleigh, 1980) and a pedagogic theory concerning the use of the program. The program is recognised by researchers as an important aid to language teaching. As one researcher observed:

> The program is unusual in involving both cognitive and affective learning, and in being able to draw into these activities pupils who are normally unable or unwilling to respond to the printed text and whose experience of in-depth reading is limited.

> These attributes, which are characteristic of programs that enhance or extend the curriculum by enabling pupils and teachers to do new things in new ways, mean that TRAY is likely to become a classic language-development program, when many if not most of the programs currently

```
= ======== ===, === == ======
====, ==== = ===== ==== == ===
===. = === ==== == ===, === ====
====== =====, === ==== == ===
=== ==== ===== === ====. = ===
=== === ==== ===== == =====,
=== ========= == ===, === =====
== =======, === === == ======, ===
===== == =======, === ==== ==
======; === ======, ===
=========, === ====== ===
========; === ====== =====
========= == === ==== == ==
====== == == === ====.
```

Score: 0   Bonus: 0

```
= f==rf=l ==n, =ll =n c==r== gr=y,
w=== = gr=== =r=n =n === l=g. =
==n w=== n= ===, =n= w=== br=k=n
=====, =n= w=== == =l= r=g ====
r==n= === ====. = ==n w== ===
b==n ===k== =n w===r, =n=
======r== =n ===, =n= l==== by
===n==, =n= c== by fl=n==, =n=
===ng by n===l==, =n= ==rn by
br==r=; w== l==p==, =n= ===v=r==,
=n= gl=r== =n= gr=wk==; =n= w====
===== c======r== =n === ==== ==
== ===z== == by === c==n.
```

Score: 27   Bonus: 5

```
= f==rful ==n, =ll =n co=rs= gr=y,
w=th = gr==t =ron on h=s l=g. = ==n
w=th no h=t, =n= w=th brok=n sho=s,
=n= w=th =s ol= r=g t=== roun= h=s
h===. = ==n who h== b==n so=k==
=n w=t=r, =n= s=oth=r== =n =u=, =n=
l==== by ston=s, =n= cut by fl=nts,
=n= stung by n=ttl=s, =n= torn by
br==rs; who l==p==, =n= sh=v=r==,
=n= gl=r== =n= growl==; =n= whos=
t==th ch=tt=r== =n h=s h=== =s h=
s==z== == by th= ch=n.
```

Score: 56   Bonus: 15

Figure 10.1 Three stages in development of a partly completed text and scores

available have long since been discarded as educationally limited or unsound.

(Johnston, 1985, p. 217)

HOW CAN TEXT COMPLETION PROGRAMS BE USED?

Before Tray can be used the teacher must choose a text. Consider first the situation where the program is to be used by a single learner. As reconstructing the text requires the identification of words and letters from their context, the words to be discovered must be within the learner's capabilities. If they are not, the teacher can adjust the initial level of difficulty of the text by showing selected words or letters from the outset. This means that the program can be tailored to the learner's requirements quite precisely. Figure 10.2, for instance, shows two possible ways of initially presenting the same text.

These programs can be used by individuals (Moy, 1985a) but are far more commonly used by groups, with or without teachers being present. The teacher's role can vary significantly. At one extreme, the teacher simply presents the program and a suitable text, tells the group how to obtain the initial instructions and then leaves them to work alone. At the other, the

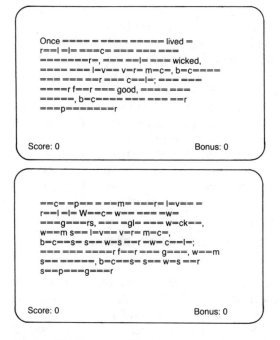

Figure 10.2 Two possible initial presentations of the same text

teacher is present throughout, directing the activity very closely. This flexibility partly explains the program's popularity, making it acceptable to teachers with a range of different approaches.

Group use has its advantages. An educationally useful Tray passage for a single learner has to fall within a narrow range of vocabulary and grammatical competences. Choosing texts for a group is much simpler, requiring only that everything in the text can be predicted by one or more of the group, and that a reasonable proportion of it will be new to each of them. Group use also opens up other possible objectives for the activity. One is to promote group problem solving in its own right, another is to encourage learners to share their knowledge of language with each other. The need for them to verbalise and defend their suggestions promotes discussion, encouraging the easier transfer of terms from the individual's oral to written vocabulary. Given that a teacher can have more than one reason for using such programs (Scrimshaw, 1986, 1987), group use is likely to be preferred. Working in groups also makes it easier to give all learners fair access to the computer over a reasonable time. It also reduces another perennial teacher problem; how to find out quickly what is going on in a learner's head. Group talk (and the changing screen display) makes it easier for a teacher to monitor progress even when he or she is working with others. The memo facility provides a similar aid to teachers, providing visual traces of the learning that has been going on in the teacher's absence. The recall and print-out options allow later discussion by the group (with or without the teacher), or private analysis by the teacher subsequently.

On a practical level, then, the program is well suited to classroom use, and allows the teacher a considerable degree of freedom in the ways in which it is used. However its design assumes that the teacher will have a sound conception of what educational potential it has, and how to realise this in terms of classroom activities. There has been a fair amount of discussion and exploration of quite what that educational potential is. Most of this has been circulated in the form of accounts of classroom work with Tray (e.g. Deane, 1984; Everett, 1984; Govier, 1984; Sawford, 1989). There have also been some studies by researchers of teachers' interpretations of its role (Scrimshaw, 1986, 1987), and methods of classroom use (e.g. Haywood and Wray, 1985; Johnston, 1985; Surgey and Scrimshaw, 1987).

WHAT CAN A COMMUNICATIVE THEORY OF LEARNING CONTRIBUTE?

These accounts present a very complex and detailed picture not easily summarised or grasped. We can therefore usefully ask whether concepts drawn from communicative theory might be helpful in structuring and interpreting this material. I would argue that three such concepts are helpful in organising the accounts given of Tray use, and making explicit the nature of the program and the activities that it supports. These are the concepts of an educational task as essentially problematic, of the zone of proximal development and the concept of scaffolding.

As we have seen from earlier chapters, the notions of the zone of proximal development and scaffolding provide a useful framework for considering specific kinds of programs and their uses. Together with the concept of educational tasks as essentially problematic, these concepts have developed as essential elements within a communicative theory of learning. The three concepts are interrelated in ways that have been elaborated as the theory has evolved. As Rogoff and Wertsch summarise it:

> First, the zone of proximal development involves the joint consciousness of the participants, where two or more minds are collaborating on solving a problem. A corollary of this notion of intersubjectivity is that the participants do not have the same definition of the task or of the problem to be solved. Through their interaction, the child's notion of what is to be done goes beyond itself, with the adult's support, and comes to approximate in some degree that of the more expert adult. Second, both participants play an important role in using the zone of proximal development, even in situations that are not directly conceived of as instructional by the participants. The child provides skills that are already developing and interests in particular domains and participates with the adult in organising the direction and pace of interaction in the zone of proximal development. The adult has particular responsibility for segmenting the task into manageable subgoals and for altering the child's definition of the task to make it increasingly compatible with expert performance. Third, interaction in the zone of proximal development is organised into a dynamic functional system oriented toward the child's future skills and knowledge. The functional system of adult-child joint participation in problem solving is organised by the task definitions, promoted activities, and hard and soft technologies available through culture.
>
> (Rogoff and Wertsch, 1984, p. 5)

THE INTERPRETATION OF EDUCATIONAL TASKS

The concept of an educational task is problematic, and necessarily so, within a communicative theory of learning. Tray certainly allows for different conceptions of the task for which it is to be used. This is a result of the relatively open design of the program, which easily lends itself, within certain limits, to alternative interpretations.

When first presented with Tray, teachers conceptualise its educational possibilities in varied ways, and characteristically see it as suitable for a variety of purposes. In one study (Scrimshaw, 1987) a group of 68 teachers were asked during an introductory session on Tray what they thought their pupils could gain from using the program. Their written responses contained over 500 aims between them, over a fifth of which were not language specific; these included such things as encouraging cooperation, problem solving or group work. The language aims included twelve major sub-categories, and many responses which fitted in none of these. Process aims such as cueing, comprehension and discussion featured, with prediction the only aim mentioned by more than half of the teachers. Interestingly, comprehension was mentioned by only a fifth. When analysed in terms of the size of linguistic unit mentioned or inferred, words and sentences were the only ones to be mentioned by more than half, and supra-text references (to, for instance, learning about genre) were mentioned by less than a tenth.

What this diversity shows is that teachers quite consciously set out to use the program in significantly different ways, and so conceptualise the specific tasks they are setting learners differently too. Such differences may, for instance, affect the texts chosen (e.g. to make a phonic skills strategy for interpretation easier (Haywood and Wray, 1988)), or they may influence the teacher roles they envisaged. Both Johnston and Haywood and Wray, for instance, accepted a variety of pupil approaches to revealing the text, including phonic strategies. On the other hand, Wisely and Duggan explicitly ruled out some of these strategies:

> The children I watched were using inefficient and weak strategies inappropriate to the activity, in that they were based on lexical and phonetic cueing systems, rather than on meaning. Are their strategies based on their age, their teacher's encouragement, early reading techniques derived from reading scheme work, or the constraints of the early version of the program? Whatever it is it 'sticks' and is definitely slowing them up. I feel that good powerful strategies can be learned, but only very slowly and am beginning to feel that this program will not look after itself; without regular care and attention within a classroom, by which I mean regular teacher-led sessions to encourage and demonstrate how powerful some strategies can be, it will become trivialised and lose some or all of its magic.
>
> (Wisely and Duggan, 1985, p. 15)

Clearly if learners do not conceive the task as being to discover the text using what their particular teacher sees as the appropriate strategies, then they may well be less successful with the task as the teacher conceives it, because the strategies to be used are an implicit element in notions of the task. Yet there is some evidence that learners approach the text in different ways regardless of their teacher's intentions (Sawford, 1989). This approach will, no doubt, be connected to their prior expectations. For instance in one French lesson in which the program was used, the teacher carefully prestructured the task and provided a number of other resources, such as pictures, to help the learners (Deane, 1984). As she was working with a number of groups, she then largely left each group to carry out the task unaided. I was observing the session and was struck by the similarities between the learners' methods of working and those they would use for a conventional translation activity. One possibility was that they were transferring these methods across because they conceptualised the computer based task as a new kind of book based translation exercise. The teacher had envisaged the task differently, and provided resources that would have helped the group to deal with the task as she envisaged it, but because their interpretation was different, the learners actually made little or no use of some of these resources.

Given this diversity of approaches, what is the best way to use a text completion program? Clearly this cannot be read off from the program itself; we need some strategic conception of the main options, within which debates about detailed aims can be set. As far as language related aims are concerned, five different but connected notions of the learner's task can be distinguished in the available accounts, namely:

1 Correctly revealing the hidden text.
2 Doing this in a way that maximises the score.
3 Doing this in ways that encourage language learning.
4 Using the program as a framework for encouraging imaginative investigation of possible, as distinct from actual, texts.
5 Using the program as a framework for investigation of the nature of a text and of the genre within which it is written.

This list brings out two important points. First, the sequence is largely hierarchical and developmental. Broadly speaking, each successive notion involves a reinterpretation of the task that absorbs and transcends the earlier ones. Secondly, of these interpretations only the last three carry much educational benefit. Yet the first two are still important, for they may often be how learners initially view their task. The teacher has to start from the conception the learners have, help them succeed at that level and then move them on to a more demanding interpretation of what is required of them. It is clear, for instance, that the conception that high scores alone are what matter is one that has to be transcended before any gains can be made. Sometimes this takes place easily (Keith and Glover, 1987; Johnston, 1985), at other times it becomes an obstacle to further development (Wailing and Loney, 1984).

A similar problem can arise when the program is used to explore possible rather than actual texts. As Robinson (1985) has pointed out, using a printed text for cloze procedures leaves open the question of the appropriate word to fill each gap. When this activity is computerised by using a Tray program, it may be difficult for learners to avoid thinking of the word programmed in as necessarily being the only correct one. This would hinder their movement to the fifth level, identified by Tweddle in an unpublished paper as one where the activity is used to explore the form and function of language. This deeper conception of the educational task is very much in line with what

Moy had in mind in designing the program. As he puts it, the danger is of achieving only:

> 'rejective' reading – that situation where the fluent reader's reading eye pulls off the words effortlessly and accurately while the same reader's mind nevertheless fails to penetrate the verbal surface and engage usefully with the ideas lurking further down . . .
>
> (Moy, in Stephens, 1985, p. 5)

One of the best ways to avoid this limitation is to accept and encourage plausible speculations on alternative possible versions of the text, an approach which leads the group on to consider why the author chose the specific words that he or she did. Provided the writing was itself deeply considered, this question would in turn lead to the ideas 'lurking further down.' Extending this position further, the text can also be viewed, as Tweddle has shown, as exemplifying a genre, the characteristics of which can be explored too. To do this, however, requires a particular approach to the session, and a greater emphasis upon the use of the memo facility. This point can be generalised, for unless teachers have a clear idea as to which general conceptions of the task they and the learners severally have, it will be very difficult to make a coherent set of teaching decisions about the detailed ways in which they want to use the program, and for what specific purposes. Some general characterisation of the task, therefore, and an awareness that the learners may not share it, are essential aids to choosing specific strategies and approaches.

The analysis above also suggests an overall teaching strategy, namely to move learners up through the hierarchy of conceptions of the overall task, and at each stage to use the program to develop the specific language competences that that conception of the task makes intelligible. This of course implies that at each point the teacher has to be aware of what the learner makes of the activity. To see how this problem might be attacked, we need to consider what goes on within the zone of proximal development.

WORKING IN THE ZONE OF PROXIMAL DEVELOPMENT

Vygotsky defined the zone of proximal development as:

> the distance between the actual development level as determined by independent problem solving and the level of potential development as determined through problem solving under adult guidance or in collaboration with more capable peers.
>
> (Vygotsky, 1978, p. 86)

The ZPD then represents a penumbra of potentialities around a learner's present achievements, but a zone that can only be entered through the joint efforts of learner and tutor. It is a zone in which the uses:

of the tools and techniques of society are introduced to the child and practised in social interaction with more experienced members of society in the zone of proximal development.

(Rogoff and Wertsch, 1984, p. 4)

Software packages, including Tray, are clearly tools in this sense, but perhaps of a very distinctive kind; so how can Tray be presented to try to ensure that the challenge it offers is within the ZPD of the learner?

In selecting texts and initial displays, the teacher is adjusting the comprehension task involved so that it falls within the ZPD of the learners concerned. The teacher's actions within the zone then take the form (as we will see more fully below) of different strategies designed to help the learner to successfully complete the task. From the analysis above, it is clear that the nature of this task cannot be precisely defined purely by the program, or even by the program with a given text and initial display chosen, without some further scaffolding of the task by the teacher.

Furthermore, it is clear that the sequence of five ways of interpreting the learner's task given above represent a broadly hierarchical sequence in terms of what the learner (and indeed the teacher) needs to understand if they are to succeed with the task. Much of the discussion of the tasks by practitioners and researchers are therefore about how to distinguish these tasks, and the problems involved in moving learners from one task conception to the next (Wailing and Loney, 1984; Johnston, 1985; Moy 1985c; Tweddle, 1991). In practical terms the problem is that each conception of the task is intended to help learners at one level of understanding, but can then become a block to reaching further levels. To help overcome this the teacher must assist the learner to go further. Each successive reinterpretation of the task by the learners draws them into their current ZPD, and challenges them to reconceptualise the task. As soon as they have successfully done this and established a secure grasp of their new understanding, they are faced by the next demand for reinterpretation. Eventually they may reach as sophisticated a view of the activity as the teacher. However for this to happen the teacher must (at least in this 'teacher-led) model, provide the scaffolding that enables this development to take place.

TRAY AS A SCAFFOLDING DEVICE

The scaffolding process has already been introduced in Chapters 3 and 5. It has been characterised by Wood, Bruner and Ross (1976) as involving six kinds of tutor activities:

- Simplifying the learning task.
- Accentuating relevant features for the learner.
- Demonstrating or modelling attempted solutions.
- Recruiting the learner's interest in the task.

- Maintaining the learner's pursuit of a particular objective.
- Reducing the frustration of the task without creating tutor dependence.

All but one of these tutor activities appear within the Tray accounts too. Furthermore, three of them may be also 'carried out' in part by the computer. Simplifying the learning task by reducing the learner's degree of freedom is done by the teacher's selection of the text, and sometimes by setting its initial presentation to encourage particular approaches by the learner. This pre-lesson control can be supplemented in the lesson by teacher direction when the learners start to diverge from the teacher's intentions (Sawford, 1989). Accentuating relevant features of the task for the learner also appears in at least two accounts (Moy, 1985b; Sawford, 1989). On the other hand, examples of demonstrating or modelling attempted solutions do not appear in the Tray accounts. This is probably because to demonstrate what letters to predict is to predict them, and to model a solution that the learner has already attempted simply involves re-entering the same incorrect letters as the learner has just tried. Strictly speaking there is no intermediate form of modelling available that tells the learner something that is more than he or she already knows, but less than everything. On the other hand, there are probably a number of partial hinting strategies that fulfil the same purpose.

The remaining three teacher activities are interesting, because here both the teacher and the program can provide scaffolding (see Table 10.1). Teachers therefore have a more complex task conceptually, as they need to integrate their actions in the ZPD not only with those of the learner but also with the 'actions' of (i.e. the feedback provided by) the program. As Neil Mercer points out in Chapter 3, in this sense the computer is an actor too. How then are the remaining three scaffolding activities divided between teacher and program in the case of Tray?

The recruitment of the learner's interest in the actual task is at first sight very much helped by the use of the computer; interest is created and sustained in some cases through the program, allowing the teacher to work elsewhere in the class. But Wood and his colleagues (Wood *et al.*, 1976) emphasise that the interest must be in the task as conceived by the tutor. As the earlier discussion indicates, it is far less clear that Tray does ensure this.

Table 10.1 Possible scaffolding roles for teacher and program when using Tray

Simplification of the learning task	T only
Accentuating relevant features of the task	T only
Demonstrating or modelling attempted solutions	T only
Recruitment of the learner's interest in the actual task	T and/or Prog
Maintaining the learner's pursuit of a particular objective	T and/or Prog
Reducing the frustration of the task without creating tutor dependence	T and/or Prog

Although it supports a hierarchy of tasks it does not seem successful in drawing learners up through the hierarchy unaided, far less interacting with them in ways that create a new conception of the task. For this a contribution from a teacher is usually needed. What the program may create is enough motivation to keep the learners 'in play', so keeping them on task, if only in terms of the conception of the task that they already have.

The same observation applies when we consider how the learner's pursuit of a particular objective is maintained. The program through its scoring system has a mechanism that may keep the learners pointed very broadly in the intended direction, but that assumes that they fully understand both the scoring system and its educational rationale. To achieve such understanding, and then to see when that understanding can be moved up to a more sophisticated level, human involvement appears to be essential. As Moy observes:

> if you just sit children at the console, boot up [TRAY] and suggest they get on with it nothing too dire will happen. They are pretty certain to find out for themselves which buttons to press. And they are equally likely to have a good time. It's even quite probable that week after week they'll clamour for more and ask to continue the lesson long after the pips have gone.
>
> But to use [TRAY] in this unsupported way is likely to squander a lot of good potential. Whatever the long and medium term situation may be, [TRAY] is a program which for a long introductory period needs very careful looking after indeed. Otherwise things can start to go awkwardly astray.
>
> (Moy, 1985c, p. 3)

Where the program does have a major scaffolding role is in reducing the frustration of the task to the learner while avoiding creating teacher dependence. Because it provides immediate (albeit inflexible) feedback in response to the learner's inputs, it can reduce the irritation caused by the very common classroom problem of 'waiting for teacher'. To the extent that 'being able to keep going' is a necessary though not sufficient condition for learning, this feature is helpful, and does reduce frustration. It also provides a source of validation for learner's interpretations that is at least apparently independent of the teacher. This may well reduce the learners' inclination to look too quickly to the teacher for validation of their own ideas.

CONCLUSION

There are real benefits to be gained from using text completion programs, but what the Tray accounts bring out is that these benefits are gained at a cost. The teachers themselves have to learn what exactly the program can do, and how to take account of its strengths and limitations. Furthermore, they need to understand themselves what conceptions of language and language learning lie behind the approaches that the program can support.

This need for teacher understanding and involvement in supporting the learning is a dominant theme in much of the material (Straker *et al.*, 1985; Straker and Schenk, n.d; Stephens, 1985). On the other hand is this requirement of increased teacher understanding an undesirable cost or a further benefit? One of the most important reasons for introducing Tray is precisely that it cannot be used to best effect unless teachers reconsider what they are using it for. Like all good curricular resources, it supports both student learning and teacher development. As Moy observes:

> The [Tray] suite of programs cannot be properly understood (and will not be used to best advantage) if the teachers concerned do not at some point grapple with the theoretical underpinnings from which it sprang and which are still shaping its developing course . . . sessions with the program itself offer a prime opportunity for putting any theory about the process of reading to the test, since the 'window' on the whole business which the moment to moment unfolding of a typical TRAY session offers, can be peculiarly enlightening.
>
> (Moy, in Stephens, 1985, p. 4)

Relating concepts from communicative theories of learning to accounts of ways of using Tray programs throws light upon both. As far as the value of the theory goes, it certainly helps to structure the accounts and the research carried out on these programs. In particular it provides and identifies a number of helpful issues for further enquiry. However, it also suggests that these general concepts are only of very limited help without the detailed accounts of the specific ways that the program is conceptualised and used by teachers and learners. Without such accounts we cannot identify what scaffolding actually involves in concrete terms, or what conceptions of the task would help us to organise the activities, and both of these are essential if the theory is to have any practical applications.

For this sort of software at least, there is little support for the view that the nature of the program determines either the teacher's role or indeed even the purpose for which it may be used. Nevertheless these things are influenced by the program's structure; in particular the design requires the teacher rather than the learner to choose the initial text and to decide in what way it should be first displayed. In these respects it is more intrinsically 'teacher-controlled' than completely content-free packages such as word processors. However this still leaves a great deal of flexibility; the design of the software creates a choice envelope of indeterminate dimensions, within which teacher and learners can pursue varied purposes more or less successfully and more or less collaboratively. Much of the discussion of Tray can be read as an attempt to define the limits of this choice envelope, and to recommend that teachers take up some particular position within it on the basis of particular views of language development and the teacher's role in supporting learning.

As we have seen, the introduction of Tray into the classroom raises questions about the role of the teacher as scaffolder. To some extent the program can contribute to scaffolding, but again what this contribution might be, and how teachers need to adjust their approaches to make the most of the opportunities created, are likely to vary greatly depending upon what precise purposes they have in mind. Here too a communicative theory of learning directs attention to the strategic issues, but it does nothing to help with the equally important matter of analysing the detailed tactics of teaching and classroom management that a reflective use of Tray requires. For this, teacher accounts and personal experimentation and reflection are needed.

REFERENCES

Chandler, D. and Marcus, S. (eds) (1985) *Computers and Literacy*, Milton Keynes, Open University Press.

Deane, M. (1984) 'Teaching French with TRAY', in Open University (1984) *P542 Micros in Action in the Classroom*, Milton Keynes, Open University Press.

Everett, P. (1984) 'TRAY with Infants', in Open University (1984) *P542 Micros in Action in the Classroom*, Milton Keynes, Open University Press.

Govier, H. (1984) 'DEVELOPING TRAY: a sample run', in Straker, A. and Schenk, C. (n.d.) (eds) *Language Development in the Primary School: the role of the micro-computer*, MEP.

Haywood, S. and Wray, D. (1985) 'Using TRAY, a text reconstruction program, with top infants', *Educational Review*, 40(1).

Johnston, V. M. (1985) 'Introducing the microcomputer into English III. An evaluation of TRAY as a program using problem-solving as a strategy for developing reading skills', *British Journal of Educational Technology*, 3(16), October.

Keith, G. R. and Glover, M. (1987) *Primary Language Learning with Microcomputers*, London, Croom Helm.

Mann, P. (1989) 'Language', in Crompton, R. (ed.) (1989) *Computers and the Primary Curriculum*, Lewes, Falmer Press.

Moy, R. (1985a) 'Developing TRAY: practical questions and possible answers', in Stephens, J. (ed.) (1985) *DEVTRAY Teaching Documents*, London, ILEA English Centre and ILLEC.

Moy, R. (1985b) 'It's gotta rhyme with night', in Stephens, J. (ed.) (1985) DEVTRAY Teaching Documents, London, ILEA English Centre and ILLEC.

Moy, R. (1985c) 'Introduction' in Stephens, J. (ed.) (1985) DEVTRAY Teaching Documents, London, ILEA English Centre and ILLEC.

Moy, R. and Raleigh, M. (1980) 'Bringing it back alive', *The English Magazine*, autumn.

Robinson, B. (1985) *Microcomputers and the Language Arts*, Milton Keynes, Open University Press.

Rogoff, B. and Wertsch, J. V. (1984) 'Children's learning in the zone of proximal development', *New Directions for Child Development*, 23, San Francisco, Jossey Bass.

Sawford, J. (1989) 'The computer and language development: using DEVELOPING TRAY in a primary classroom', in Sawford, J. (ed.) (1989) *Promoting Language Development through IT*, Coventry, MESU .

Scrimshaw, P. (1986) 'Teaching TRAY to teacher', Open University Cal Research Group, *Technical Report No 56*, Milton Keynes, Open University Press.

Scrimshaw, P. (1987) 'Learning from TRAY: teachers' perceptions of possible uses for a text disclosure program', *Language and Education: An International Journal*, 1(1).

Straker, A. (1989) *Children and Computers*, Oxford, Blackwell.

Straker, A., Robson, C., Wagstaff, A. and Wilson, S. (eds) (1985) *Infant and First Schools: the role of the micro*, MEP.

Straker, A. and Schenk, C. (eds) (1984) *Language Development in the Primary School: tutor guidelines and resources for a short course for primary teachers on the use of the microcomputer in the infant or first school*, MEP.

Surgey, P. and Scrimshaw, P. (1987) 'Who Controls CAL? The case of TRAY', in Scanlon, E. and O'Shea, T. (eds) (1987) *Educational Computing*, Chichester, John Wiley & Son.

Tweddle, S. (1991) 'Developing TRAY revisited' unpublished paper.

Vygotsky, L. S. (1978) *Mind in Society: the Development of Higher Psychological Processes*, edited by Cole, M., John-Steiner, V., Scribner, S. and Souberman, E. and translated with assistance from Lopez-Morillas, M. and Luria, A., Cambridge, Mass., Harvard University Press.

Wailing, D. and Loney, H. (1984) 'Ripples in the pool: some ways of using TRAY', in Straker, A. and Schenk, C. (eds) *Language Development in the Primary School: Tutor guidelines and resources for a short course for primary teachers on the use of the microcomputer in the infant or first school*, MEP.

Wisely, C. and Duggan, K. (1985) 'Primary DEVTRAY', in Stephens, J. (ed.) (1985) *DEVTRAY Teaching Documents*, London, ILEA English Centre and ILLEC.

Wood, D., Bruner, J. and Ross, G. (1976) 'The role of tutoring in problem solving', *Journal of Child Psychiatry*, 17, Oxford, Pergamon Press.

Chapter 11

Computer-based approaches to second language learning

Diana Laurillard and Giorgio Marullo

INTRODUCTION

Second language learning will assume a new importance over the next few years as the reality of closer links between the UK and Europe forces us to rethink our attitude to foreign languages. As industry and commerce begin to confront the disadvantages of our relatively poor linguistic competence there will be questions as to why our counterparts in Europe fare so much better, and a rush to blame the schools, where currently 50 per cent of all 14 year olds give up foreign languages (DES, 1990, p. 89). The NCC working party report warns that more government resources will be needed because there is a serious shortage of specialist teachers even at this level of pro- vision. But more resources are unlikely to be forthcoming, at least in the short term. Teachers will be asked to shoulder new burdens, teaching more students, more languages, with scarcely increased resources. As with the other aspects of language competence dealt with in this book, there is a long-standing hope that computers will be able to assist in this difficult task. In this chapter, we consider what kind of role they might play. There is no expectation that they can solve all the problems, but there is an imperative to look at how they might help.

METHODOLOGIES OF SECOND LANGUAGE TEACHING

Methodological developments in second language teaching have usually had a basis in linguistic theory, socio-linguistics and psycho-linguistics, but the theoretical underpinnings often transmute into little more than rhetoric by the time materials and techniques reach the classroom. The audio-lingual method, a prescribed sequence of drills and exercises, was derived from a structuralist view of language, which stresses the interrelationships between segments of language and the linguistic functions of individual elements of language. However, the behaviourist approach to learning, with its notions of practice, mastery and control, dominant during the pre-war development of the audio-lingual method, excluded teaching about the function of linguistic devices, because of the implication that language is an instrument of communication and thought. Behaviourism could not admit such cognitivist ideas as a basis for a teaching methodology, and this meant the audio-lingual method tended to be stripped of its structural underpinnings, and was left with an impoverished collection of unmotivated exercises.

The communicative approach, now in widespread use in schools and colleges in the UK, derives from a functionalist view of language, with greater emphasis on the social context of language, where function concerns not just linguistic functions of language, but also social and situational functions. The functionalist view, originally expressed by Firth and later Halliday, was used as the theoretical basis for the Council of Europe's Modern Languages Project, which established a curriculum for teaching a second language with the communicative method. It:

> takes the communicative facts of language into account from the beginning without losing sight of grammatical and situational factors. It is potentially superior to the grammatical syllabus because it will produce a communicative competence.
>
> (Wilkins, 1976, p. 19)

As Berns has argued, however, many of the materials and techniques developed for the communicative method reflect the theoretical philosophy 'in surface features of teaching and not in the deep structure of the theoretical underpinnings' (Berns, 1990, p. 83). Some teachers use 'communicative drills', where students respond 'truthfully' to teachers' questions, which is the only concession to a communicative act in an otherwise traditional skills-based approach. Other teachers focus on entirely communicative functions and offer no systematic treatment of grammatical forms. Canale has defined four components of communicative competence – perhaps it is the awesome range of the communicative method that makes it difficult for modern language teachers to implement (Canale, 1983):

- Grammatical competence: knowledge of the sentence structure of a language.
- Sociolinguistic competence: using language appropriate to a given context.
- Discourse competence: recognising different patterns of discourse.
- Strategic competence: compensating for incomplete knowledge of the rules.

There is no hierarchical or linear relationship between these: they all interact, they are all essential. If teachers are trying to cover this range of competences within the constraints of the school timetable, which offer at best only 2 hours per week on any one language, then perhaps it is not surprising that examiners discover serious inadequacies in pupils' grammatical competence:

The main weakness of candidates was their failure to use verb tenses and forms correctly.

(Southern Examining Group, French, 1989)

When problems of communication did arise, it was often shaky grammar that caused them, because the use of the wrong tense or the wrong person of a verb made what the candidate was trying to convey unclear through ambiguity.

(Southern Examining Group, Spanish, 1989)

The implementation of the communicative approach does not achieve Wilkins' hoped-for superiority. Communicative competence remains elusive for most learners.

The original theoretical definitions of the structuralist, functionalist and communicative approaches all acknowledge a range of essential requirements for learning a second language, but they give prominence to different aspects, and this has distorted their implementation in the classroom. We are now approaching an enlightened broadmindedness where the broader theoretical position is reflected in the consensus view of language teaching methodology. The current proposals from the DES for foreign languages in the National Curriculum give predominantly communicative exercises as examples of good practice, but also suggest:

Once they have thoroughly absorbed a set of related chunks of language, learners need to explore and if necessary be shown how the underlying model works, not told about it.

(DES, 1990, p. 54)

Although the document quotes Widdowson's view that communicative competence is 'essentially a matter of adaptation, and rules are not generative but regulative and subservient' (p. 54), it is the generative, grammatical rules that it finally acknowledges as of greatest value, rather than the arbitrary, experientially derived socio-linguistic rules that govern appropriateness of use in context. By 'underlying rules' it means the 'framework of structures which forms the skeleton of any language':

If learners can be helped to see the common features of the chunks of language which they have learnt, they will be better able to adapt them to the demands of different situations and increasingly to check their own production.

(Ibid., p. 56)

Thus the preferred current strategy, if we may take this document as the best expression of a consensus on language teaching methodology, is that once learners have absorbed some chunks of language and patterns of communication, they should be given access to the underlying model via a guided discovery approach that uses both learner-controlled exploration and teacher-controlled demonstration.

THE VYGOTSKYAN PERSPECTIVE

Chapter 3 has argued that Vygotsky's communicative theory provides a comprehensive approach for the study of computers in classrooms, emphasising the importance of studying learning from the computer in the broad social context of the classroom activities. Certainly, the communicative approach to second language learning ought to find support from Vygotsky's analysis of how language is utilised in social interaction, and, given its perceived value for the study of computer-based learning in general, we should consider the implications of the theory in this particular learning context.

Vygotsky (1962) describes the development of first language in a child as a progression from socially determined functional speech to functionally differentiated egocentric speech, and sees the latter as fundamental to thought: 'Egocentric speech, splintered off from general social speech, in time leads to inner speech which serves both autistic and logical thinking' (p. 19).

The development of speech therefore plays a crucial role in the development of the child as both a social being and an individual. The process has been described also as a progression from 'object-regulation' when the child is controlled by the environment to 'other-regulation', when the child is controlled by a person, to 'self-regulation' when speech is used to control oneself and others (Foley, 1991). The importance of this developmental sequence for cognition, especially the final stage of self-regulation, is used as the basis for a critique of traditional approaches to language teaching. Within the Vygotskyan perspective a pedagogically sound approach has to exploit the learner's capacity for self-regulation. It is argued that there is little opportunity for self-regulation in the structuralist drills or in the functionalist exercises and what second language teaching needs, therefore, is a task-based approach that accords self-regulation its proper place:

> self-regulation is not achieved at a particular point in ontogenetic maturation, as an individual can have achieved self-regulation in one task but not in another. Thus at any stage in an individual's life (such as learning a new language) the individual externalises the inner order so that he may regulate himself once again, externally, in order to recover self-regulation . . . What the Task-based approach does . . . is to use these same psychological principles in second language pedagogy.
>
> (Foley, 1991, p. 73)

The aim, therefore, is to re-create in the second language classroom the conditions under which individual learners acquired their first language. Vygotsky's theory of language development is very general, general enough to be described by Bruner, in his introduction to the English translation, as a theory of education (Vygotsky, 1962), so it is quite legitimate to attempt to apply it to the learning of anything. There are difficulties in applying it to second language learning, however. Vygotsky is talking about *language acquisition*, i.e. being immersed in a society using the target language, and this must be distinguished from *language learning*, i.e. through classroom instruction. The assumptions must be made that (1) second language learning is like second language acquisition, and (2) second language acquisition is like first language acquisition. Let us examine these assumptions further.

If the communicative approach tells us anything, it tells us that language and language usage is context dependent. The social context within which we hear, see and produce language affects what we process and how. That is why it is seen as so important to preserve the learner's experience of the relation between context and use, and to avoid the artificial drills and exercises of earlier methodologies. However, the social context of the language classroom, where we do second language learning, is fundamentally different from the social context of a social encounter with native speakers of a foreign language, where we do second language acquisition. In both situations the individual's overriding concern is probably to avoid looking like a complete fool, but this takes different forms. In the first case you have to avoid imitating that funny accent too closely or your friends will laugh; in the second you have to do your best to make it sound right to avoid getting that funny look. In the first case you need good marks in the exam; in the second you actually need some bread. Those who recognise the importance of contextualising language cannot deny that the individual's experience of it must be quite different in the two cases: second language learning is likely to be experienced differently from second language acquisition.

There is certainly nothing in Vygotsky's analysis to suggest that second language learning is like first language acquisition. In fact he explicitly states (in the same book) the exact opposite. He differentiates between the development of spontaneous everyday concepts, such as 'brother', and scientific concepts, such as 'exploitation':

> The inception of a spontaneous concept can usually be traced to a face-to-face meeting with a concrete situation, while a scientific concept involves from the first a 'mediated' attitude towards its object.
>
> (Vygotsky, 1962, p. 108)

The two types of concept are developed differently, bottom-up and top-down in latter-day terminology, and Vygotsky's focal problem is to understand how the two interrelate. Learning a foreign language is an example of the development of scientific concepts:

> learning a foreign language . . . is conscious and deliberate from the start. In one's native language, the primitive aspects of speech are acquired before the more complex ones. The latter pre-suppose some awareness of phonetic, grammatical and syntactic forms. With a foreign language, the higher forms develop before spontaneous, fluent speech.
>
> (p. 109)

This is one manifestation of the problem of how an individual develops new systems that are structurally analogous to ones developed earlier, such as:

> written speech, foreign language, verbal thought in general. The experimental evidence yielded by our studies disproves the theory of shift, or displacement, which states that the later stage repeats the course of the earlier one . . . All our evidence supports the hypothesis that analogous systems develop in reverse directions at the higher and at the lower levels, each system influencing the other and benefiting from the strong points of the other.
>
> (p. 110)

Therefore a second language develops in the reverse direction to the first language. We have to remember that Vygotsky's 'experiments' were conducted at a time and in a culture where the structuralist 'mediated' approach to teaching a foreign language would have been the unquestioned norm, and students would have had little choice about acquiring the 'higher' grammatical concepts earlier than fluent speech. Even ignoring his experimental evidence, however, his theoretical approach does not admit the reading that second language learning might be like first language acquisition. Learning a foreign language is conscious and deliberate: learning it as a set of spontaneous concepts could only occur in the special circumstances of immigrants or pidgin speakers; and coming second means that it cannot play the same part in the development of the individual's sense of self that the first language does. Furthermore, it is the process of 'self-regulation' in language acquisition that produces the interim grammars of second language learners, the 'interlanguage' and 'pidgin' forms, with their own generative rules and routinised chunks. Second language teaching methodology will do the same if it relies on the same process. Therefore we want to clarify that for teaching purposes we cannot necessarily rely on the processes of language acquisition, and this is important when we come to consider how we can best make use of existing theory.

Vygotsky's own analysis of second language learning cannot be used, therefore, to support the communicative approach, although considering it in the wider context as a theory of teaching and learning, it would certainly raise some interesting questions about the context within which a language teaching program was to be used. We shall return to this point in the concluding section.

A PSYCHO-LINGUISTIC PERSPECTIVE

There is considerable research in psycho-linguistics that is relevant to our concerns but it has not yet been consolidated as a theory of second language instruction (Klein 1986; McLaughlin 1987). The bulk of this research relates to second language *acquisition*, which refers to the spontaneous learning of a language, e.g. by immigrants, and contrasts, therefore with second language *instruction*. Klein argues that there is a long way to go before we can provide evidence for a particular form of language instruction (p. 55) and that psycholinguistic research cannot yet even define 'how the human language processor functions in language acquisition'. None the less, some of the theoretical analyses and experimental results from this field could be used to constrain the way we formulate teaching methodology, even if they cannot determine precisely what it should be.

Klein describes four problems that face the spontaneous language learner, and they are interesting to the language teacher because they give an indication of the kind of work that must be done by the learner who has to learn grammatical rules inductively from a sequence of inputs, albeit a carefully controlled sequence. The four problems are defined below, and each is re-interpreted for the classroom-based learner.

Analysis

'Analysis' requires the learner to segment the acoustic signals of an utterance and relate them to parallel non-linguistic events, such as body language, in order to derive meaning. How the analysis is done depends critically upon the learners' previous knowledge. Consider the example of learning the words 'book' and 'table' from a real-world context. It requires that learners know about the gender of the article. If not, or if the concept is at all shaky, there is a risk that they could segment the sound 'una tavola' as 'un atavola', by assuming that the article 'un' is constant. It requires other contexts for the word 'tavola' to enable them to sort this out, e.g. 'le tavole' (the tables). However, here again, unless article agreement and pluralisation were already well understood, this utterance may be simply incoherent. Notice also that while the teacher may regard 'un libro' and 'una tavola' as illustrative of the concept of gender agreement with the article, the learner who has not segmented the sound correctly will be unable to apprehend this concept from this example. In a different example, the learner who produces the following from dictation[1] is unable to use these utterances to derive the form of the perfect tense:

Chantal a telephoner a 10 heures et elle ma dit que . . .

(Chantal a telephone à 10 heures et elle m'a dit que . . .)

It is clearly fallacious to expect that this learner can induce the forms of the perfect tense from hearing it expressed in utterances of this type. The success of an inductive approach to analysis is heavily dependent, therefore, on a well-constructed sequence of tasks, that introduce only one new item in the context of other well-understood knowledge. The cognitive load experienced by the learner who has to hold several uncertainties simultaneously, waiting for confirmation or disconfirmation of any one, is too great for most language learners.

Synthesis

'Synthesis' requires the learner to use the syntax derived from their analysis of the spoken target language to produce their own utterances. However, as Klein points out, the complex syntax of the correctly spoken language is not necessarily reproduced by the learner. In language acquisition, it is common to find learners using simplified forms of the syntax they hear, known as 'morphs', which reduce morphological complexities to their simplest possible form, and rely on word order and information to give structure and therefore meaning to their utterances. For example, a spontaneous learner, who has mastered no conjugation, uses very few finite verbs, no auxiliary or modal verbs, and few function words, and relies mainly on learned names and constructed pragmatic rules, rather than acquired syntactic rules for structuring sentences. They will produce forms such as:

I not come Germany – Spain always farmer work.

(Klein, 1986, p. 84)

meaning 'before I came to Germany I used to work in Spain on a farm', where topic order and 'not' do the work of 'before', 'always' does the work of the modal form 'used to', and 'farmer work' combines two names to express 'work on a farm'. Such syntax can never be derived from hearing the target language. It is developed from a series of pragmatic rules concerning topic order, word order, etc., that appear to be common to many speakers who learn the language in this way.

The problem of synthesis is not so great for second language learners who are receiving instruction, because there is explicit focusing, even within inductive methods, on syntactic forms, and the input they are exposed to is carefully managed to ensure that the forms they meet are not too complex. For this reason, it is more common to find that the pragmatic rules the classroom learner resorts to depend much more on transliteration from their first language, as in:

Il prend trente minutes aller a l'école.

('aller' = literally 'to go'; it should be 'pour aller' = literally 'for to go'; 'trente' should be plural to agree with 'minutes', an error due not to transliteration, but to an overgeneralisation of the lack of agreement in English)

Je finnissent mes examens sur dix huit Mars.

(literally 'on 18 March'; it should be 'le dix-huit Mars' = literally 'the 18

March'; the verb should be 'finis', pronounced without the 's' sound, rather than the third person plural form used – probably not an attempt at transliteration, except possibly as a way of providing a voiced ending as in English)

The most common equivalent of the 'morph' for classroom learners seems to be the use of the infinitive form of the verb, as in:

Je faire au tennis.

Je passer une semaine . . .

Je aller faire de course.

although this could also be seen as a type of transliteration, where learners transfer the lack of conjugation in English, and select one form of the verb. Either way, these learners also appear to use pragmatic rules of some kind, and generate forms never used by native or expert speakers.

The problem of synthesis is quite different for the classroom learner, and we cannot expect to find the same pragmatic rules used by spontaneous learners, mainly because the latter's task is much harder: they do not have enough of the target language to be able to do transliteration. It is clear from the above examples, however, that it is possible to find common forms of the problem of synthesis from an analysis of target-language output by classroom learners. We shall return to this point later.

Embedding

'Embedding' refers to the ability of the learner to use contextual information to elaborate the meaning of an inadequate utterance. For example, the hearer can easily interpret the nonsensical utterance 'me bread' as 'I would like some bread' if it is uttered in a bakery by a customer to the assistant. As the learner's language competence develops, they can gradually become less dependent on context to convey and interpret meaning. The communicative approaches to language teaching often takes the trouble to create situational contexts for learners, to support them in conveying and interpreting meaning, so that the language constructs they meet in that situation can be understood, with help from the context, and their structure and form inferred. Support from the situational context is clearly helpful within that situation, but the problem for the classroom learner is that their goal is not the pragmatic, situation-specific goal of acquiring bread. Their goal is language competence. So their problem is one of 'disembedding' – of being able to abstract the particular language construct from the situation, so as to be able to use it in other contexts. The teaching methodology has to provide for this as well – a point that we shall return to later.

Matching

'Matching' is the problem the spontaneous learner must solve in order to gradually reduce the gap between their own utterances in the target language and those of a native speaker. The gap is perceived and used as a means of learning the correct forms via three types of control mechanism:

- *Monitoring* enabling the learner to modify their speech production.
- *Feedback* delayed control resulting in self-correction, or correction by others.
- *Reflection* retrospective control of language performance, not coincident with speech production.

(Klein, 1986, p. 142)

Clearly, the classroom learner has a considerable advantage over the spontaneous learner in the sense that the teacher will usually be a conscientious corrector, providing feedback that the learner may not be able to provide for themselves. But the assumption of the communicative approach is that the 'matching' problem should be solvable by the classroom learner without the constant intervention of the teacher giving the right answer. So it is relevant to consider Klein's analysis of just how difficult the matching problem is. Suppose the student who wrote:

Nous suis aller fair de course.

(should be: 'Nous sommes allées faire des courses; literally: 'we have been to make some purchases')

utters this sentence in a communicative context, such that their interlocutor wishes to provide corrective feedback, not explicitly, but in a way that allows them to reflect on their utterance, match it to the native speaker's and deduce the correct forms of the rules that they got wrong. Klein describes three types of error that can be made: phonological, morphological and syntactical. Since this was originally a written sentence we have no information about the student's phonology, but how would the morphological errors 'aller' and 'de course', and the syntactical error 'suis' be corrected (assuming fair' is a simple spelling mistake)? To begin with 'aller' sounds like 'allees', especially for a non-native speaker, and probably would not get corrected at all. Suppose the native speaker offers:

vous êtes allées faire des courses?

as feedback. To act as a correction, the student has to recognise that 'êtes' is part of the conjugation of 'être' and agrees with 'vous' and therefore they should have used a different part of the verb to agree with their 'nous'. Given that they can produce 'nous suis', this is expecting a lot. Secondly they have to hear the phonological distinction between 'de' and 'des', interpret it as 'des' and not an alternative pronunciation of 'de', and in addition deduce that therefore 'courses' must be plural and have an unspoken 's' at the end. It is a considerable task to cope with all that, and it demands dedicated reflection by the student on their existing morphological and syntactic rules to cope with just one of the corrections.

In reality, many teachers give much more direct corrective feedback, and in the above example would give written corrections on the original written sentence. Even in that situation, however, it is difficult for the learner, if they look at the feedback and not just the mark, to derive the general form of the rule that 'être' must be conjugated. If, for example, they are using 'suis' as a kind of morph, looking for a simple form of the conjugation to mirror the English form (of regular verb, that is, not the irregular 'to be') then from this correction they may simply learn to substitute 'sommes' as the morph for all parts of the conjugation. The difficulty with the assumption of the communicative approach – that the learner can learn the rules of syntax and morphology by induction – is that it requires an extremely dedicated and insightful learner to accomplish this task. Even with restricted input and corrective feedback, it should be clear from the above examples that the task of generating the current rules puts a tremendous cognitive load on the student. Even the most diligent learner will have trouble sorting out the confirmatory evidence for their various current hypotheses from the implicit use of the correct rules in the native speaker's language.

REQUIREMENTS FOR A TEACHING METHODOLOGY FOR A SECOND LANGUAGE

From the above discussion, we can conclude that some of the requirements for a teaching methodology must be as follows.

1 The problem of analysis suggests that the sequence of taught linguistic items must be carefully constructed so that only one new item is introduced at a time, and is embedded in other well-understood forms.
2 The problem of synthesis suggests that classroom learners construct their own synthetic rules, dependent more on transliteration than on the pragmatics of real communication, and that these rules are discoverable from empirical studies, and could be used to inform the process of instruction.
3 The problem of embedding becomes the problem of 'disembedding' for classroom learners, and suggests that the teaching methodology must explicitly decontextualise the language constructs to be learned, if the learner is to acquire them in a form that is generalisable for multiple contexts. Furthermore, because embedding takes place in an artificial context in the classroom, the normal motivation to convey and interpret meaning is lost (role-playing a customer is importantly different from actually being one), and the learner may therefore need a more explicitly stated goal, which will tend to be a meta-linguistic one (e.g. to become

competent in asking questions), rather than a pragmatic one (e.g. to acquire some bread).

4 The problem of matching shows that even classroom learners need considerable support to enable them to use the gap between their own output and that of a native speaker to formulate the correct syntactic and morphological rules.

The general conclusion of this section is that the communicative approach, with its reliance on induction as the principal means of learning linguistic forms in the target language creates too great a cognitive load for most learners. The requirements outlined above would be extremely complex for a classroom teacher, or even an individual tutor to handle. We conclude, therefore, that the classroom learner will be better served if we preserve the complexity that language competence entails, and the communicative methodology is supplemented by an explicit 'deductive' method, where the underlying grammatical rules are taught, in order to overcome the classroom versions of Klein's four problems.

Computers in second language teaching

Computers have been used in second language teaching for over fifteen years and there is now a proliferation of language teaching programs. Because it is difficult for such a medium to handle the uncertainties and ambiguities of natural language, language teaching programs have almost never been developed within the communicative methodology. Currently, as Chapter 10 illustrates, experiments are now beginning with the new communication tools, such as computer-mediated conferencing, video conferencing, satellite broadcasting, etc., which facilitate the practice of communication skills with native speakers. However, computer-based tutorial programs have usually been didactic, using the more traditional grammar-based methods. It might seem, therefore, that computer-based tutorials would contribute the supplementary teaching argued for at the end of the previous section. Unfortunately they do not. They have never been recognised by the majority of language teachers as exemplifying good teaching, and remain peripheral to the core of classroom teaching. In this section we attempt to account for this by demonstrating that the design of these programs often violates the requirements we derived in the previous section.

We have argued elsewhere (Laurillard, 1990) that a teaching program must have the following design features in order to support a self-contained learning process:

- *Information*: describes the new content to be learned.
- *Goal*: motivates the learning.
- *Integration*: provides the connection between new and known content.

- *Performance*: requires the learner to demonstrate their knowledge.
- *Feedback*: enables the learner to improve their performance.

By applying this analysis to any supposedly self-contained teaching program, it is possible to see which design features are missing or inadequate, and therefore to predict how it might fail.

In the previous section, we derived a number of requirements for a language teaching methodology, and these further constrain the form these design features must take for a computer-based language teaching program:

- *Information*: must introduce syntactic and morphological rules explicitly.
- *Goal*: must be supplied in order to motivate performance and reflection on performance, and therefore attention to feedback as a way of improving performance.
- *Integration*: the information and performance exercises must be sequenced in a way that introduces new linguistic items only in the context of known items.
- *Performance*: is required to allow matching against the target form to take place; it must be elicited in a sequence that allows progressive de-contextualisation to occur; it must be capable of eliciting any standard misconceptions or idiosyncratic rules the learner has; together with the feedback, the performance required must be capable of taking the learner further towards the intended goal.
- *Feedback*: must deal explicitly with any diagnosed misconceptions or mal-rules; must provide help with analysing the gap between learner performance and target form in terms of the information supplied, or in terms of previously mastered items.

Applying this analysis to many current computer-based language teaching programs reveals all too easily that they are lacking or inadequate in one or several of these features. The point is best illustrated if we take one of the better current programs and attempt to demonstrate that it too violates some of these principles.

Let us consider a program that teaches the syntax of object pronouns for French. It begins with a demonstration of how the different pronouns are substituted for different types of noun or noun phrase, and how on substitution they change position. For example, it begins by presenting the sentence:

Nous donnons le livre au professeur

then animates the change of 'le livre' into the pronoun 'le':

Nous donnons le au professeur

and animates its movement into its proper position before the verb:

Nous le donnons au professeur

The program then supplies further information by displaying the following table:

Object pronouns

1	2	3	4	5
me				
te	le			
se	la	lui	y	en
nous	les	leur		
vous				

At this stage the program has offered no explicit goal, and the information relevant to the rule being taught is incomplete, because the ordering of the pronouns is only implicit in the table: it does not make it clear that it would be incorrect, for example, to put 'lui' before 'le' as in 'Nous lui le donnons'.

The next stage of the program begins with a cleared screen, so the initial information is no longer available, and sets a task for the learner to perform, e.g.:

Ils offrent le bal au garçon

what's the pronoun for au garçon? *lui*

correct

The program does require performance by the learner, but it is the computer that does the matching against the target form. The sequence of tasks does allow decontextualisation of the individual pronouns because 'lui' occurs in the context of both 'au garçon' and 'au professeur', and others. It also allows for decontextualisation of the re-position rule, as this is practised with every task set.

It is clear, however, that the program has not been designed with reference to standard misconceptions or learner-generated pragmatic rules. In order to do this, it would have to set certain kinds of exercise to elicit these, give feedback that is specific to the particular misconception elicited, and use this information to generate further exercises which would either elaborate the nature of the misconception, or provide further practice and reinforcement for the new learning. When a standard error is committed, however, e.g.:

Nous offrons de la monnaie à la dame

What's the pronoun for à la dame? *elle*

the program responds with:

I don't recognise your answer

Would you like to try again?

There are not so many standard errors for any one rule that it is difficult to design the program to recognise them. However, in this program the feedback does not deal explicitly with standard misconceptions because it cannot recognise them. What other help does it offer? Does it help the learner analyse the gap between their performance and the target performance? It appears that the program only analyses it as either 'does or does not match'. However, it does provide a hint, after the student has got the answer wrong three times in succession:

> sorry that's not right: lui is the indirect object singular.

This ought to be helpful as it provides an analytical description for the learner. However it is not expressed in terms of the information initially supplied, which did not distinguish explicitly between direct/indirect or singular/plural, nor even define 'object pronouns'. It may be that the learner is expected to have mastered these terms already, but there is no pre-test to check this, and it must usually be the case that students of French are uncertain about these grammatical forms. Uncertainty will make this feedback meaningless to them.

This is not an unusually bad program – we began this analysis by stating that it is one of the better ones: it includes information, requires performance and provides feedback, which is more than many language teaching programs can claim. The problem is that we have derived quite strict criteria for the form the various design features must have if the program is to address some of the critical problems the language learner faces. We have found no computer-based language teaching programs that meet these criteria. In the next section we describe an attempt to build one.

Design for a computer-based language teaching program

To better illustrate the requirements for a CAL methodology, we describe in this section a program that attempts to meet the stricter criteria outlined in section 4. The program is designed to teach some basic aspects of grammatical structure, namely subject pronouns, in order to be able to build on this knowledge to teach verb morphology explicitly. The teaching is therefore aiming to deal explicitly with the underlying grammatical rules, but the program is meant to be used as a supplement to a communicative approach, once learners have absorbed some patterns and routines of communication.

More explicitly, the goal of the tutorial program is to help the learner develop an automisation of the general concept of personal pronoun and the particular forms it takes in the target language. The role of automaticity in the acquisition of language skills has been demonstrated, for example, by Schneider and Schiffrin (1977) for reading, and by Tarone (1982) for speaking, where automaticity is: 'the relative access the learner has to the knowledge, irrespective of its degree of analysis' (Bialystock, 1982, p. 183).

The learner progresses from controlled, and therefore slow, performance, to a speedier, automated performance. The increased access afforded by automisation is characterised by the learner being able to reduce their discrimination time, pay more attention to higher order features, and ignore irrelevant information (McLaughlin, 1987, p. 142). Thus the goal of the tutorial program is to facilitate this process for subject pronouns and verbs. The information presented introduces explicitly the grammatical information needed, namely the syntactic form of the pronouns in terms of their

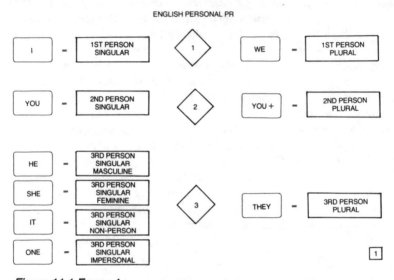

Figure 11.1 **Frame 1**

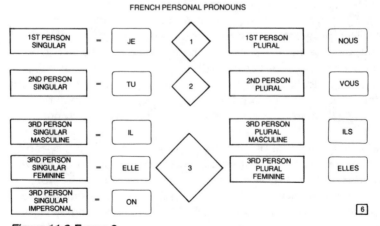

Figure 11.2 **Frame 6**

'grammatical description' (GD) in the first frame (Figure 11.1) and the lexical (and phonological, since each French word is spoken) items themselves, once the syntactic forms have been mastered (Figure 11.2).

The arrangement of these two frames helps to emphasise the internal structure of person (1st, 2nd, 3rd) and number (singular, plural), and the complexity of the 3rd singular form. That is all the information needed throughout the program.

Integration of new information with known items is achieved by leaving nothing to chance. The reason for beginning with subject pronouns is that they are necessary to explain the morphology of verb conjugation – how else do you explain why verb endings change? But the explanation will be meaningless unless the concept of 'pronoun' is already well understood. Within this program, we cannot begin at Figure 11.2 without establishing an understanding of the syntax of pronouns because students must understand the components of person, number and gender to be able to cope with explanations about agreement of verb endings. If the French pronouns are associated only with their English equivalents, the learner's tacit knowledge of person, number and gender implicit in the English usage will not be tapped, because these components play a lesser role in English than they do in French. Therefore, the information needed to integrate verb morphology with pronouns, must be mastered here.

Performance is elicited in a sequence that allows progressive de-contextualisation, by sequencing the tasks as follows:

1 Learners are asked to select the pronoun corresponding to a given grammatical description (Figure 11.3).
2 They are asked to select a grammatical description corresponding to a given pronoun.

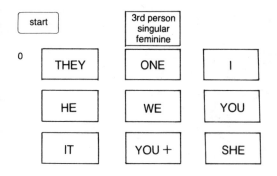

Figure 11.3 Frame 2

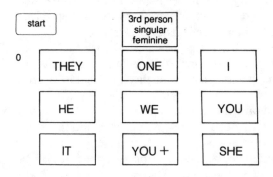

Figure 11.4 Frame 4

3 The pronouns are randomly ordered, and they are asked to select a pronoun corresponding to a given grammatical description (Figure 11.4).
4 The grammatical descriptions are randomly ordered and they are asked to select a grammatical description corresponding to a given pronoun. The French version proceeds through similar stages to the final stage (Figure 11.5).

Thus both English and French versions are intended to progressively decontextualise any association between spatial position and pronoun, and emphasise the automisation of the concepts in their most general form.

Within each of the above tasks, the learner is required to respond correctly to each of the nine items within a given time in order to demonstrate automaticity, where the time criterion is calibrated from times taken by

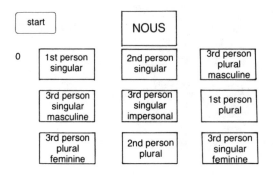

Figure 11.5 Frame 10

expert and novice speakers. The design includes two ways in which they can match their own performance to the target: (1) the French pronoun is spoken for a correct response or flashes for an incorrect response; (2) the learner's actual average time is continuously marked on a rule showing the target response time, thus visually displaying the gap between their own performance, and the target one.

The program does not, at present, attempt to diagnose standard misconceptions or mal-rules. This is because there has so far been little research to establish what these are. Teachers and examining bodies know that learners have difficulty with the morphology and syntax of verbs, and that they have sparse knowledge of 'subject pronouns', if for no other reason than this kind of description of language is no longer taught. They certainly have a tacit knowledge of all these aspects of language because they use them in their own language, but the extent to which this is articulated, accurate, and accessible enough to help them in coping with the structure of a foreign language is not known. The program therefore assumes they know nothing, and teaches the relevant concepts as if from scratch. This reflects our own ignorance, however, more than that of the learners. Clearly they know something, but what precisely, and how this might affect the teaching is an issue that awaits further research. Till then, the program must fail on the criteria of addressing learners' existing misconceptions.

For the same reason, the feedback is not designed to cope with misconceptions or pragmatic rules, and only sets out to assist the student in matching their performance to the target, where all items are presented in the same form in which they appeared in the initial presentation.

The match between *performance* required and intended goal is achieved by incorporating an algorithm in the program that decides which items are to be presented next in the following way:

1 It introduces new items only when some have already been mastered (an aspect of 'integration').
2 It rehearses recently learned information before it has time to fade completely.
3 It moves to the next level of difficulty (i.e. putting the items into a different context), only when mastery of all items is achieved at the prior level.

This procedure is intended to help the students attain automaticity for their use of subject pronouns. Whether it does, what the optimal criteria for mastery are (in terms of speed and accuracy of response), whether students remain sufficiently motivated to remain attentive, and whether the mastery of the concepts in this way transfers to their use in the context of verb morphology, are all empirical questions. Initial pilot studies suggest that students find the program highly motivating, if somewhat exhausting (some have spent as much as one hour continually on the program). The design of the program is adaptive to the learner, using information about the speed and accuracy of their responses at each stage to determine how much more practice they need in order to achieve automaticity. If it can achieve this, in such a way that the knowledge can be used effectively for learning to cope with the morphology and syntax of verbs, then this kind of computer-based program could be a very useful adjunct to the standard communicative methodology by offering precisely what that method cannot offer, i.e. the basic structural hooks to assist learners in analysing and synthesising their communicative experience of the language. This aspect is tested via a pre- and post-test that assesses the degree of transfer students can achieve on the same concepts in different contexts. The ultimate test would be to follow through further teaching to see if they can now learn about morphology more efficiently, as a result.

One of the interesting features of this kind of adaptive tutorial program is that the number of linguistic items attended to is very high. By the end of the tutorial, the student will have focused on nine linguistic items and nine meta-linguistic descriptions, the former at least 13 times each, the latter at least 11 times each. That is on the assumption that they do everything correctly and fast enough, in which case the whole procedure takes approximately 12 minutes. More typical figures would be around 18 times for each item, the whole procedure lasting about 30 minutes. Similar figures should be achievable for the extension program that would attempt to automatise the conjugative process. The advantage of such highly concentrated attention on a few linguistic items should be that combinations such as 'nous suis' and 'je faire' should be rendered almost impossible. One problem with the communicative approach is that the constantly rich communicative context cannot offer such a high concentration of experience of standard forms. Having to cope with elaborate contexts, students develop their own strategies for dealing with information overload, and these common errors could well be the result of that. If adaptive tutorial programs can counter that by giving 'nous sommes' a high frequency in their experience of the language, then that will be a further way in which they can complement the communicative approach.

CONCLUSIONS

This chapter has attempted to build some basic principles for the design of language teaching programs by considering both the basic research on how novices confront a new language, and the design characteristics of good computer-based tutorials. By combining the two we hope to have justified some of the criteria for language teaching tutorials by which existing programs can be judged and future ones designed. It is by no means an exhaustive analysis: it applies only to certain kinds of tutorials; it has nothing to say about pre-requisites, nor how diagnosis and remediation should be handled; it does not look at integration with other media or follow-up exercises. In the light of discussions in earlier chapters in this book it would be interesting, for example, to explore how a Vygotskyan analysis of the social context of learning would critique the use of language tutorials designed to help learners develop linguistic concepts: how does language serve as a medium of thought about language? There is much still to do. However, we would argue that the criteria developed earlier provide the basis for further work to build on because they are already powerful enough to yield a substantial critique of one of the more elaborate program designs in this field. By developing further this kind of approach we believe it will be possible to radically improve the standard of language teaching tutorials.

NOTE

1   We are grateful to Patricia Manning for permission to use extracts from her data for this chapter.

REFERENCES

Berns, M. (1990) *Contexts of Competence: social and cultural considerations in communicative language teaching*, New York, Plenum Press.

Bialystock, E. (1982) 'On the relationship between knowing and using linguistic forms', *Applied Linguistics*, 3(3).

Canale, M. (1983) 'From communicative competence to communicative language pedagogy', in Richards, J. and Schmidt, R. (eds) *Language and Communication*, London, Longmans.

DES (1990) *Modern Foreign Languages for Ages 11 to 16*, London, National Curriculum Council.

Foley, J. (1991) 'A psycholinguistic framework for task-based approaches to language teaching', *Applied Linguistics*, 12(1): 62–75.

Klein, W. (1986) *Second Language Acquisition*, Cambridge, Cambridge University Press.

Laurillard, D. M. (1990) 'Unit 2: how computers can assist learning', *EH232 Computers and Learning*, Milton Keynes, Open University Press.

McLaughlin, B. (1987) *Theories of Second Language Learning*, London, Edward Arnold.

Schneider, W. and Schiffrin, R. M. (1977) 'Controlled and automatic processing 1: detection, search and attention', *Psychological Review*, 84: 1–64.

Southern Examining Group (1989) *Chief Examiners' Reports, Summer 1988 Examinations*, Guildford, Southern Examining Group.

Vygotsky, L. S. (1962) *Thought and Language*, Cambridge, Mass., MIT Press.

Wilkins, D. (1976) *Notional Syllabuses*, Oxford, Oxford University Press.

Chapter 12

Reading, writing and hypertext

Peter Scrimshaw

INTRODUCTION

Hypertexts and hypermedia are today being widely discussed by educators interested in information technology. Great claims have been made for their educational potential, and systems are becoming available in schools (Cumming and Sinclair, 1992) following a number of years in which they have been evolving in higher education. This chapter considers three questions:

1 What is a hypertext?
2 What kinds of hypertexts are most relevant to language development?
3 What, given a communicative theory of learning, are the relative strengths and weaknesses of each of these kinds of hypertext?

WHAT IS A HYPERTEXT?

As it appears to the user (see Figure 12.1), a hypertext consists of a set of screen displays, linked together by 'buttons' on the screen. When the cursor is placed over a button and activated (e.g. by clicking a button on the mouse) the user is taken to another linked screen.

All hypertexts are created on computers, using one of the many specialised systems now available. These systems provide, in effect, a programming language through which any number of hypertexts can be created and viewed, rather as a word processing package allows the user to create and display any number of different texts. Available packages include HyperCard (for the Macintosh), Guide, Linkway and Hyperties (for IBM compatibles), and Genesis (for the Acorn Archimedes). While these packages (and there are many others) vary greatly in detail and sophistication, they all share certain features. As one writer on the role of hypertexts in literacy puts it:

a hypertext consists of topics and their connections, where again the topics may be paragraphs, sentences, individual words, or indeed

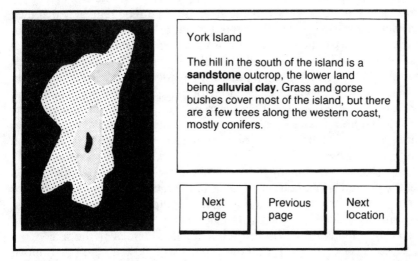

York Island

The hill in the south of the island is a **sandstone** outcrop, the lower land being **alluvial clay**. Grass and gorse bushes cover most of the island, but there are a few trees along the western coast, mostly conifers.

| Next page | Previous page | Next location |

Figure 12.1 This hypertext screen contains five buttons: the three at the bottom right and the words in bold in the text. Clicking on any of these five buttons takes the reader to an appropriate screen

digitised graphics. A hypertext is like a printed book that the author has attacked with a pair of scissors and cut into convenient verbal sizes. The difference is that the hypertext does not simply dissolve into a disordered bundle of slips, as the printed book must. For the author also defines a scheme of electronic connections to indicate relationships among the slips. In fashioning a hypertext, a writer might begin with a passage of continuous prose and then add notes or glosses on important words in the passage . . . the glosses themselves could contain glosses, leading the reader to further texts. A hypertextual network can extend indefinitely, as a printed text cannot.

(Bolter, 1991, p. 24)

In its most general formulation, then, a hypertext can be defined as an open-ended set of topics connected by variable links. The topics may be presented in a passive form (e.g. as text, pictures, diagrams, graphs) or an active one (e.g. as runnable computer programs, animation sequences, short musical or voice sequences). Hypertexts containing these more active elements are often called hypermedia, but for simplicity we will use hypertext as the generic name. For present purposes, we will mainly consider only those hypertexts made up of passive text and some supporting graphics used to develop reading and writing competences, although one or two examples of hypermedia will be mentioned later. So what are the basic common features of all such hypertexts, and how can they be used to promote literacy?

The central concepts in hypertext are topics, links and networks. Topics, as we have seen, can be of variable size; the main requirement is that they form units of meaning, and the central issue for the author is what unit of meaning they wish the reader to focus upon. To the extent that the author sets these units of meaning small, control over the reading inclines towards the author. If they are larger, they allow the reader to skip and reread within a single screen, allowing more freedom for the reader. However, there is no reason for the size of this unit always to be the same. As with printed texts there can be links from individual terms to passages, to an index or chapter headings, or cross-links from one passage to another, or indeed to a completely different text.

Links too can be of many kinds; and here the hypertext has advantages over the printed book. Authors presenting an argued case could for instance provide links from a given topic to examples, counter-examples, supplementary details, a synopsis, an alternative formulation or a refutation of the claims being made. Using a set of labelled buttons on the screen, the reader could choose which of these aspects to follow up, and then move easily back to the main topic to choose another aspect, or press on into a new topic.

The networks that the links produce may also be very variable, in both structure and complexity, as Figure 12.2 illustrates. At one extreme, one might have a linear pattern of links, as in Network A. This is actually far more prescriptive than a printed book can be, allowing only forward movement, until the final topic is reached, then returning the reader to the starting point. Apart from deciding when to go on to the next topic, users have no control over the sequencing of their reading. At the other extreme, every topic may be connected to every other, as in Network B. Here the author decides only the material and the topics into which it is divided. Users then make their own decisions as to which topics to consider, and in what sequence to do this. All sorts of intermediate structures are feasible too. A hierarchical pattern is one possibility, as in Network C, in which perhaps the lower level contains more detailed treatments of the issues outlined in the level above. Users of this hypertext are always constrained to read the simpler account first, but can choose whether to go on to look at a more detailed treatment, or to return to the top level topic (perhaps a contents page) and select another issue to explore. Clearly many structures are possible, in which writer and reader share control over the reading sequence between them, and therefore share control over the nature of the actual texts that the readers construct from the material available. Hypertexts differ, therefore, in the balance between the freedom allowed to, and the support provided for, the reader.

So far we have considered 'read only' hypertexts, in which the topics and links are fixed and unchangeable. But these packages also allow the user to make their own hypertexts, or alternatively to modify all or part of a text or

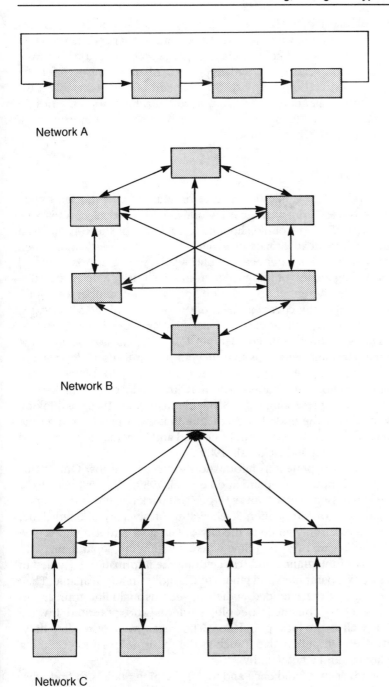

Network A

Network B

Network C

Figure 12.2 Three kinds of hypertext networks

the network of links that has been provided by another author. So hypertexts can be designed in three ways; as texts to be read unchanged, as texts that can be modified or extended by users to some degree, or as a tabula rasa, upon which users write their own hypertext. All three cases offer the possibility of individual or group use. So what sort of hypertexts might we find in these three categories, what learning and teaching opportunities do they present, what are their limitations, and how far do they support a communicative approach to learning?

Hypertexts for reading

One major kind of text is that designed to provide information for a wide diversity of purposes. Print analogues include encyclopaedias, newspapers, instruction manuals and trouble-shooting guides. All of these have been converted into hypertext formats of varying levels of sophistication. Such texts contain information extending beyond what any one user is expected to need, providing a bank of knowledge from which users select what they require. There is therefore no pressure to limit the number of topics included; the greater the coverage the more widely useful the hypertext is likely to be. However, there is a real risk that increased size creates a network of links so complex that readers get 'lost in hyperspace'; losing track of where they are, and what it is that they are trying to do (Edwards and Hardman, 1989). The problem can be reduced by looking for better ways of presenting route choices to readers. This may involve investigating the best way of marking and presenting links (Schneiderman *et al.*, 1989) or thinking through very clearly the underlying structure that the topics have, and the implications of this for the type of links needed and how they are organised into a network (Wright and Lickorish, 1989).

One example of hypertext as information source is Glasgow Online (for a preliminary description see Baird and Percival, 1989). The first version of this hypertext was built using Apple's HyperCard package. It was developed by the Department of Information Science at the University of Strathclyde, and offered an electronic guide to the city of Glasgow and its culture. The designers were a team of 31 part-time workers within the department, who saw it as a way of integrating and restructuring the information provided in the various books, pamphlets and guides to Glasgow already available. They had a clear idea of the intended audience, seen as including tourists, researchers, teachers, business people, students and potential inward investors, as well as the local population. The system was for reading only, and was available in public places such as the tourist information centre, a reference library, and a hotel lobby.

Given the diversity of audience and topics, helping readers to find what they were looking for was a major problem. The approaches the team considered illustrate something of the range of options that hypertext authors more generally have available:

• A guided tour along hierarchical lines, under the control of the author.
• A system of explicit signals that directed, but did not force, the user along non-hierarchical routes through the topics.
• 'Subliminal' signalling, using, for instance, underlining, highlighting and italics, to nudge the user along routes chosen by the author.
• The use of metaphors (such as that of the book or of physical travel) to make the structure of the hypertext intelligible to users.

Another early example of a hypertext-style reference source was the BBC Domesday system, a multi-media source of information organised into a set of linked topics that has been tried out in schools. The way in which the system was used in six British schools have been evaluated (Freeman, 1990).

The system includes two videodiscs whose contents are displayed selectively on a monitor screen, under computer control. The discs contain maps of the UK at various scales, pages of photographs and text on many locations shown on the maps, and statistical information and articles on life in Britain in the early 1980s. The statistical information can be displayed in a variety of ways and superimposed upon the video images. Readers can move around the screen with a tracker ball, choosing what to do next from a menu of items. To find information the reader can either work down through a hierarchical tree structure of menus, or input one or more key-words to identify all the items to which they applied. Teacher's reactions to the system were interesting. As Freeman reports it:

> Teachers . . . are used to software that allows them to enter and organise their own or the children's data, but the Domesday system cannot satisfy all these aims. It is essentially an information providing mechanism, a compendium of resources, transferring a body of knowledge to the user. It is difficult to make the interaction into a personal learning experience, by creating and testing their own models of information. A high level of interactivity, therefore, means interactivity with the interface, rather than the information. The user is reacting to the system by understanding how to use it and find his way around, rather than proacting with the system by reorganising what is there or entering new data.
>
> (Freeman, 1990, p. 192)

The teachers evolved a range of ways of using this novel resource. Freeman identified four models of use:

• *The didactic model*, in which each group was set a directed exercise by the teacher to find, read, comprehend and record the material on a set topic.

- *The task model*, in which the teacher set an achievable goal and the students worked out together through discussion and experiment the best way to achieve it.
- *The partnership model*, in which a more complex task was set, the teacher being available to respond as required to the students initiatives, and helping them to realise the full significance of the information that they are uncovering. Freeman notes that there was no other delivery mechanism within the schools that had the power to present such a wealth of information from a student-led enquiry.
- *The library model*, in which the system was available for all to use for whatever purposes they wished; these included individual browsing, following up an enquiry arising from topic work or individual study, or training in the use of the system itself.

A comparison of the Glasgow Online and Domesday systems brings out a number of important issues about read-only hypertexts. The assumption behind Glasgow Online is that most users will need some help in finding what they want, and that the system will have to provide this; hence the emphasis upon finding ways of building guidance into the system. On the other hand there appears to have been no expectation that those looking for information would want to add to or modify what was provided. Users then were seen as independent individuals, defining their own needs, but requiring help built into the system to explore what it could provide for them. From this perspective the different forms of guidance that the designers considered could be seen as a range of scaffolding devices from which users could choose, depending upon their own assessment of how much support they required at that stage.

The models of use that Freeman identified form a sequence in which teacher involvement in setting aims and procedures is progressively reduced. A teacher who worked through that sequence with a group entirely new to the system could be seen as taking a scaffolding role as far as their learning was concerned. In particular classroom situations this support might be necessary because students (unlike the volunteer users of Glasgow Online) saw no purpose in using the Domesday system at all, so that both purpose and motivation had to come from the teacher. More interestingly, teacher involvement could also be needed to encourage students to tackle more complex (and thus more educative) tasks than they might think of doing alone. Whereas Glasgow Online meets users' self-defined needs, the teachers using the Domesday system seem to have seen it as a resource, together with their own skills and knowledge, that would enable students to succesfully tackle more complex tasks. Indeed, even in the apparently teacher-independent library model we might anticipate some teacher involvement in setting topics or raising questions away from the system that encouraged its use.

The examples discussed above have been of hypertexts that contain factual information. Yet there is no reason why fictional material should not be dealt with in this way too. Adventure games are the most widely known genre within interactive fiction. They present the children with a closed and very simple world, into which they step as actors. The actions they can take, and their results, are predefined within the game, unless a minor random element has been added for interest. Usually the world presented is a fantasy one, but there are games which simulate realistic (but still greatly simplified) worlds within which they decide where to go and what to do. Within this world some overall task is set to give direction to their choices, and the children then move through it looking for objects or information that will help them with the task. In concrete terms the games require children to read a page of text on the computer screen (sometimes with accompanying pictures) and then decide what action to take, usually selecting from a limited range of options provided. They then enter their choice which moves them on to the appropriate page, and the process is repeated.

Although not always recognised as such, most adventure games are basically hypertexts with fixed links and a built-in dictionary to enable the program to respond appropriately to the keyboard entries of the user. They are very widely available; Costanzo (1989) reports that one American publisher has an estimated total sale of over a million copies of such games. Playing these games does make demands on the user, and they therefore have some educational potential. Costanzo notes:

> When the story consists entirely of words . . . the reader must translate linguistic information into mental images. Each detail of a scene becomes important because it may hide essential clues. The ability to picture scenes is a survival skill. Even when the text is accompanied by graphics . . . the reader must form mental maps to keep track of relationships. Stories that contain scores of locations and dozens of movable objects and characters call for some sophisticated mental mapping. If television short-circuits the visual imagination, as some educators believe, interactive text may provide a challenging antidote.
>
> (Costanzo, 1989, pp. 77–8)

On the other hand, as he points out, the instructions that the user types in have to be kept simple enough for the program to handle. The text of the stories too is generally easy to read, and presented in short sections on the screen. Costanzo suggests that this will change as more serious writers begin to experiment with the medium and produce more complex and interesting texts. However, it may not be this straightforward. First, these texts are commercially produced, typically for young male readers, and reducing the ratio of action to reading may not be popular. Secondly, the successful navigation of the adventure depends upon picking up clues from the text, and usually the text of the story is carefully pared down to make these easier to locate. If there is a lot of detail that is irrelevant to this instrumental purpose, successful guesses as to what to do next become harder. This may reduce the typical reader's motivation to continue with the adventure (and subsequently to buy more). What would be needed to sustain both more complex tasks and this competitive motivation to complete them would be adventures in which the task itself is conceived in more complex ways, so that the increased level of detail is instrumentally useful in solving the task.

Another strategy would be to look for kinds of interactive fiction that do not require the completion of a stereotyped task. Here the purpose of reading is the pleasure and insights that the experience gives, rather than any extrinsic motive. In his reflective book on hypertext and writing Jay Bolter (1991) argues that a hypertext format is well suited to modern fiction, which is very open to experiment. In particular, this format overcomes the practical obstacles that conventional book design placed in the way of earlier experimental writers, such as Sterne and James Joyce.

He takes as his main exemplar a hypertext fiction called 'Afternoon', written by Michael Joyce (1987). This has over 500 episodes and some 900 links. As with an adventure game the reader has to make choices after reading each episode, but these are not choice of actions. Instead the reader may ask to read more about a topic, or select one of a number of key words in the episode, each choice introducing a different continuation. If none of the offered choices appeals, the reader can press Return and will be taken on to yet another episode. As Bolter observes:

> There is no single story to which each reading is a version, because each reading determines the story as it goes. We could say that there is no story at all: there are only readings. Or if we say that the story of 'Afternoon' is the sum of all its readings, then we must understand the story as a structure that can embrace contradictory outcomes. Each reading is a different turning within a universe of paths set up by the author.
>
> (Bolter, pp. 124–5)

This sort of structure, as we shall see later, raises interesting problems for supporters of collaborative learning.

Hypertext systems as writing aids

If the focus is shifted from hypertexts as things to read to hypertexts as things to write, a different range of possibilities appear. There are many situations in which we need to plan writing, and record notes and ideas for future use. In Chapter 8 outliners were mentioned. These allow a writer to draft ideas and organise and reorganise them until a suitable preliminary plan for the text has been produced. These programs are essentially designed to help the writer produce and adjust a hierarchical structure of headings and sub-headings, to which, in many versions, blocks of substantive text can be linked, being revealed only when required. This is very close to a hier-archical hypertext system; which suggests that we could look for other kinds of writing aids by considering what role different types of hypertexts might play.

One route would be to move away from the hierarchical framework of outliners towards a much looser approach, in which the hypertext is en-visaged as a modern version of the commonplace book. Here its role would be to act as a repository for all sorts and sizes of pieces of text, graphics or whatever on a subject of interest. New items would be linked to others as they were added, on the basis of whatever intuitive connections or associ-ations the writer sensed might exist. Such links would be subsequently deleted, added to or moved as the writer's thinking evolved, and a clearer conception of the subject emerged. The structure of the developing hyper-text would thus model the author's current pattern of thinking about the subject, and would be likely to lead to a network with many links rather than few, and with no obvious hierarchical structure. This approach fits well with a view of writing as an intensely personal activity, in which the aim is to crystallise and express the writer's viewpoint as authentically as possible, without imposing unnecessary external constraints. However it has its difficulties. One is that hypertexts written in this way, if they are of any complexity, run into the problem of being difficult to read; not least because with most hypertext systems readers may find it hard to know when they have actually read everything provided. This difficulty may even extend to the author, after the passage of time. Another problem is that, as a non-linear presentation of the text, it is not something that can easily be transferred into printed form; indeed the function of headings and subheadings in outliners is precisely to ease the transition from a complex web of initial ideas to their presentation in a linear form. An unstructured hypertext offers no such constraints, and thus no such support.

This suggests another strategy. Just as we can envisage a looser format than that provided by outliners, so we could envisage a tighter one. If, for instance, one starts from a definite theory about what the process of good writing involves, it might be possible to create a program that guides the writer through the stages of composition that the theory posits. An interesting example of this approach has been described by a group of American researchers at the University of North Carolina (Smith, Weiss and Ferguson, 1987, and Smith and Lansman, 1989). They developed a system for writers that they describe as follows:

Our system, which we call the Writing Environment or WE for short, helps writers transform loose associative networks of ideas into a hierarchical structure and then write a document in accordance with that structure. The product that results can remain in electronic form but it can also be printed out to produce a paper document. Thus, the system can be used

> both as a conventional hypertext system and as an authoring system with advanced graphical, direct manipulation structure editing capabilities.
>
> (Smith, Weiss and Ferguson, 1987, p. 2)

The WE system provides the author with the choice of working in any one of four kinds of formats, moving between them as required. In network mode the system allows the creation of loose networks of ideas; these are displayed on the screen and they can be linked together in the usual way. If the author moves to tree mode he or she must start selecting items from the network and indicating where in an evolving hierarchical structure they are to go. Thus the original loose network is gradually transferred into a hierarchical structure. In edit mode, the author selects an item from the hierarchy and writes the text to go with it. Finally, in text mode the system takes the text written and reorganises it automatically into a linear form for printing, using the hierarchy as a guide to the order in which each section of attached text should be included.

The North Carolina team believe that the best structure for a text is one which has a hierarchical structure, and point to the research evidence for this claim. In their 1987 paper at least, it is clear that they are making this claim only for some kinds of writing. They suggest that:

> hypertext in its most fundamental form . . . is most consistent with one particular mode of thinking – exploration. Exploratory thinking usually occurs early in the development of a set of ideas. Such thinking is an integral part of the overall cognitive process not just for writing but for many forms of productive, professional work. But it is an end in itself only for certain situations. Great for an aesthetic experience – James Joyce, or more likely, John Fowles, would have loved it as a literary medium. Great for an undirected, free-flowing learning experience, analogous to spending an evening browsing through an encyclopaedia. But as a tool for professionals, hypertext, we believe, will become a supporting utility over which more constrained applications will be developed rather than the primary application system, itself. To be truly effective, hypertext applications must match additional power with additional control and structure. In the long term, constraints may turn out to be more important than raw power.
>
> (Smith, Weiss and Ferguson, 1987, p. 2)

These two ways of using hypertext systems to support the development of writing are quite different. Favouring the commonplace book approach appears to assume an active, self-confident and individualistic view of learning; the constructivist model discussed in Chapter 2 comes to mind. The sort of question that must be asked of its supporters, however, is how learners are to gain and check their material, and what role there is for the teacher. Indeed, what can we expect a learner to learn from creating only their own links and text items? Making explicit what one already knows is far from trivial, but can this approach offer anything more?

Conversely, the WE system assumes that the nature of a good text and, to an extent, the processes by which it is best produced, are sufficiently well established to make the creation of such support tools valuable. There the picture is of a writer being helped to practise and internalise a carefully researched but still externally defined model of good writing. The questions we might raise here concern the validity of the model of writing used, the capability of any hypertext system to fully convey that model to learners, and a query about the possibility that frequent use of such systems might involve some loss of imagination and flexibility in writing.

Hypertext as context for collaboration

So far we have looked at hypertexts largely as something to be written or read by individuals. Similarly, the emphasis has been upon ways in which they might help with reading or writing considered separately. But in a communicative approach to language teaching and learning, the emphasis is put upon seeing all aspects of literacy as interrelated, and looking to groups as one potentially very valuable learning environment. The mostly rather individualistic approaches discussed so far, useful though they are, do not emphasise group work. What would a collaborative approach to using a hypertext system look like? To start with, nearly all the kinds of hypertexts discussed so far could be used or created by groups. This would fit well with a communicative theory of learning, which assumes that learning requires the shared construction of knowledge. However, many of the issues about group use that arise, as the discussion of the Domesday system illustrates, are similar to those already discussed in relation to other kinds of software, so will not be taken further here.

An interesting exception, however, is the reading of interactive fiction. Adventure games do lend themselves quite well to joint exploration, but this is probably because they have a predefined purpose built in, and require the solution of clearly defined sub-tasks as the exploration proceeds. The program thus gives both a long-term focus for the group's activities and a series of immediate puzzles to solve, where cooperation gets an immediate reward. But what about the other kinds of interactive fiction? It is not clear that these can sensibly be read jointly in any obvious way. Reading such a text involves choices, but they seem likely to be made on the basis of implicit rather than explicit criteria which would not lend themselves to brief discussion. The fact that the reader must choose a personal route through the text, probably reading only some of it (and in an order that other readers may not replicate) affects the sort of critical discussion that can subsequently take place. With a conventional text the sequencing and structure is itself an aspect that can be discussed, but here this possibility disappears. Similarly, discussion of a conventional text often assumes that the whole text has been read by all the group. Where this is not so, the shared experience upon which a common knowledge of the text can be developed is missing. Also missing is the basis for a teacher to lead and enable such discussions. Indeed, one way at getting a clearer view of the educational problems and potentials that these texts present is to try to envisage in concrete terms how a teacher might enable a group to study them more productively; this may not be too easy.

This dilemma may mean that traditional ideas of textual criticism, like our ideas of texts, will have to change as interactive fiction becomes more widely read (for a very interesting development of this point see Landow, 1992). On the other hand, perhaps it serves as a way of marking out a limitation in the scope of a communicative theory of learning. By its nature, such a theory emphasises the public and shared aspects of learning, playing down the inner experience. Yet in the case of aesthetic education these inner experiences are central, and not necessarily explicitly transmissible. It is perhaps no coincidence that a communicative approach to language development emphasises the linkages between speech and writing on the one hand and reading on the other, and uses that linkage to present reading as a very public activity.

On the other hand, although group learning can take place around a single computer, hypertexts can in principle be shared across a network of machines. This network might be, for instance, within a school, or be a national or international public network, like the electronic mail and conferencing systems discussed by Bernadette Robinson in Chapter 9. Where the hypertext is only designed to be read, the distinction between single and multiple use is of minor importance, as the multiple users have no way of interacting with each other through their computers. However, if the network is used to provide a communal hypertext that can be modified independently by its different users, then distinctive problems and possibilities are presented. Suppose also that we initially provide on this network a hypertext that contains a great deal of information relevant to subjects of mutual interest to the users. Let us also envisage that expert teachers are included as users themselves. Then we have something very close to the sort of learning and teaching situation that a communicative theory of learning would suggest is optimal. Such a system would support both collaboration amongst learners and scaffolding by teachers, working with an extensive body of potentially relevant knowledge. A well documented example of a system of this kind (Landow, 1992) is provided by the Intermedia network of Brown University in the United States.

In 1987 a 3-year research project was started to introduce a computer based component into (amongst others) an introductory English literature course at Brown University (Yankelovich, Landow and Cody, 1987). The intention was to develop students' critical thinking by placing a greater emphasis upon class discussions initiated and directed by the students themselves, while still ensuring that these discussions took place within the framework of an adequate and easily accessible source of background information. The computer based material was a large hypertext, comprising around 1,000 text and graphics files, connected by some 1,300 links. Fourteen computers were networked together in a single room, and were available up to midnight every day for the 45 students taking the course in its computer enhanced form. As well as exploring the hypertext, students had set readings, a weekly lecture, self-directed class discussions, writing assignments and examinations.

The subject of the hypertext was a survey of English literature from 1700 to the present. Topics covered included timelines for individual authors and general topics such as political history, literature and the women's movement. Biographies of authors, essays on literary technique and discussions of contextual topics such as technological developments and social philosophies were also included, as were primary materials and annotated bibliographies. The links between these topics were made explicit in a series of overview files. Each of these could be called up onto the screen, where it appeared as a diagram showing the local connections within the network. Thus the overview for Alfred Tennyson showed links to detailed texts on his life and main works, as well as to more general texts on religion, science and technology, other arts, literary techniques, cultural context and literary relations. These overviews were seen as a way of presenting a body of complex ideas in a simpler way, so that students would better understand them. They also emphasised a key teaching point for the course, that all these ideas and processes impinge upon individual authors, periods or literary movements. This assumption was, of course, one that made a hypertext format especially suitable for presenting the structure of ideas in the course.

The introduction of the hypertext element was evaluated through observation, interviews, surveys and student diaries. The results of the project were encouraging (Landow, n.d.). Students with access to the hypertext system gained a markedly better grasp of the materials, and introduced more kinds of data into their discussions and written work. The number of students participating in discussion, and the total number of student contributions, increased by around 300 per cent. Student comments in the discussions were more precise and more often consisted of factual statements or critical judgements, rather than generalised observations. The change also helped many students to learn how to use books more effectively. Hypertext use also persuaded many that, because the topics were so strongly marked as interlinked, they could not, as previous groups had done, ignore any of the set reading. Examination results were also rated more highly by the marker. A very important factor producing these effects may have been that the students were also invited from the outset to contribute suggestions for additional links and other improvements to the hypertext. As Landow observes:

> Having been asked their opinion once, they proceeded to give it freely ever afterward. Throughout the semester students thus offered proof reading and criticisms of the nature and placement of links as well as requests for documents on subjects like labour history or critical theory that they believed useful.
>
> (Landow, n.d., p. 8)

The Intermedia network can be seen as an electronic supplement to, or partial replacement for, the library, lectures, publishing networks and face to face exchanges that go on within a conventional scholarly community, in which the shared field of knowledge evolves by replacing, extending or modifying current ideas. What the Intermedia project does is to make this process visible to students, while inviting them to take part, to some extent, in the process for themselves. To set up such a system and to decide what it should contain and how it should be used required the lecturers involved to be very explicit about their intentions. At the same time the network and its contents and rules for use make the lecturers' aims highly visible to the students. This may be an important factor in the results achieved.

CONCLUSION

Designers of learning environments like Intermedia have to be very clear about the position they take on the nature of knowledge and learning. The examples we looked at earlier bring out a crucial divergence in the epistemological assumptions that different supporters of hypertext may make. For some the strength of hypertexts are that they allow us to escape the artificial linear constraints of printed texts and allow us to choose topics and design links in ways that map on to the (non-linear) structure of the domain of knowledge with which the hypertext is concerned. The best structure, therefore, is predetermined by the concepts and logic of the subject concerned. For others, the strength of hypertexts are that they can be progressively developed by the user as an externalisation and record of his or her individual understanding and thought; the links are those that the user sees as important, the topics those that the user chooses to explore, described and assessed in the terms that the user values. While hypertexts can be designed to meet one or other of these demands, no one version will simultaneously meet both. The first presupposes a preordained structure built into the hypertext before the user receives it, the latter a blank hypertext screen that awaits the user's own ideas. In one, users should be readers of the right text, on the other, users are the writers of the text they read.

A similar divergence of assumptions arises when we think of hypertexts as educational tools. On one view, learners are pretty much alike, and so an optimal learning route through a set of topics can be found and set up. The links are then naturally restricted so as to prevent the learner going wrong; this gives an instructional and highly directive kind of hypertext. However, if one assumes that learners vary, albeit along a relatively few dimensions, such as their preference for graphical as against textual presentations of material, then we might expect to see hypertexts in which parallel routes through are provided, with some device for helping the individual learners to choose what is best for them. A third position would be to assume that learners are very different; this would suggest that the hypertext should be as open ended as possible, with all sorts of possible routes through. It would also involve assuming either that the learner can find the best route alone, or that there would be a mentor available to assist in, but not direct, this choice.

In this chapter the emphasis has largely been upon the computer related aspect of collaborative learning. But as the Intermedia case illustrates, the use of a network of computers need not exclude face to face discussion and teaching. The 'virtual classroom' that Robinson mentions briefly in Chapter 9 is not, in my view, a desirable aim, even were it practicable. Nor, as has emerged earlier, is there any reason to think that using hypertext systems on a single computer need mean that group work becomes unnecessary. Indeed it is important to recognise that not everything worth learning can be conveyed through a computer-based medium, even ones as flexible as hypertext and hypermedia. What this suggests is that the integration of a networked hypertext system into a face to face learning culture would have considerable potential, allowing learners to develop their ideas by interacting with others (including teachers) within and across the two contexts. So what might such a system for school use look like?

What would be required is a conferencing system linked to a large database, both presented in a hypertext format. Each learner would need at least some opportunities to contribute both to the debates carried on the messaging system, and to the evolution of the common database of information. Such a system could also carry assignments and provide learner-supporting programs (such as Tray and others that we have looked at earlier in this book) for learners to use as required, alone or in electronic or face-to-face groups, with teacher support. Users would also need face to face contact with at least some of the contributing group, and access to teachers, both directly and through the conferencing system. From this nexus of information, activities and discussion with others, learners would be able to evolve their own electronic commonplace book of ideas, examples and evidence, drawing as required from the shared network, and contributing their own ideas back to it as they developed. Yet simply creating such a system would not ensure active, shared learning. The extent to which it became an active learning system would depend also, for example, upon the number of contributors, the patterns of communication between them, the structure of the hypertext, and the distribution of authorship rights within the group.

In essence, what the medium of hypertext provides is an infinitely adjustable level of control over the relative power of the user and the designer to determine the text that is read. What their relative roles are depends upon how the hypertext is designed, and who is involved in the design process. In that respect it is radically different from the other forms of software that we have looked at in earlier chapters, each of which had built into it a broadly given level of control over the user, varying from open ended packages such as word processors and computer conferencing systems, through intermediate cases such as text disclosure programs, to the relatively highly structured, and therefore directive second language learning program described in Chapter 11. Hypertext is, by contrast, a protean device, that can be structured to be most things to most people. Its widespread popularity rests therefore upon a mistaken aggregation of benefits from what are in reality quite different kinds of hypertexts. Fully exploring and verifying its educational potential will be a massive but essential task.

REFERENCES

Baird, P. and Percival, M. (1989) 'Glasgow Online: database development using Apple's HyperCard', in McAleese, R. (ed.) (1989) *Hypertext: theory into practice*, Oxford, Blackwell Scientific Publications Ltd.

Bolter, J. D. (1991) 'Writing space: the computer, hypertext, and the history of writing', New Jersey, Lawrence Erlbaum Associates Inc.

Costanzo, W. V. (1989) *The Electronic Text: Learning to Write, Read, and Reason with Computers*, Educational Technology Publications, Englewood Cliffs, New Jersey.

Cumming, A. and Sinclair, G. (1991) 'Conceptualizing hypermedia curricula for literary studies in schools', in Delany, P. and Landow, G. P. (eds) *Hypermedia and Literary Studies*, Cambridge, Mass., MIT Press.

Edwards, D. and Hardman, L. (1989) '"Lost in hyperspace": cognitive mapping and navigation in a hypertext environment', in McAleese, R. (ed.) (1989) *Hypertext: theory into practice*, Oxford, Blackwell Scientific Publications Ltd.

Freeman, D. (1990) 'Multimedia learning: the classroom experience', *Computers in Educaton*, 15(1–3).

Joyce, M. (1987) 'Afternoon: a story', Cambridge, Mass., Eastergate Press (computer hypertext program).

Landow, G. P. (n.d.) 'Hypertext in literary education, criticism, and scholarship', Department of English and the Institute for Research in Information and Scholarship (IRIS), Providence, Rhode Island, Brown University.

Landow, G. P. (1992) *Hypertext: the convergence of contemporary critical theory and technology*, Baltimore, Johns Hopkins University Press.

Schneiderman, B., Brethauer, D., Plaisant, C. and Potter, R. (1989) 'Evaluating three museum installations of a Hypertext system', *Journal of the American Society for Information Science*, 40(3).

Smith, J. B. and Lansman, M. (1989) 'A cognitive basis for a computer writing environment', in Britton, B. K. and Glynn, S. M. (eds) (1989) *Computer Writing Environments: theory, research and design*, New Jersey, Lawrence Erlbaum Associates Inc.

Smith, J. B., Weiss, S. F. and Ferguson, G. F. (1987) 'A hypertext writing environment and its cognitive basis', TextLab Report TR87–033, University of North Carolina at Chapel Hill, Dept of Computer Science, Chapel Hill, NC.

Wright, P. and Lickorish, A. (1989) 'The influence of discourse structure on display and navigation in hypertexts', in Williams, N. and Holt, P. (eds) (1989) *Computers and Writing: models and tools*, Oxford, Blackwell Scientific Publications Ltd.

Yankelovich, N., Landow, G. P. and Cody, D. (1987) 'Creating hypermedia materials for English literature students', in *SIGCUE Outlook*, 20.

Chapter 13

Researching the electronic classroom

Neil Mercer and Peter Scrimshaw

INTRODUCTION

The chapters of this book support the view that computers have opened up some interesting lines for the development of educational activities. More-over, the variety of uses for computers in education multiplies rapidly, as do the number of computers in schools, and the frequency with which they are used. In almost every school in Britain and the United States we now expect to see children doing computer-based activities on a regular basis. The nature of educational software is also in a rapid, continuous process of development. But, as many of the authors in this book have argued, there has not been a corresponding rate of development of our understanding of how computers really do function in the context of classrooms and other learning environments. This presents us with three central questions which we will consider in turn:

- How do computers actually function as components of classroom activities, and with what results?
- What methods of investigation would best enable us to answer that question?
- What theoretical framework would best help us to interpret the information we obtain?

HOW DO COMPUTERS FUNCTION WITHIN CLASSROOM ACTIVITIES?

As new kinds of software emerge, apparently offering new educational possibilities, we must realise that these possibilities only become realities for curriculum based education when the software is incorporated into educational activities. By 'activity' here we mean all or part of a scheme of work carried out by learners, through which they are expected to achieve some curriculum-related goals. We believe that this is both a necessary and inevitable condition of using computers in a classroom (other than as some recreational, extra-curricular, pastime). A further implication of this belief is that one cannot assume that the same educational software will generate the same educational activities in different classrooms (any more than one can assume that, say, the same textbook, novel or poem will generate the same activity). This may seem self-evident but it does not seem obviously reflected in the design of educational software, or in the kind of psychological and educational research that has influenced that design (as the chapters by Light, Mercer and Jones make clear).

Equally important to our understanding of how computers function in real-life learning environments is an appreciation of the growing body of experience in using computers amongst teachers and pupils. This makes new kinds of activity practically possible, as well as creating a more know-ledgeable and critical environment for the introduction of new software. The broad implication here is that, as mentioned above, research into computer use – and more precisely of how teaching-and-learning is done with com-puters – must keep pace with software developments. We believe that the chapters of this book contribute towards our understanding of this matter, but they inevitably leave many questions unanswered. One thing that they do make clear is that the consequences of using computers in teaching-and-learning are never predictable from the design of the software; and another is that it is dangerous to generalise about learning with computers from what happens in non-computer based activities. Indeed there are signs that, for instance, word processors, computer conferencing and hypertext systems are not simply functioning as more (or less) effective means of achieving conventional ends. It is quite possible that introducing them into classrooms and elsewhere is beginning to redefine what constitutes reading, writing and discussion. The educational implications of such redefinitions are considerable.

A very interesting aspect of the developing use of computers in class-rooms is the ways in which computers are incorporated into the existing classroom culture. Here, as Eunice Fisher points out in Chapter 6, issues of access and opportunity will be important. Because activities are not defined by software alone, but also by the contexts in which the software is used, children in the same class doing the 'same' computer-based task may in fact be doing quite different activities, and so be offered quite 'unequal' educa-tional opportunities. An obvious example is when children are collaborating in a task and a dominant partner defines the roles which children take and the extent to which they influence proceedings. As Paul Light shows in Chapter 4, collaboration at the computer is a complex process, and one which needs careful study and evaluation. And beyond the process of computer use, we still know relatively little about whether computer-based activities really do make the learning of some things – geometry, essay writing, a second language, communication skills – easier or more effective in some way than similar non-computer based equivalents. That is, we still have too little evaluative evidence of the consequences of incorporating computers into teaching-and-learning activities.

From what we do know, it seems necessary to endorse the view expressed by Bernadette Robinson in Chapter 9, that software design (and hardware design too, to the extent that this is commercially possible) should be driven by educational, rather than technological goals. For example, if children are going to be collaborating, shouldn't they have software and hardware well-designed for doing so? This is where a closer relationship between the research communities of computer design and the study of teaching and learning could provide real benefits. Findings of research on actual computer use in educational settings could provide the most valuable and significant feedback to enable software designers to provide better programmes. Taking these ideas seriously could allow the development of a more systematic and effective 'creativity cycle' as represented in Figure 13.1.

WHAT METHODS OF INVESTIGATION ARE NEEDED?

We certainly want more empirical data about how computers are used and can be used in educational settings. Is it possible to say what kinds of enquiries are most likely to yield the most useful information to feed the 'creativity cycle?' In this book authors have referred to data gathered through at least five different methodologies; experimental studies, questionnaire

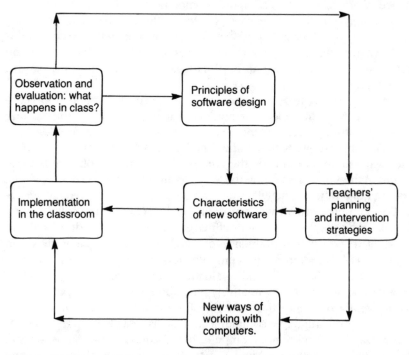

Figure 13.1 A creativity cycle for improving computer-based learning and teaching

based surveys, teacher's accounts, action research projects and obser-
vational/ethnographic studies. Each approach has its distinctive strengths
and weaknesses, and we believe that each has something to contribute.

Because they are abstracted from real-life educational settings, experimental research studies into learning processes may often appear to be
designed only to advance theoretical understanding. However, many of their
advocates can point to the ways that their findings can be used to improve
practice too. This approach has been discussed in Chapter 1 and Chapter 4,
and some of the research findings on word processing discussed in Chapter
8 come from such studies. One of the strengths of this approach is that it
allows research to focus upon particular factors, and to test hypotheses
about their significance for the outcomes of the learning process. As Paul
Light's chapter shows, experimental methods throw up particular patterns of
data which rightly demand explanations, and which would seem to have
direct implications for the organisation of collaborative learning in schools.
From the perspective of practice, however, the findings of experimental
studies may have little apparent validity for teachers, if the experiments
appear to screen out too many factors which operate in real classrooms,
making its findings only partly applicable there. In short, for practitioners,
experimental studies often provide a spur to reflection and further enquiry,
but not a source of answers to problems of classroom implementation.

Questionnaire based surveys have a rather similar role in guiding practice,
but for quite different reasons. They also systematically simplify the situations they deal with, by constraining respondents in terms of the length and
direction of their answers. While this element of constraint can be reduced
by the use of open ended questions, this then leaves the researcher with the
task of interpreting the answers of people who are not available to verify any
interpretation. Especially if used in isolation from other methods, questionnaires tend either to prejudge what issues are important, or to leave the
researcher with daunting problems of interpretation. Our view is that, at
present, we know too little of the variety of circumstances in which
computers are used and the ways that teachers make decisions about how
and when to use them in curriculum-based activities; but to design good
questionnaire enquiries about such matters would require a more adequate
database of findings from observational research in schools than is at present
available. Survey results are also often hard for individual teachers, heads or
principals to apply to their own situation without further investigation. It
would not help to know that, for instance, most teenagers have a positive
attitude to computer use in schools, unless you also know whether the
teenagers in your school are typical in that respect, and if they are, how this
positive attitude can be directed towards educational goals. Surveys are
valuable prompts for further enquiry, but without this they can only give
very uncertain guidance in specific situations. Perhaps their most useful
contribution is in policy guidance where the policy maker has a

responsibility for the whole class of people or institutions sampled for the survey. For instance, the national and state surveys on differential access to computers discussed in Chapter 6 may not have a direct message for every school, but they certainly do for national and state governments.

Teachers' accounts of their classroom experiences have featured strongly in this book, especially in Chapters 8, 9 and 10 on word processing, computer managed communication and text completion programs. Unlike, for example, journal articles on experimental research, there are no particularly strong conventions about what such accounts should include or exclude. However, they are usually in the form of a narrative, which includes the teacher's own feelings and intentions as well as an account of what took place, as they saw it. They may also contain some evaluation of the results or the process, examples from children's work, comments by children on the activity, extracts from curriculum plans and so forth. The strength of these accounts is twofold. First, for the teacher producing them what is discovered in the process of preparing the account has direct applicability. Secondly, such accounts are likely to use a language and framework of values that will be recognised by some, if not all other, teachers; these accounts are usually high on intelligibility for practitioners. On the other hand, they are specific accounts of particular places, and individually cannot be used to sustain any claims about classrooms or schools in general. So how can other teachers make use of them? The only way that we can see is by readers making direct comparisons and contrasts with their own situation, thus bypassing the issue of generalisability completely. Thus it could be that another teacher's account of a problem makes explicit to some readers the nature of a similar problem that they face but had not clearly recognised for what it was. Conversely, an account of some strategy that is quite novel to the reader may provide the spark for a rethinking of an apparently insoluble problem. Yet this is something of a hit and miss affair; it may well be that an otherwise useful account does not include the additional item of information that a particular reader needs to see the account's relevance. In part this is a function of the conditions under which teachers usually have to produce such narratives. Without any time provided for investigation, observation or writing up it is difficult for teachers to go into the detail that they might wish.

One way of trying to avoid these limitations is to look to outside researchers to conduct very detailed qualitative or quantitative observational studies. Quantitative studies of classroom life – i.e. those using coding schemes or similar tools to measure the relative incidence of different kinds of classroom events – share many of the strengths and weaknesses of questionnaire studies. We will concentrate here upon qualitative research based upon observation, interview and analysis. For the reasons given in Chapter 3, this approach has much to offer at a time when one of the key issues for research is to find out just what is going on in classrooms. Of course it has its weaknesses. One is that it is time consuming and difficult to carry out, which means that the number of specific studies that can be made of computer based work using this approach is bound to be limited in practice. If only a small sample of classrooms is observed, representativeness and generalisability of findings are going to emerge as problems. More profoundly, there is also the risk (so often pointed out to observational researchers by colleagues who favour more systematic experimental/ quantitative research methods!) that researchers' preconceptions, theories and hypotheses will lead to a selective interpretation and presentation of specific examples from the riches of observational data to support their case. A further problem of interpretation is that, if carried out by people other than practising teachers, there is always the danger that the research will pull away from teachers' concerns, making implementation of the results more problematic.

If none of these options is entirely suitable, can they be combined in any productive way to serve our current research needs? We would suggest that they can. Quite how this is done will, amongst other things, depend upon the extent to which the research is intended to be 'applied' in the sense of how directly it is intended to inform classroom practice. This is the kind of approach that we have tried to develop in the SLANT (Spoken Language and New Technology) Project (see Mercer, Phillips and Somekh, 1991, for an outline of the project and its rationale), in which research expertise in socio-linguistics, discourse analysis and educational evaluation is combined with an active teacher involvement in the selection of observational settings and the analysis of findings. At the time of going to press this project is just beginning to publish its first, preliminary, findings.

Behind the SLANT approach lies the belief that the long-term aim for applied educational research must be to negotiate a closer relationship between teachers and academic researchers not by denying the distinctive contribution either of academic research or practitioners' insights, but by establishing a joint educational research and development community in which contributions of both kinds can be integrated. A more specific aim is to create a theory of computer assisted learning visibly relevant to the improvement of practice; and correspondingly, a practice that was informed by, and critically responsive to that theory. The obstacles to such a pro-gramme are considerable, but the ever expanding numbers of teachers taking higher degrees, the concern for practical relevance within such degrees and the growth of the action research movement all suggest that the general conditions for such a development exist.

WHAT SORT OF EDUCATIONAL THEORY DO WE NEED?

To sustain a research community of the kind described above requires a broadly shared language and conceptual framework within which research can be planned, findings can be interpreted, and – most importantly –

disagreements can be articulated and tested out in practice. We need, in short, a theoretical framework for understanding and evaluating what is going on, and for locating the results of individual studies within the emerging picture. Amongst other things, such a framework ought to handle the realities of learning as it really goes on – as a socially and culturally grounded activity – rather than as an 'abstract' process. More specifically, it ought to be able to handle the peculiar 'three-way' relationship which may exist between a learner, a teacher and 'active' software. It also needs to link with the concerns of teachers and a body of academic researchers, without being entirely defined by either of them.

There are a number of possible frameworks available for such a theory, some of which have not figured significantly in this book. (One interesting possibility, for example, would be the sort of grounded theory advocated by Strauss and Corbin (1990). The contributors to this book have, with varying degrees of conviction, expressed the view that the most relevant and coherent framework is that offered by the kind of 'socio-cultural' or 'communicative' theory which is currently being constructed from the early work of L. S. Vygotsky. The main argument in its favour is that it alone can handle the nature of learning as an educational activity. In a wide ranging discussion of the centrality of talk in education, Gordon Wells (1992) suggests that the strengths of this theoretical perspective can be articulated in terms of three basic principles, each of which is empirically well supported. Our own summary formulation of the principles offered by Wells is as follows:

1 'Knowledge' is not an abstract commodity, but a state of understanding constructed by every 'knowledgeable' individual.
2 Knowledge construction is essentially social and cultural in nature.
3 Knowledge construction is always mediated and facilitated by cultural practices and artifacts.

As examples of 'cultural artifacts', Wells lists 'wheels, levers, clocks and microscopes: 'tools' which, as members of the culture, we 'inherit', but which were invented by problem-solvers in previous generations' (p. 3). He might well have added 'computers' to that list, for they are certainly the most imaginative and powerful recent additions to our culture's problem-solving toolbox. But, very significantly, Wells goes on to say:

> Of all these culturally inherited mediating tools, it is generally agreed, the most important is *discourse* – that is to say, the interactive and constructive meaning-making that occurs in purposeful linguistic interaction with others.

> (p. 3, our italics)

It has to be admitted, however, that 'communicative' theory is far from coherent or complete: and certain of its central concepts require more precise definition and empirical exemplification (see, for example, Maybin,

Mercer and Stierer, 1992 for a discussion of the concept of 'scaffolding' learning in the classroom). Our belief is that the theory will best be developed through being incorporated into a self-consciously 'applied' research programme of the kind outlined above. We will conclude, therefore, by posing some specific questions for further research which we feel represent the essence of the development of the relationship between our empirical knowledge about the use of computers in real-life learning settings and of the construction of an educationally relevant theory of the learning process:

- In what respects do models of communication in the classroom need rethinking to take account of the existence and potentialities of computers? What retrospective light does this throw upon the nature of conventional curriculum materials, seen as communicative devices?
- Is the computer best conceptualised as a tool, as an active participant in the learning process, or something in between? Is the answer to this going to be the same for all kinds of software, and for all kinds of classroom activity?

We have summarised in this chapter the basis for our belief in the actual and potential significance of the issues dealt with in this book: the theme of 'language, computers and education' embodies the relationship between two of the most important and powerful problem-solving resources of our culture. There is much more to discover about that relationship, and the future development of educational policy and practice may hinge on the nature of such discoveries.

REFERENCES

Maybin, J., Mercer, N. and Stierer, B. (1992) '"Scaffolding" learning in the classroom', in Norman, K. (ed.) *Thinking Voices: the work of the National Oracy Project*, London, Hodder & Stoughton for the National Curriculum Council.
Mercer, N., Phillips, T. and Somekh, B. (1991) 'Spoken language and the new technology: the SLANT Project', *Journal of Computer-assisted Learning*, 7.
Strauss, A. and Corbin, J. (1990) *Basics of Qualitative Research: Grounded Theory Procedures and Techniques*, London, Sage Publications.
Wells, G. (1992) 'The Centrality of Talk in Education', in Norman, K. (ed.) *Thinking Voices: the work of the National Oracy Project*, London, Hodder & Stoughton for the National Curriculum Council.

Index